To my wife, Renate Peters

The Blues Lyric
Formula

MICHAEL TAFT

Routledge
Taylor & Francis Group
New York   London

Published in 2006 by
Routledge
Taylor & Francis Group
270 Madison Avenue
New York, NY 10016

Published in Great Britain by
Routledge
Taylor & Francis Group
2 Park Square
Milton Park, Abingdon
Oxon OX14 4RN

Printed in the United States of America on acid-free paper
10 9 8 7 6 5 4 3 2 1

International Standard Book Number-10: 0-415-97499-2 (Softcover)
International Standard Book Number-13: 978-0-415-97499-8 (Softcover)
Library of Congress Card Number 2005024931

Library of Congress Cataloging-in-Publication Data

Taft, Michael.
    The blues lyric formula / Michael Taft.
       p. cm.
    Includes bibliographical references (p.) and index.
    ISBN 0-415-97498-4 (hb : alk. paper) -- ISBN 0-415-97499-2 (pb : alk. paper)
    1. Blues (Music)--Analysis, appreciation. 2. Blues (Music)—History and criticism. I. Title.

MT146.T34 2006
781.643'01'4--dc22
                                               2005024931

Taylor & Francis Group
is the Academic Division of Informa plc.

Visit the Taylor & Francis Web site at
http://www.taylorandfrancis.com

and the Routledge Web site at
http://www.routledge-ny.com

Contents

Acknowledgments

I began formulating the ideas presented in this study more than thirty-eight years ago, when I was a student of Robert P. Creed, and I thank him for his inspired teaching. I broadened my thinking on the blues (and many other subjects) as a student and colleague of Neil V. Rosenberg, to whom I am eternally grateful. As well, I thank the entire faculty of the Folklore Department at Memorial University of Newfoundland, especially the late Herbert Halpert, John D.A. Widdowson, and Peter Narváez, and my thanks as well to linguists Harold Paddock and Lawrence Smith of the linguistics department at the same university. I owe a great debt to Michael J. Preston of the University of Colorado for introducing me to the world of computers and the humanities and for his encouragement of my work over the past three decades. Two blues scholars, Jeff Todd Titon and John Barnie, were especially supportive during the time when I was trying to articulate my ideas about blues formulaic structure. I also want to thank David Evans for his great body of blues scholarship, which has informed all aspects of the present study. Finally, I thank my wife, Renate Peters, for her unflagging support.

Introduction

It is difficult to imagine what North American popular music would be like if there had been no blues. This African American song form, a phenomenon of the last decade of the nineteenth century, which evolved and flourished in the southern United States and African American enclaves in the urban North, has become an integral part of the fabric of twentieth-century popular and commercial music traditions. Jazz, country, bluegrass, rock, and pop songs would not exist in their present forms without the influence of the blues. That the blues, almost since its inception, has existed simultaneously as a form of American folksong and a commercial form of popular song partly explains its pervasiveness and its strength.

As well as catching the ear of the American public (both African American and European American), the blues quickly came to the attention of scholars, and the number of books and articles written on the blues over the years makes this song form one of the most well-studied traditions in American folklore. Like others before me, I became intrigued with the blues as soon as I heard it sung, and like previous scholars, most notably David Evans (1982, p. 9), I immediately associated blues lyrics with Parry Lord theories of the formulaic nature of oral poetry.

Evans's discovery led him to years of fieldwork among blues singers, and he has published a body of work unrivaled by other scholars. His culminating book, *Big Road Blues*, is a classic, but in the final part of his book, Evans cautioned against the application of Parry Lord theories to the blues (1982, pp. 315–16). His years of study led him away from the early, intuitive connections he had made between blues lyrics and the structure of epic poetry. The considerable differences between the long, orally composed narrative verses of epic poetry and the short, aphoristic, lyric structure of the blues convinced Evans that any detailed, Parry Lord analysis of the blues formula was little more than an academic exercise.

Yet, where Evans saw differences between the blues and epic poetry, I continue to see similarities, if not in the function, history, or metrics of these poetic traditions, then in their similar use of the "formula," however that is to be defined. As I will demonstrate, formulaic structure is a prosodic form that extends beyond its usual associations with epic verse and long, narrative poetry; it functions as well in the blues as it does in Yugoslavian epics or in Old English verse—perhaps better. The road taken by Evans led him to a folkloristic analysis of the traditional, orally performed blues; my road has led me to reevaluate the lyric structure of popular, mass-mediated, commercially recorded blues.

This study, then, is a structural analysis of the formulaic composition of blues lyrics, specifically the blues lyrics recorded by African American singers for pre–World War II commercial recording companies. While some scholars, Evans among them, have worked in this area, there has never been a rigorous and detailed exploration of exactly how blues singers used formulas in creating a commercially acceptable form of song. My intention is to give a step-by-step description of the rules implicit in the formulaic structure of the blues; my goal is to reanimate the discussion of blues lyric structure and to flesh out the intuitions of previous scholars.

Interestingly, while there has been little rigorous structural analysis of blues lyrics, scholars have examined in detail the music of the blues. As evidenced by the record notes to many reissue albums of prewar blues, musician-scholars have been quick to point out the peculiarities of blues musical composition. Ethnomusicologists are well equipped to describe, in a scientific manner, the musical structure of the blues, and Titon's book *Early Downhome Blues* (1977) is a landmark in this respect. In fact, Titon's description of "skeletal tunes" and his use of linguistic theory and terminology points (as he clearly understood) toward a similar approach to blues lyric structure.

The structural study of blues music has progressed more rapidly than that of blues lyrics largely because of the advanced state of musicology. The musicologist has a system of theories and methodologies that can be readily applied to the study of blues music. It may be an oversimplification to say that music is a logical and well-ordered mathematical construction (see Clough and Douthett, 1991), but the fact remains that the physical properties of music can be measured and recorded in a most exacting and scientific fashion.

By contrast, the student of blues lyrics has no readily accessible set of theories and methodologies. Blues lyrics, like all poetry, involve the clever use of language; they are dependent on special phonological, lexical, syntactical, and semantic limitations and options that overlay the general rules of everyday language. This being the case, the proper approach to the structural analysis of blues lyrics must lie in the discipline of linguistics. Windelberg and Miller, among others, have certainly recognized that a rigorous, linguistic approach must be taken to any analysis of poetic formulas (1980), and Rosenberg similarly stated that, in discovering the nature of the formula, "the linguist will yet tell us much" (1978, p. 3).

In comparison with musicology, however, linguistics is still at an early and elemental stage of development. If language is, like music, a logical mathematical system, linguists have yet to understand its massive complexities. All linguistic theories are tentative and precarious, and the scholarly literature in this field is largely composed of redefinitions, new paradigms, theoretical disputes, and debates on the most basic and elemental aspects of language. Chomsky's words ring as true today as they did forty years ago: "The tentative character of any conclusions that can now be advanced concerning linguistic theory, or, for that matter, English grammar, should certainly be obvious to anyone working in this area" (1965, p. v).

The problems for the student of blues lyrics go beyond the "tentative character" of linguistic theories. For the most part, linguists have studied competence rather than performance in human language (see Chomsky, 1965, pp. 3–4). The blues scholar, however, is more concerned with performance than with competence; that is, actual speech acts rather than ideal situations are the primary interest of the blues scholar. In addition, the special rules that govern poetic speech are quite different from those that govern language as a whole, although poetic rules are almost never inflexible, and the study of lyrical structure is the study of what is more or less "acceptable" within the framework of the poetic form. As Chomsky pointed out, however, acceptability "is a concept that belongs to the study of performance, whereas grammaticalness belongs to the study of competence" (1965, p. 11). There is, thus, a major difference in the way linguists and blues scholars view language, and the application of linguistic theories to actual speech events, such as blues lyrics, must take this difference into account.

This study is concerned primarily with blues performance rather than blues compositional competence. I transcribed almost all of the hundreds of lyric examples in this study from actual blues performances. The rules of formulaic composition that I have derived, therefore, come from these examples rather than from hypothetical, ideal blues structures. It is deceptive, however, to state that this study is entirely divorced from the examination of blues competence. My intuitions about blues structure were initially based on notions of competence and were subsequently developed and clarified through the study of blues performances. As Chomsky wrote, it is neither possible nor desirable to ignore competence in empirical investigations (1965, p. 4).

Of necessity, my description of the blues formulaic system relies on generalizations and on an understanding of what the "ideal" blues lyric would comprise. Thus, in the following chapters, I suggest rules of compositional competence, but I cite actual blues lyrics as examples. The problem, of course, is that I could not always find the perfect examples to illustrate my points. Conversely, there were always blues lyrics that contradicted the rules of competence that I was trying to formulate. The linguist could call these contradictions "errors (random or characteristic) in applying his knowledge of the language in actual performance" (Chomsky, 1965, p. 3), but I could not so easily dispense with the anomalies and peculiarities of actual blues performance.

The result of this conflict between ideal forms and real texts is a description of the blues formulaic system that becomes clearer and more exacting as one moves one's focus from the structure of the entire corpus of the blues toward specific blues lyrics. As I explain in subsequent chapters, the whole concept of the "formula" is as much a theoretical construction of the analyst as it is a reality of the blues composer's craft. This paradox relates directly to the question of competence versus performance: my definitions and descriptions of blues structure become more precise when I apply them to performed texts than when I discuss them in the abstract.

Bearing this in mind, this study should not be considered a linguistic or, more specifically, semantic analysis. I use linguistic and semantic theories (considerably simplified) as a tool to help in describing the formulaic nature of the blues, and thus these theories are a means rather than an end. As is now obvious, I rely on the theories of generative and transformational grammar, first outlined by Chomsky, to describe blues formulaic composition. In this respect, I am following the lead of other formula scholars, such as Haggo and Kuiper (1983), who used Chomskyan models in their description of conversational formulas. My simplified use of generative semantics is indebted to the readable and usable work of Geoffrey Leech (1974).

As Spraycar and Dunlap have noted, the larger one's sample size, the more accurate one's analysis of formulaic structures (Spraycar, 1981; Spraycar and Dunlap, 1982). Thus, I have chosen a large corpus for analysis: more than two thousand commercially recorded blues, sung by more than three hundred and fifty singers. In the next chapter, I define in greater detail the commercial blues that make up this corpus, but I should explain that my source for these songs was not the original

78rpm discs on which they were produced. Rather, I used the extensive collection of blues reissue albums that have made these songs available to researchers over the past fifty years.

There is a problem, however, in relying on reissued songs for a corpus. In effect, the reissue record companies, by selecting which songs they would rerecord, imposed an unwanted set of criteria on my study. Whether because of the personal aesthetics of the reissue record producers or because of the rarity of some of the original recordings, some blues artists have been poorly represented on reissue albums. Thus, I have purposely searched for recordings that do contain lesser-known (or lesser-liked) singers to balance my selection. Still, despite my searching, there are no examples in the corpus from such prolific artists as Leothus Green, Viola McCoy, and Lucille Hegamin. Other singers, such as Buddy Moss, Mamie Smith, and Charlie Spand are not represented in proper proportion to the number of records they made.

The size of my corpus, perhaps one-fifth of all the blues songs commercially recorded before World War II, functions to smooth out any of the statistical irregularities mentioned earlier. Of course, not all of the songs that I analyzed are represented in these pages, because I have given only examples that illustrate my thesis. (I have published the entire corpus separately; see Taft, 2005.) Yet without analyzing every song in the corpus, I would not have been able to reach the conclusions that I present in the following pages.

In analyzing these blues lyrics, I have followed the lead of other formula scholars, especially Duggan (1969, 1973), in using the computer to reorder the blues lyrics into a concordance (Taft, 1977, pp. 19–24; 1984). The result of this process was that I was able to see, quite clearly, how singers used the same phrases in different contexts. By analyzing these phrases—in actuality, manifestations of blues formulas—I was able to discover the compositional rules of blues formulaic structure.

What follows is what I have found.

CHAPTER 1

Defining the Commercial Blues

One might speak of the blues as a single song form or genre, because virtually all blues share certain qualities of lyric and music, or at least share a sentiment that is, in some sense, "blue." Yet within any genre there are subgenres, and this is certainly true of the blues. As I make no claim that this study describes all blues in all its forms and in all its contexts, I am obliged to define the corpus of those songs that I have included in my analysis and on which I base my theory of formulaic composition.

Obviously the commercial blues defines itself as a subgenre of the blues; more specifically, however, they are those blues recorded between 1920 and 1942 by commercial record companies expressly for the African American record-buying public. These recordings came to be known as "race records," both within the recording industry and among those interested in the blues (see Dixon and Godrich, 1970, p. 17). The blues also were performed in a variety of other contexts: as field hollers by agricultural workers; in jam sessions among singers and their followers; at community picnics and other social gatherings; in juke joints, barrelhouses, dance halls, and brothels; in cabarets and on the vaudeville stage; in circuses, tent shows, and medicine shows; in work camps and prisons; at private parties; at song festivals and contests; for the benefit of folk-song collectors; on radio; in the street; in rehearsal before public performances; and in private with no audience other than the singer. The blues performed in a recording studio by a commercial record company is allied with all these other blues, but because context is so central to performance, the recording studio context created its own demands on this tradition (which I discuss later in this study).

The recording companies were not interested in the blues to the exclusion of all other types of performance, however, and their "race record" series included a number of different song forms. A large part of this commercial repertoire was religious material: mostly gospel songs and sermons. As well, these series included jazz pieces, novelty songs, ballads, popular Tin Pan Alley compositions, skits, and instrumental music. Selecting blues songs from among this potpourri, therefore, is still a matter of definition.

The most obvious and identifiable aspect of a song genre such as the blues is its texture—its use of rhyme, stanzaic structure, and line structure. In fact, most previous scholars have used these gross textural characteristics in defining the blues as a genre. As Keil stated, "The analyst is usually well advised to concentrate on form, structural regularities, syntactic rules. Indeed, blues and non blues can easily be distinguished in these terms" (1966, p. 51).

The emphasis on such textural characteristics is partly on account of the generally held opinion that the lyrics, rather than the music, are the basis of the definition of the blues. Singer Rubin Lacy said, "The blues is sung not for the tune. It's sung for the words mostly. A real blues singer sings a blues for the words" (Evans, 1967, p. 13). In more scholarly language, Szwed made the same point: "There is greater concern for textual message and meaning: the blues are information oriented" (1970, p. 222).

It is not the entire blues lyric, however, but the stanza that defines the texture of the form—an idea accepted by such varied scholars as White (1928–29, p. 207), Hyman (1958, p. 306), Charters (1973, p. 4), and Ferris (1970a, p. 34). As well, most scholars are in accord as to the structure of this stanza. Niles may well have been the first to set down the basic structure of the blues stanza:

> The thought would not necessarily be expressed in a single line, twice repeated without variation. There might be and usually was one repetition, but instead, the second line would slightly modify, by way of emphasis, the first, while the third would introduce something new. (Niles, 1926b, p. 2)

Two years later, White gave a slightly more precise definition, when he wrote, "Typically [the blues] consisted of either one line sung three times or a line sung twice (either with or without a modification of the second line), and an entirely different third line" (1928, pp. 387–88).

A number of scholars since the twenties have agreed with this definition (see, for example, Ames, 1955, pp. 253–54; Courlander, 1963, p. 126; Locke, 1936, p. 32), while others have expanded this definition to include the stanza's metrical characteristics—twelve bars of music with each of the three lines occupying four of the twelve bars (see, for example, Blesh, 1958, p. 103; Brakeley, 1949; Chase, 1955, p. 452; Jones, 1963, p. 68; and Oster, 1969b, p. 22).

A further expansion of this definition includes the criterion of rhyme, as singer Leonard "Baby Doo" Caston explained:

> In the blues they'd be making these recordings, you're playing the twelve bar blues, you have to do these things in order for maybe whomsoever listen to this particular thing wouldn't hear it the first thing you said. And so they would add the rhyming thing at the end. So this would make you do your first line two times and your rhyme would come after. Well this got to be a thing where people listening would expect that; so they still do. So in order to get things across they would do it. (Titon, 1974, p. 24)

Of course, many scholars share Caston's criteria (see, for example, Brown, 1953, p. 287; Cook, 1973, p. 24; Guralnick, 1971, p. 22; Keil, 1966, p. 51; and Rust, 1962), but Caston makes the important point that these are not merely academic criteria, but folk criteria as well. Perhaps of equal importance is Caston's view that the recording context helped to shape and solidify this particular stanzaic texture.

This texture is quite obvious to anyone familiar with the blues, whether singer or scholar; perhaps so familiar and obvious that most writers on the subject have not bothered to describe fully the features of blues texture. Is there any doubt, for example, that Courlander or Locke would include rhyme in their definitions? They simply did not state the obvious. The following textural definition by Dankworth sums up the points made previously and is probably in accord with the views of most writers on the subject:

> The words of the blues are simple rhyming couplets ... the first line being repeated (either exactly or with slight variation) before the second is stated, thus making three lines in all. Each line of the poem takes four bars of music, hence the term "twelve bar blues." (1968, p. 47)

Most writers have designated the typical blues stanza as an "AAB" form—one line repeated twice with an accompanying, rhymed third line, although such a form does not clearly indicate that the A line and the B line do rhyme. Scholars have had less to say about the texture of the individual line in the stanza. Several, however, have recognized that the blues line is divided into two parts, usually separated by a caesura: "Each couplet represents, as a rule, four parts, each line two divisions, each division a single phrase" (Odum and Johnson, 1925, p. 267). A few others have noticed this caesura, although they have labeled it a pause, a break, or simply a division in the line (see Gruver, 1972, p. 8; Kent, 1971; and Nicholas, 1973, p. 1), while one scholar, Jahn, described the stanza as six lines, rather than three, because of the presence of the caesura (1968, p. 166).

Only three writers, however, have explored in any detail the placement and nature of this caesura. Metfessel scientifically measured the durations of the caesuras in various songs sung by African Americans; for example, in the blues "You Don't Know My Mind," Metfessel (1928, pp. 109–10) recorded the following caesuras, measured in hundredths of a second:

Take me back daddy [.62] try me one mo' time [.47]
Ef I doan do to suit you [.29] I'll break my back bone tryin'.

Titon described the caesura in terms of the music of the blues, where singers accomplished this pause through "a rest ... an end pitch held longer than a quarter note ... or an intervallic skip, usually upward, of at least a minor third" (1977, pp. 142–43). Carruth noted that the caesura might be "a pause that is either metrical or ametrical" (1986, pp. 112–13). Whatever form the caesura takes, it is quite noticeable to the listener.

There is a danger, however, in accepting all of these criteria in defining the blues. Although they hold for most blues songs, there are so many exceptions to the AAB, twelve-bar stanzaic form that a more flexible definition must be found that will include these exceptions as blues songs. Perhaps the least constant criterion is the twelve-bar nature of the stanza. Odum and Johnson were probably the first to point out that the blues is capable of considerable metric variability (1925, p. 291), and most subsequent writers have agreed that stanzas of eight, eleven, sixteen, twenty-four, or, theoretically, any number of bars are possible in the blues.

Indicative of this metric flexibility is the fact that the number of bars in a blues song does not correspond in any way to the number of vocal syllables singers used in their stanzas. As Jean Wagner pointed out, "A more or less indefinite number of unaccentuated syllables can be put between the stresses, which make a blues verse quite lengthy, so that it can be represented typographically in two lines of equal or unequal length" (quoted in Jahn, 1968, p. 167). This being the case, the metrical criterion seems rather superfluous to any definition of the verbal texture of the blues. Roxin went so far as to state that the "time of each verse is built not by seconds, but by the repeating cadences and sung lines. A song is not three minutes long, but five verses long; a verse is not fifteen seconds, but three lines long" (1973, pp. 10–11).

The AAB criterion is less easily dispensed with. That the lines of a stanza should rhyme is fairly well accepted by singers and their audiences alike (see Taft, 1978). The number of repetitions of the lines in a stanza, however, can vary considerably, and AAB is only one of many stanzaic forms acceptable in blues performance. The textural definition of the blues stanza, therefore, must be broadened to include any number of variations on the basic rhymed couplet AB.

Oster, among others, recognized the basic couplet as the common textural feature of all blues:

> In making use of such clever, richly evocative figures of speech, blues singers rely heavily on conventions of rhetorical structure. In both talking blues and blues which are more rigid in structure most lines are made up of two sections of approximately equal duration with a caesura (a pause) in between, more or less in the middle. Often there is a striking contrast between the first half of a line and the second half, and/or between the opening line of a verse and the last line. The results of these elements in combination is a quotable verse, complete in itself, often aphoristic, rhythmically appealing as the words trip easily off the tongue and readily remembered roughly analogous to the heroic couplet of the eighteenth century, if we disregard the repetition of a line in the blues.
>
> True wit is nature to advantage dressed
> What oft was thought, but ne'er so well expressed.
>
> The final line completes the thought initiated by the first, in a way which is clever, witty, dramatic, or strikingly imaginative. (Oster, 1969b, p. 70)

I will discuss later Oster's thoughts on the contrasts between two half lines or between two lines, but this description is correct in stressing the couplet as the essential stanzaic structure of the blues.

What are some of the variations of this basic couplet? The most common variations involve repetitions of the first line, last line, or both lines of the stanza—the AAB repetition being by far the most frequent form:

1   I'm flying to South Carolina; I got to go there this time
    I'm flying to South Carolina; I got to go there this time
    Women in Dallas, Texas, is about to make me lose my mind
    (Blind Lemon Jefferson, 1929e)

But the unembellished AB blues stanza is also quite common:

2   Good Lord, good Lord, send me an angel down
    Can't spare you no angel; will spare you a teasing brown
    (Blind Willie McTell, 1935b)

The first line of the stanza is more commonly repeated than the second, the singer sometimes using an AAAB form:

3   If you want a good woman, get one long and tall
    If you want a good woman, get one long and tall
    If you want a good woman, get one long and tall
    When she go to loving, she make a panther squawl
    (Wiley Barner, 1927)

But singers also repeated the second line of the stanza, as in this ABB form:

4   I tell you girls, and I'm going to tell you now
    If you don't want me, please don't dog me around
    If you don't want me, please don't dog me around
    (Robert Wilkins, 1929)

Singers also repeated both lines in an AABB structure but more commonly repeated the entire couplet twice, as in the following ABAB stanza:

5   Well I solemnly swear; Lord, I raise my right hand
    That I'm going to get me a woman; you get you another man
    I solemnly swear; Lord, I raise my right hand
    That I'm going to get me a woman, babe; you get you another man
    (Son House, 1930a)

Theoretically, any combination of these forms could occur in the blues, so that AAAAB, AABBB, ABBB, ABABAB, AABAAB, and other such structures were possible, if not probable. Perhaps the strangest and rarest form of line repetition in the corpus is ABA, as in the following example:

6   I got something to tell you just before I go
     It ain't nothing, baby; turn your lamp down low
     I got something to tell you just before you go
     (Otto Virgial, 1935a)

Not all stanza variations involve repetition, however. Singers quite often added refrains to an AB couplet. These refrains varied from short taglines to multilined structures, but whatever the form of the refrain, it did not have to conform in any way to the textural constraints of the blues couplet. Note the following examples:

7   Look here, woman; making me mad
     Done bringing me something somebody done had
     [refrain]:
     Carry it right back home; I don't want it no more
     (Ed Bell, 1930b)

8   You say you done quit me; now what should I do
     Can't make up my mind to love no one but you
     [refrain]:
     I don't like that
     No I don't
     I don't like that
     No I don't
     You know it kill me dead
     I don't like that
     (Pillie Bolling, 1930a)

The structure of both of these examples might be represented as ABr. This is the most common type of couplet and refrain structure.

The refrain, however, might also take the form of a blues couplet. Following the same rules of blues texture variation, the refrain can be either a simple blues couplet or a couplet involving the repetition of the first or second line. The following two examples represent ABr(AB) and ABr(AAB) stanza forms, respectively:

9 Early one morning just about half past three
  You done something that's really worrying me
  [refrain]:
  Come on; take a little walk with me
  Back to the same old place where we long to be
  (Robert Lockwood, 1941b)

10 I got a gal; she got a Rolls Royce
  She didn't get it all by using her voice
  [refrain]:
  I'm wild about my 'tuni; only thing I crave
  I'm wild about my 'tuni; only thing I crave
  Well sweet patuni going to carry me to my grave
  (Willie Baker, 1929f)

Just as the refrain can manifest itself in a number of different forms that may bear little or no relationship to the structure of the blues couplet, the couplet can become a refrain, chorus, or blues-like interjection in what is essentially a nonblues song. This textural phenomenon most often occurred in the songs of female vaudeville singers. Such songs might begin with a Tin Pan Alley, popular song texture, such as an ABCD stanzaic form, but then break into a different rhythm, and the singer might sing one or two blues couplets before the song returns once again to its nonblues structure.

In the following song, sung by vaudeville singer Trixie Smith, the first stanza exhibits a nonblues ABCD structure; the second stanza has an ABC structure with internal rhyme in its second line; the third stanza, although it exhibits a blues-like AB structure, does not have a caesura in its lines. The fourth and fifth stanzas, however, are definitely blues couplets, with proper AB structures and midline caesuras:

11 Now some folks long to have a plenty money
  Some will want their wine and song
  But all I want is my sweet loving honey
  I cry about him all night long

  Once I had a dear sweet daddy, but I didn't treat him right
  So he left town with Mandy Brown
  That is why I'm blue tonight

  So I'm leaving here today
  When I find him he will say

Please come back and love me like you used to do; I think about you every day
You reap what you sow in the sweet bye and bye, and be sorry that you went away

Oh, baby, I'm crazy; almost dead
I wish I had you here to hold my aching head
(Trixie Smith, 1925)

In this song there is a definite instrumental and vocal break as Smith shifts into a blues texture. The last line of the third stanza, "When I find him he will say," also seems to act as an introduction to the blues stanzas that follow. This song is typical of the semiblues songs (as defined in this study) that female vaudeville singers recorded in the hundreds during the prewar era of commercial recording.

In addition to repetition, refrains, and "embedding" in nonblues songs, singers could embellish their couplets with certain stylistic and vocal devices. Shouting, talking, or singing in falsetto were three such devices. Another device, similar to variations in repetition, was what might be called "staggering," wherein singers repeated parts of a line or half line in an incremental fashion:

12 When you hear me walking, turn your lamp down, turn your lamp down, lamp down low
    When you hear me walking, turn your lamp down low
    When you hear me walking, turn your lamp down low
    And turn it so your man'll never know
    (Bobby Grant, 1927a)

Example 12 is an AAAB stanza with staggering in the second half of the first line.

On rare occasions, singers sang only a partial blues stanza; that is, they would not sing a B line after singing (and perhaps repeating) an A line. In theory, these partial stanzas should not be considered blues stanzas at all, but they generally occur within the context of blues songs, where other stanzas conform to the texture of the blues. Such partial stanzas as AA, AAA, AAr, and so on, were more common in less-structured, noncommercial blues and might hearken back to those early forms of the blues sung before the era of commercial recordings. In the commercial blues, the "incomplete" nature of such stanzas is implicit in the overall structure of the song.

Singers were not limited to variations within the stanza; they could also vary the structure of their stanzas, from stanza to stanza, within the same song. In other words, singers felt no need to maintain a consistent stanzaic form within the same song. In the following song, for example, the structure of the stanzas is AA, AA (two partial stanzas), AB, and ABB, respectively. Note also that staggering occurs in the last two stanzas:

13   I'd rather be the devil, to be that woman's man
I'd rather be the devil, to be that woman's man

Oh nothing but the devil changed my baby's mind
Oh nothing but the devil changed my baby's mind

I laid down last night, laid down last night, I laid down last night; tried to take my rest
My mind got to rambling, like the wild geese from the west, from the west

The woman I love, the woman I love, the woman I love, Lord, stoled her from my best friend
But he got lucky; stoled her back again
But he got lucky; stoled her back again
(Skip James, 1931a)

The combinations possible within the confines of the simple blues couplet are many. If one adds to this the possible combinations of stanzaic types within the same song, the varieties allowed in blues texture seem endless. Blues singers, however, were remarkably conservative. Most possible textural structures never appear in the corpus under analysis. This conservative tendency is especially clear when one considers that perhaps 80 percent of all the songs in the corpus follow a strict AAB pattern throughout. Thus, although there was considerable room for creativity within the texture of the blues, singers preferred to concentrate their creative efforts on the inner structures of the blues couplet—the formulas.

Texture alone, however, does not entirely define the commercial blues. Religious songs or ballads in the commercially recorded repertoire might share the same textural structures with the blues, but the nature of their texts separates them from the kind of song under analysis here. Abrahams and Foss showed that songs fall on a continuum between "action oriented" and "emotion oriented" texts (1968, pp. 37–60), and the blues—clearly a lyric rather than a narrative song—falls well to the emotion-oriented side of this continuum.

Although some blues are narrative, or contain several stanzas that are chronologically sequential (to be discussed later), and others follow a specific theme from stanza to stanza (see Evans, 1982, pp. 131–44), most blues are fairly free of such constraints. As lyrics, they are commentaries on some situation, rather than narratives about some situation. If there is an implied narrative in blues songs, this narrative is usually developed in an indirect fashion through pithy and aphoristic statements on the effect of the narrative on the persona, the persona's reaction to the narrative, or the emotional atmosphere that surrounds the narrative.

I do not intend to describe in detail the implied narrative (or narratives) that underlies the blues lyric. The formulaic analysis, which makes up the main part of this study, will in fact reveal the major themes and concerns of the blues and thus serve to define the textual aspects of the blues better than if I attempted, at this point, to give some random thoughts on the "meaning" of the blues. Yet some generalities about the text of the blues are in order. Perhaps the most important defining feature of the blues text, other than its basic lyric nature, is that it is a secular song; that is, the blues is a commentary on secular issues in African American society rather than on religious issues. This division between sacred and secular black culture was well understood by the record-buying public, who might have bought both blues records and gospel records but who always remained aware of the distinctions between these two major forms of African American music.

As a secular, lyric form, the blues could comment on an incredibly wide range of social issues. And, in fact, it is possible to find songs about poverty, drunkenness, racism, gambling, partying, politics, the family, or almost any other aspect of everyday life. Yet there is one theme whose overriding presence in the corpus makes it a part of the definition of the blues: namely, the theme of love. Love is the major topic of the blues: faithfulness, jealousy, adultery, sexuality, lust—all aspects of love are grist for the blues mill. Again, this finding came early in blues scholarship—Odum and Johnson (1925, p. 160) to Charters (1963, p. 8) to Courlander (1963, p. 130), to name only a few. Singers, as well, have seen the theme of love as a defining feature of their songs. James "Son" Thomas said, "It ain't very many blues made that ain't made up about a woman. It's a few ain't made up about a woman, but most of them is 'my baby this' or 'my baby that'" (Ferris, 1970b, p. 13). Robert Pete Williams was even more categorical: "Love makes the blues. That's where it comes from. There wouldn't be no love and there wouldn't be no blues if there was just men" (Cook, 1973, p. 40).

Singer Henry Townsend's bittersweet outlook is blues-like in its form and speaks very much to the interrelationship between love and the blues: "You know, that's the major thing in life. Please believe me. What you love the best is what can hurt you the most" (Charters, 1963, p. 14). But the blues explores both the hurtful and the joyous aspects of love—it is a love lyric.

One final part of the definition of the commercial blues concerns its place in the continuum of orality and literacy. No formulaic study can avoid this question, and I will return to it later, but the literary nature of the commercially recorded blues deserves to be included in this definition, if only because this particular feature of commercial blues separates it from those blues performances that were improvised, orally composed compositions.

The image of blues singers as deliberate and careful composers who prepared their songs in advance of their recorded performances contrasts with the popular, romantic stereotype of these artists. A widely held perception of blues singers is that of performers who, without prior practice or thought, sang impromptu compositions into the recording microphone. Longini believed that the songs found on commercial recordings were purely oral in composition (1939, p. 97), while Middleton wrote that the "literate bluesman is rare, and playing off paper is felt to be incompatible with playing from the heart" (1972, p. 51). In actual fact, however, commercial blues artists were not above committing their songs to print and were considerably more literate than the popular stereotype would lead one to believe.

This is not to say that there was no improvisation in blues performance. In other performance contexts, spontaneous composition was common. LeDell Johnson recalled that his brother Tommy Johnson would "just set there and follow with his box, and he could make up a song in ten minutes" (Evans, 1971, p. 22), and James "Son" Thomas said, "If I'm playing and don't know the song, I can add verses as I play. It come to me, the right verse of what to say and everything" (Ferris, 1970a, p. 42).

Indeed the talent to improvise is a common boast among blues singers. Blind Jimmie Brewer stated,

> I sit down and make up a thousand songs. ... Anybody ask me what I did, I don't know, so you just got to give 'em a name. ... Because I don't know what it is, I'll just sing and play something. ... Funny thing playing music as long as I'm playing somebody else's records, I know what I'm gonna play, but when I gonna play something of my own, I don't know what it's gonna be until I start and playin' it. (Ahlstrand, 1967, p. 12)

Aaron T-Bone Walker similarly boasted,

> I didn't know the words because there weren't any set words. I made them up as I went along. That's the way we do, you know. Right today I can make up blues faster than I can sing them. I could sing the blues for you a whole day and never repeat a verse. (Shapiro and Hentoff, 1955, p. 249)

Singer Furry Lewis also boasted of his improvisational prowess, but at the same time he gave some indication of the workings of a singer's mind:

> I can sing a song that I know already. But I can just sit here and sing a song I never sung in my life before, a song about this bed, that bottle of beer there, a song about this television, anything. And the guitar got to keep up, 'cause I'm gonna make it. I just make up the words right quick, "Well, that ain't gonna match that." Then something come into your mind, and it's gonna get it to a T. (Olsson, 1970, pp. 72–73)

These artists were not, however, thinking in terms of the recording context. While they might have been perfectly willing to improvise when playing in an informal context, they would have been more reticent about singing an unrehearsed, spontaneous blues in the recording studio. Even in some nonrecording contexts, singers might have felt the need to write down and preserve their lyrics. Booker White recalled that, while imprisoned at Parchman Farm, he "was writing songs and sticking them in a crack somewhere until he got out" (Evans, 1966a, p. 8).

Even though White was quite capable of improvising, in the recording studio he created his blues from written notes that he had previously made to himself (Evans, 1966b, p. 7). White's written cue cards indicate that some of his songs were partially spontaneous; that is, he knew in advance what he was going to sing about, and he might have even written down bits of lyric, but the exact form and content of the song remained fluid until he actually started singing. A few singers, of course, did improvise in the recording studio; for example, Willie Trice was quite "disturbed by Decca's habit of recording a number, playing back the 'mother' (thereby destroying it) so that the artist could see any weaknesses and then cutting another exactly the same. Easy for some, but not for Willie, who had difficulty remembering what he had sung on the first take!" (Bastin, 1971, pp. 36–37).

Titon showed that the widely divergent takes of "Match Box Blues" recorded on the same day by Blind Lemon Jefferson indicate spontaneous, unrehearsed composition (1977, pp. 38–42). Yet the fact that Trice, Jefferson, and many others were given several chances to sing their songs made these performances different from true impromptu composition. The expectations of the record company officials and the atmosphere of the recording studio militated against improvisation and favored carefully prepared texts.

Some commercial blues artists wrote down their blues simply to aid their memories as they sang, as did Mary Johnson: "I wrote down my own numbers at the time; I composed my own blues and I would just write them down and throw them away and I wouldn't think no more about them" (Oliver, 1965, p. 115). But other singers were more methodical and were very much aware that committing their compositions to print was the first step toward achieving copyright. The Memphis Jug Band obviously had more than aiding their memories in mind when they wrote down their lyrics:

> [Ralph] Peer would usually write to Son [Will Shade] about two months in advance of a recording date, giving him time to rehearse the band. They'd go over to Son's house and work all day on a tune, singing it over ten and fifteen times, until they had it right. Jennie [Clayton] would write down the words and when they had timed it, Son would write his "ok" on the words, put the title on top and his name on the bottom, so that Peer's Southern Music Corporation could copyright it. (Charters, 1959, p. 115)

Even those singers who, in other contexts, were not used to writing down their lyrics or rehearsing their songs often felt the need to do so before recording. Singers who were illiterate, or nearly illiterate, would employ amanuenses to write down their lyrics. This was the case with Tommy Johnson, when he was preparing for a recording session.

> Of course, he may have been asked by Speir to practise this time, but, for whatever reason it was, he went to Crystal Springs and engaged the help of some of his sisters and sisters in law. Clarence [Johnson]'s wife Gertrude recalls helping Tommy on three songs. He would sing a line or stanza, and she would write it down and read it back. If Tommy didn't like it he would have her cross it out, and he would think of another until the song met with his satisfaction. (Evans, 1971, p. 62)

In some cases, the scribes would become cowriters, or at least creative helpers to singers. Broonzy said of Sonny Boy Williamson's wife, "She helped him write his songs and helped him to learn how to sing them. She could rhyme a song and had wonderful handwriting" (1955, p. 121). The helper could even be a record company official; H.C. Speir claimed to have helped Kokomo Arnold write "Milk Cow Blues" (Evans, 1972, p. 120).

Writing a blues song could also be a truly communal effort, especially among the more sophisticated urban recording artists. The team of Georgia Tom Dorsey and Tampa Red wrote blues in this way, as Dorsey recalled:

> We'd do it together. I wrote most of the songs. I'm the one could write the music down. See I made the manuscript like that. Well, we both wrote lyrics. Tampa come up with some of the lyrics and if we didn't have no music, I'd write the music. (O'Neal and O'Neal, 1975, p. 26)

Leroy Carr and Scrapper Blackwell not only used their own talents to create songs, but also sought help from others, such as singer Pete Franklin's mother, Flossie Franklin (Lornell, 1972), or Blackwell's sister, Minnie (Anon., n.d.). In fact, the communal compositions of Carr and Blackwell were highly sophisticated.

> As Scrapper describes it, the making of these blues resembled cultivated poet craft rather than casual folk composition: they would sit for hours at a big dining room table, adding and taking out verses, crossing out and changing, getting the rhymes correct ("if you can't rhyme yourself, get a rhyming dictionary"), and finally, giving each blues a title. (Rosenbaum, 1961)

Rural singers also made use of the communal method of song composition; for example, Robert Hicks, while on his way to a recording session, collaborated with another train passenger on the composition of "Mississippi Heavy Water Blues" (Lowry, 1973, p. 15).

Not only did blues singers engage in communal composition, but also even the most creative artists sang songs that had been composed for them by someone else. This "ghostwriting" could be an informal sharing of material, or it could be a more organized Tin Pan Alley affair, in which record companies hired lyricists to write songs for their artists. Certainly, in the case of the female vaudeville singers, a large proportion of their songs were of the Tin Pan Alley variety. Thomas Dorsey, as well as writing songs for his own performances, was one of the finest Tin Pan Alley blues composers. Dorsey

> studied music at the Chicago College of Composition and Arranging, learning the skills he parlayed into a loose connection with Paramount Records' music publishing arm. In this capacity he wrote lead sheets (at $3 apiece) of recorded material

for copyright purposes and sometimes submitted works to Paramount's star attractions, who were nearly all vaudeville singers like Ma Rainey and Trixie Smith. Between 1923 (when he began arranging and writing for Paramount) and 1932 Dorsey was to author some two hundred blues songs. (Calt, 1972)

Tin Pan Alley composition represented perhaps the least spontaneous type of performance before the recording microphone. They were carefully arranged and written by one artist and rehearsed and memorized or read in the studio by another artist. Yet even with these songs, there could be a certain amount of improvisation. Bessie Smith would often sing Tin Pan Alley blues but slightly alter the lyrics during recording to suit her specific style of performance (Albertson, 1972, p. 50). The written lyric, therefore, was not entirely inflexible and did allow a certain amount of spontaneity.

It is also interesting to note that written blues did not necessarily mean that those lyrics achieved any sort of permanence in the repertoires of singers. As noted previously, Mary Johnson disposed of her manuscripts shortly after recording them and soon forgot the words that she had written. This same attitude toward written blues was expressed by a number of singers, among them Victoria Spivey:

> In those days it was a matter of the dollar, all of us could write those blues a dime a dozen. [Lester] Melrose would talk to me tonight and tomorrow I would have him six tunes and the very next day knowing that we wouldn't get any royalties we forgot about them and would write six more. Those were the days. (Godrich, 1965, p. 10)

The "disposable" written text opens up an interesting area of research into the differences between written and oral traditions. Where writing is simply a tool for the transmission and memorization, but not for the preservation, of a song, the lyrics of that song might remain almost as changeable and fleeting as an orally composed piece. The fact that many commercial blues were written, therefore, does not necessarily ensure their stability in tradition. The real stabilizing factor was the phonodisc, which gave permanence to the song, whether it had been improvised in the studio or carefully worked out with pen and ink beforehand. The phonodisc added a further stability to the tradition by creating a popular market for songs that the record-buying public would expect performers to repeat in blues contexts outside the recording studio (see Evans, 1982, pp. 115–31, on this point).

There were other means, of course, of getting song material besides the methods described previously. One method was "covering," in which singers sang the same songs already recorded earlier by other singers. This was a common practice among vaudeville artists, but singers of all sorts indulged in it. For example, Robert Johnson's "32-20 Blues" (1936d) is a conscious cover of Skip James's "22-20 Blues" (1931g). As we shall see, Garfield Akers's "Dough Roller Blues" (1930a) is an almost word-for-word cover of Hambone Willie Newbern's "Roll and Tumble Blues" (1929b).

A less ethical means of obtaining material was a direct outgrowth of the written composition of blues texts. One singer might simply steal a written song from another performer. There is no way of knowing how common this practice was, but it was reported that "one of the famous blues singers of the 30s had a penchant for stealing songs and used to haunt the studio when they [Carr and Blackwell] were recording to look at their lead sheets; he became known as the 'studio ghost'" (Anon., n.d.).

Whether a commercially recorded blues song was carefully written down and rehearsed or more or less improvised in the recording studio is difficult to determine from listening to the resulting recording. Certainly, as will be demonstrated, from the point of view of formulaic structure, there seems to be no difference in this respect. For example, one would imagine that Robert Johnson would be a good improviser of the blues because of his "down home" style of performance, yet alternative takes of his recorded songs are almost identical to each other, indicating that he either worked from written texts or memorized every word of his songs before stepping into the recording studio. What is even more surprising is the fact that even in nonrecording contexts, Johnson shunned spontaneous versification, as David "Honeyboy" Edwards recalled:

> He didn't change his numbers much. Just like he'd play his first number he recorded, he's play it the same way all the time. Every number that he played, it was just like he played it the same way all the time. He never would do no changing much. He could play lots of numbers he had never put on record, some songs that he'd make up, or some of the old records that guys call for that somebody else had recorded. Just like we'd do. Request a song. But on his own he would play his own numbers. People liked them. (Welding, 1968, p. 9)

It seems that Johnson was quite aware of how recordings tended to solidify the blues tradition.

While the antecedents to the commercially recorded blues were primarily forms of oral literature, the same cannot be said of blues songs composed for the purpose of commercial recording. The commercial blues is certainly a good example of what Foley called "orally derived" literary poetry (1981a, pp. 129–31), and whether its formulaic structure is a result of its oral roots or not (a question that I discuss later), the commercially recorded blues is a literary formulaic form of poetry.

The overall definition of the blues under analysis in this study (that is, the commercially recorded blues) includes the following features: its texture is the rhymed couplet in which each line is interrupted by a caesura; its text might best be described as a love lyric; its context is the recording studio; and its form of composition is, in a majority of cases, a written, rehearsed, nonspontaneous poetic creation.

* * *

In the introduction, I outlined the source of the corpus under analysis. All blues examples in the following chapters come from that source (unless otherwise stated), and all of the examples conform to the definition given earlier. Consequently, my analysis is concerned with the essential component of the blues—the blues couplet. I have not included an analysis of refrains (unless they conformed to the blues couplet structure), spoken interjections, or other parts of the lyrics that lie outside the blues couplet structure. For example, my analysis of those vaudeville blues, in which the blues couplet is embedded in another form of song, covers only those parts of the songs that take a blues couplet form.

Essentially, then, this analysis is not of the blues song but of the blues couplet. In most of the examples that I will give, I have reduced blues stanzas to their basic couplet form. This means that I have eliminated repeated A or B lines for the purpose of clear transcriptions. In this matter, I have followed the transcription methodology that I used in my anthology of this corpus (Taft, 2005). Where the repetitions of a line contain substantial variations, however, I have transcribed the repetitions to show these variations.

I have not tried to reproduce pronunciation, emphasis, or other such phonological features in these transcriptions, and I have not opted for an "Uncle Remus"–type reproduction of these lyrics. My aim was to reproduce the lyrics as accurately as possible but also as clearly as possible (for a more detailed discussion of my transcription methods, see Taft, 1984, p. xiii). In those instances where I could not decipher lyrics, I have used a series of three question marks (???). Where I was unsure of a transcription, I have enclosed that transcription in asterisks (*).

CHAPTER 2

Defining the Blues Formula

Whether improvised before the microphone or meticulously written down and memorized, blues lyrics conform to one structural pattern: they are formulaic, and the basic unit of blues composition is the whole-line or half-line formula. The idea, however, that blues lyrics are made up of formulaic units is not new. In fact, most scholars who have commented on blues lyrics recognized, either tacitly or explicitly, its formulaic structure. Not all used the word *formula* in describing this phenomenon, and not all were in agreement on the size or nature of the basic formulaic unit in the blues. But all recognized that there was a traditional storehouse of lyrical material on which singers drew in constructing their songs.

As early as 1911, Odum used the term *formula* in describing blues-like work songs:

> The real work song, and that from which many of the negro songs originally sprang, is the work song phrase. The formulas by which they "pull together" are often simple expressions of word or phrase originated in communal work. (1911, p. 389)

Longini also used the term and gave examples of formulas in the blues, although she saw the formula not so much as the basic structural unit of the blues but rather as a filler or stopgap in an otherwise innovative song form: "Further changes are wrought thus: if in the singing of a song, a line is forgotten, pat phrases or formulas are inserted, e.g. 'that's all right mama, that's all right for you, just anything you do,' or 'I believe to my soul'"(1939, p. 97n). Brown also used the term *formula* when he wrote that "formulas of loving and leaving are numerous" in the blues (1953, p. 289), but whether he was referring to lyric structure or simply to poetic imagery is difficult to determine.

The majority of blues scholars, however, have not used the term *formula*. Van Vechten called these units "favorite phrases" (1925, p. 57), whereas Niles preferred the terms "common property line" (1926a, p. 292) and "common property verses" (1926b, p. 10). Chase referred to "current tag lines strung together in the moment of improvisation" (1955, p. 453), while Oster resorted to an architectural metaphor: "the basic element of the blues ... are standardized bricks which can be used to construct a wide variety of buildings" (1969a, p. 267).

Some writers had a rather low opinion of blues formulas, believing that their repetitive, noninnovative nature indicated bad poetry. Ames (1951, p. 167), Oliver (1968, p. 42), and Calt (1973, p. 25) revealed their feelings toward the formula by using the rather pejorative term *cliché*. Still others acknowledged the presence of formulas only tacitly in their comparative notes. For example, Odum and Johnson noted analogous lines and phrases between one song and another (1926), while White showed how the phrase "a good looking woman" was used in conjunction with various end-of-line formulas in different blues (1928, pp. 313–15). In his notes to Charley Patton's recorded repertoire, Fahey pointed out many analogous phrases in other recorded songs, but as with Odum and Johnson, and White, he did not explicitly label these structural units (1970, pp. 72–107).

Just as there has been little agreement on what to call these basic structural units, there have been a number of opinions as to how large a section of the blues lyric constitutes this basic element of composition. Words, phrases, lines, and stanzas all have been called formulaic by one writer or another. The following passage is indicative of the fuzziness and imprecision that has marked studies of the blues formula:

> Blues was an improvised music in which singers created either their own songs or new versions of old songs by impromptu imagination, free association, and the use of what folklorists call "floating" verses (lines that crop up time and again in a wide variety of songs), for example: "I'm a poor boy, long ways from

home," "Laughing just to keep from crying," and "I got a woman, she's six feet tall/Sleeps in the kitchen with her head in the hall." (Roberts, 1972, p. 181)

Note that the above writer first chose a line, then a half line, and finally an entire stanza as examples of formulas; furthermore, it is not at all clear what he meant by "verse" in this context.

This imprecision is common. In one article, Ames wrote that the blues is composed of "traditional phrases" (1950, p. 202), while in another he included words as well as phrases in his definition of blues formulas, giving the following potpourri as examples of basic units: "'Don't you leave me here,' 'mistreat,' 'lonesome,' 'worry my mind,' 'how long?' 'weary,' 'call my name,' 'baby,' 'man of mine,' 'can't keep from crying,' 'too damn mean to cry,' 'hung his head and cried'" (1943, p. 250). Similar vague descriptions have been given by such writers as Clar (1960, p. 173), Evans (1974, p. 245), Kamin (1965, p. 55), Keil (1966, pp. 52, 71), Newton (1959, p. 157), Oliver (1965, pp. 5–6), and Jarrett (1984, pp. 161–62).

Other scholars settled on the stanza alone as the basic unit of blues composition, although, again, because most of them used the more imprecise term *verse*, it is difficult to know exactly what they had in mind. Guy B. Johnson described the stanzaic formula rather colorfully: "Like certain modern household appliances, which are 'guaranteed to fit any standard fixture,' these stanzas are available for adoption into any song which they happen to fit" (1935, pp. 552–53). Two other scholars resorted to biology in writing of a "'genetic pool' of verses" (Kent and Stewart, n.d.), while Charters (1963, pp. 6, 23), Roxin (1973, p. 10), and White (1928–29, p. 207) also described the stanza as the basic unit, though in less flamboyant terms.

Ferris (1970a) was the most articulate proponent of the blues stanza as the basic formulaic unit, although at the same time he perceived part stanzas or half lines as being units in themselves. He called these part stanzas "commonplaces," however, and did not discuss them as integral units of blues structure. The very fact that Ferris recognized traditional units smaller than the stanza (i.e., the "commonplace") seems to work against his theory that the stanza is the basic structural unit; Pearson's review of Ferris made this very criticism (1972, p. 194). Evans has also tended to see the stanza as the essential formulaic unit of the blues, although in his major work *Big Road Blues* (1982), he shied away from any detailed, structural formulaic analysis beyond pointing out, throughout his work, that blues singers continually borrow stanzas and parts of stanzas from one another in composing their blues.

Ferris and Evans were two of many who failed to look beyond the blues stanza in the search for the formula. For example, Oster, in the notes to one of the songs in his collection, wrote, "The second to last stanza affords a significant example of how a blues singer often takes a standard verse and alters it slightly to fit his own personal situation" (1969b, p. 323). The "slight" alteration was, in fact, the substitution of one half-line formula for another.

Such vague and imprecise theories stem from a lack of rigorous and detailed analysis of blues lyrics. Most scholars merely paid lip service to the "traditional storehouse of lines, phrases, and verses" in the blues and then went on to discuss aspects of the blues that were of greater interest to them. Compared to what scholars have attempted and accomplished in the study of epic poetry, what blues scholars have done is little more than state a hypothesis.

This is not to say that blues scholars have not been urged to pursue their gut reactions. In a review of Lord's *The Singer of Tales*, D.K. Wilgus wrote, "The investigator may well find closer analogies [to Lord's formulaic system] in blues and even blues ballads" (1961, p. 44), but no one answered his challenge. Similarly, Bruce Jackson called for a rigorous formulaic analysis:

> The structural units in Negro folksong are the metaphor and line, not the plot or part of plot. Instead of weaving narrative elements to create a story, the Negro song accumulates images to create a feeling. ... Negro songs *are* formulaic, however, and the study of the incidence and configurations of formulae would be profitable, if arduous. (1965, p. xi, emphasis in original)

Oliver also called for "greater study" of the blues formula (1968, p. 189), while Wolfe specifically proposed an index of blues formulas (1971–72, pp. 159–60).

The formula has received more detailed attention from at least two analysts. Titon devoted a chapter in his book to the subject (1977, pp. 178–93) and, unlike Ferris, was more rigorous in his use of linguistic, generative theory to explain variations in formulas. Yet his analysis is only a few pages, while the bulk of his chapter is concerned with the meaning of the formulas rather than their structure. Titon was considerably more rigorous in his analysis of the structure of blues music (1977, pp. 138–77), his description of blues lyric structure suffering by comparison. John Barnie (1978a, 1978b) followed Titon's lead in his analyses of the blues formula, but his studies concentrated on a few formulas only, rather than on developing an overall, systematic description of blues formulaic structure. Research in this area by both Titon and Barnie might best be described as cursory and preliminary.

The problem is that any orderly description of this aspect of the blues involves the quantitative analysis of a huge corpus of material. As Evans wrote, "There are thousands of traditional textual and musical elements altogether, and no comprehensive attempt has ever been made to organize this body of material for study" (1982, p. 145). Choosing a small number of texts, or choosing a limited number of formulas, for analysis will lead only to a limited understanding of the formulaic system. In the more general area of formulaic scholarship, Duggan rightly objected to poetic samples that were too small, too concentrated, or random (1973, p. 19). Similarly, Spraycar and Dunlap have found serious statistical flaws in small corpus formulaic studies; their contention is that as an analytic sample approaches the size of the entire corpus of a poetic tradition, the results of formulaic analysis become more accurate and meaningful (Spraycar, 1981; Spraycar and Dunlap, 1982).

Duggan's solution as he applied it to his formulaic study of the *Chanson de Roland* was a computer analysis of the lyrics (1969); more specifically, he used a computer-generated concordance to reorder the medieval French epic so that he could see linguistic variations and congruencies in the text. Likewise, Foley has devised a computer program for generating formulaic analyses in a variety of different poetic forms (1985). In a sense, both Titon (1977, p. 181) and Evans (1982, p. 145) have awaited the present study for a full, rigorous, and computerized analysis of the blues formulaic system.

It is evident that for the purposes of this study, the concept of the blues formula must be clearly and rigorously defined. Although formulaic scholarship, in general, has existed for well over one hundred years (Hainsworth, 1968, pp. 4–5), there is no one definition of the term *formula* on which all scholars agree. The disagreements are caused, in part, by the different types of poetry that have been studied as formulaic systems: classical Greek epics, Old English and Middle English verse, and modern Yugoslavian epics, among others. Obviously, different kinds of poetry require different types of formulaic structures.

It is not my intention to construct a paradigm that will describe all formulaic systems, nor is it my aim to establish the only possible definition of the blues formula. Different approaches to blues scholarship require different definitions of blues structure. Thematic criteria might be of primary importance for some types of analyses, while folk categories might be more significant for other studies. Because the aim of this study is to show how commercial blues artists constructed their songs,

I will establish an operational definition of the formula that will be of the most use in this type of analysis. Even within the boundaries of this study, however, an inflexible paradigm is impossible, because, as will be shown, the formula is a theoretical construction that may be shaped, to some extent, to fit particular structural analyses.

All the various definitions of the formula are based on the concept of recurring patterns of speech within a poetic form. The length of these patterns, their linguistic properties, and their functions within the text, however, have been subject to various interpretations. In whatever ways earlier scholars defined the formula, Milman Parry's definition has been the traditional starting point for modern formulaic studies:

> In the diction of bardic poetry, the formula can be defined as an expression regularly used, under the same metrical conditions, to express an essential idea. What is essential in an idea is what remains after all stylistic superfluity has been taken from it. (1928, p. 11)

Since 1928, however, scholars have stretched and twisted this definition beyond anything Parry might have recognized, as H.L. Rogers pointed out:

> Parry's "regularly employed," itself unsatisfactory, has been interpreted to mean "approximately repeated." Parry's "under the same metrical conditions" has been interpreted to mean "under no metrical conditions." Parry's definition of the formula as a "group of words," one finds, has also been relaxed: on the one hand, it is held to include single words; on the other, it is extended to cover not only lexical features (collocations), but grammatical features as well. (1966, p. 98)

In an attempt to make the definition of the formula more exacting, some scholars have made use of linguistic theories and terminologies. In this way, they hoped to eliminate many of the vagaries in Parry's definition. The use of linguistic terminologies alone, however, does not ensure a clear and unambiguous definition. Note the following passage:

> The formula is a habitual collocation, metrically defined, and is thus a stylization of something which is fundamental to linguistic expression, namely the expectation that a sequence of words will show lexical congruity, together with (and as a condition of) lexical and grammatical complementarity. (Quirk, 1963, pp. 150–51)

Quirk's concept of "lexical congruity" or for that matter of what is "fundamental to linguistic expression" is as vague and variable as Parry's nonlinguistic criteria. Other scholars, however, have been much more precise in determining when two phrases may be seen as members of the same formula. These scholars may be grouped into two linguistic schools: those who define the formula primarily by its syntactic properties and those who define the formula primarily by its semantic properties.

The "syntax school" of formula scholars (called "syntacticians" by Foley, 1981b, p. 67) sees sentence structure as the main criterion for regarding two phrases as members of the same formula or formula group. One of the earliest proponents of this school was Waldron, who, in describing the structure of Middle English alliterative verse, conceived of generalized formulas with innumerable lexical substitutions: for example, "as soon as the (NOUN)(VERB)" or "the first (NOUN) that he (VERB)" (1957, pp. 798–99). Creed similarly defined the Old English formula as a "syntactic entity" made up of "an article and its noun, or a noun or pronoun and its verb, or a verb and its object" (1959, p. 446). Fry described Old English formulaic systems using the same model as Waldron and stated quite categorically that "formulas of a system are related semantically only in the loosest sense" (1967, p. 203; see also Gattiker, 1962). The syntactic school of Old English scholars continues to have its proponents (see, for example, Bolton, 1985), and at least one scholar has proposed that syntactic features are the basis of blues formulas (Jarrett, 1978, pp. 32–36). Linguist Kiparsky (1976) also took the syntactic position in his study of Homeric epics; his exploration of the similarities between idiomatic speech and epic formulas was perhaps the most fruitful of all the syntactic investigations, but his study suffers from a lack of semantic considerations.

This disregard for the role of semantics in the definition of the formula has not gone unnoticed. Hainsworth wrote, "I conclude that very severe difficulties must be surmounted before it will be possible to make sentence structure the sole criterion of formulaic status" (1964, p. 160), while others have been less charitable in their objections to the syntax school (Green, 1971, p. 92n; Minton, 1965; H.L. Rogers, 1966, p. 102).

The problem with the syntactic definition of formulas is not that such patterns do not exist in poetry but that syntactic patterns are not peculiar to a poetic form; rather they are patterns inherent in the language itself. Finlayson made this very point:

> To speak about a syntactic grammatical structure as the "mould" into which meaning can be poured is to say no more than that the English language has a discernable syntactic

structure. The phrase, "I shall ... the (you) ... ," is a formula only in the sense that any phrase or sentence is a formula. All language is in this sense a formula. (1963, p. 375; see also Rogers, 1966, p. 100)

Those of the syntax school have failed to realize that the pattern that is specific to a poetic form is a subset of the rules of language—a language within a language—and it is this subset of linguistic rules wherein the definition of the formula lies. Lord, in discussing Yugoslavian epic poetry, made this point when he wrote, "In studying the patterns and systems of oral narrative verse we are in reality observing the 'grammar' of the poetry, a grammar superimposed, as it were, on the grammar of the language concerned" (1960, pp. 35–36), while Ashby, writing on the *Chanson de Roland,* stated, "The singer mastered a poetic language or set of rules which govern formula production" (1979, p. 41). Others have similarly realized this basic fact, as it applies to Old English poetry, modern English balladry, and American folk sermons (Conner, 1972; Buchan, 1972, p. 146; Rosenberg, 1970b, p. 15, respectively).

Bearing this in mind, a scholar's approach to formulaic analysis should not be purely linguistic but be more properly stylistic, because stylistics is the study of special subsets of language. This language within a language may very well have special syntactic rules; that is, a poetic form may include sentence structures that would be considered odd or incorrect in everyday speech, but this is not always the case. As in the case of American folk sermons, blues lyrics exhibit few, if any, extraordinary sentence constructions. Poetic language, however, is almost always made up of images and ideas that are usually not associated with everyday language. Epics abound with descriptions of heroic deeds and fantastic events; folk sermons deal with religious symbols and images; blues lyrics are concerned mostly with love. It is the poet's need to continually articulate these select images and ideas within a restricted poetic form that gives rise, in some cases, to formulas: recurrent patterns of language that evoke certain word pictures, sentiments, or philosophies.

The aspect of language that carries the bulk of imagery is its semantic structure. The semantics school of formulaic study is smaller than the syntax school, but significantly the arguments of its proponents were concurrent with those of the syntax scholars. In reference to Homeric epic, Whitman defined the formula quite simply as "a semantic unit identified with a metrical demand" (1958, p. 109). Following Whitman's lead,

Wayne A. O'Neil applied semantic criteria to his definition of the formula in Old English poetry (1960a). Nagler proposed that each individual formulaic phrase in Homeric poetry be considered an "allomorph, *not of any other existing phrase,* but of some central Gestalt," which clearly calls for semantic rather than syntactic analysis (1967, p. 281, emphasis in original). Likewise, Ashby has looked to "sememes" as the basis of medieval French epic formulas (1979, p. 48), while Schwetman has reiterated the semantic nature of Old English poetic formulas (1980, p. 98).

In this all-too-brief survey of formulaic theory, it is interesting to look back to Parry's definition once more. Although he did not use linguistic terminology, his conception of the formula as expressing "an essential idea" clearly puts him in the semantics school. Essential idea or meaning is discovered through semantic, rather than syntactic, analyses. Thus, despite more than seventy years of defining and redefining the formula, scholars have done little better (and in some cases far worse) than did Milman Parry in getting at the heart of the formula.

The blues formula is a semantic unit. More specifically, each blues formula is composed of at least one complete semantic predication. Leech described a predication in the following manner: "If a sentence (according to traditional definition) 'expresses a complete thought,' then a predication can be informally characterized as a 'complete thought' that a sentence expresses" (1974, p. 90; see also his detailed discussion, pp. 126–56). A predication is composed of at least one predicate and up to two arguments and might be visualized in a hierarchical tree diagram in which the predication (PN) is shown to include within its structure one or two arguments (A1 and A2) and a predicate (P):

PN

A1   P   A2

In turn, each predicate and argument is composed of a number of semantic features that ultimately generate a word or phrase from the speaker's lexicon. In the following diagram, only a few of the possible semantic features are represented:

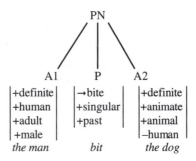

Although a predication might look like a "simple sentence," it should not be thought of as one. A predication may indeed be expressed, syntactically, as a simple sentence, where arguments are nouns and the predicate is a verb, but it may also take the form of an adverbial, adjectival, prepositional, or noun phrase. To understand this, one must realize that a predicate names any relationship between two arguments, whether that relationship involves a subject and object linked by a verb:

the man *bit* the dog,
I *walked* to town;

A prepositional relationship:

the house *on* the hill,
a tale *of* two cities,
a man *about* town;

A coordinating conjunction relationship:

to *and* fro,
John *and* Mary,
tired *but* happy,
good *or* bad;

A subordinating conjunction relationship:

fire *when* ready,
I would run *if* I were able;

or any other relationship between two arguments. Note in these examples that the arguments linked in a relationship by the predicate do not have to be nouns but can be any part of speech, from verbs to adverbs to entire clauses. I will describe different manifestations of this semantic structure later, but for now it is important to know that the fundamental formulaic unit of the blues is the semantic predication.

If the blues formula is a predication, how is it expressed within the confines of the poetic structure? Parry and Whitman, among others, defined the formula in terms of its metrical function within the poem, but the blues is rather free of metrical constraints. The blues formula may be defined, therefore, not by its "metrical demand" but by its placement within the blues line.

To make this clear, briefly review the structure of the blues couplet. It is made up of two lines that rhyme with each other, each line is divided into two half lines by a caesura, and each line comprises at least one complete thought without any enjambment from one line to the next. The following couplet is typical:

1   I walked from Dallas; I walked to Wichita Falls
    After I lost my sugar, I wasn't going to walk at all
    (Blind Lemon Jefferson, 1926a)

The formula, because it is a predication (one complete thought), always remains within the confines of one blues line. In a majority of cases, there are two formulas for each line, corresponding roughly to the two half lines of the stanzaic structure. This is the case with couplet 1. The first half line contains a complete formula, which might be represented by the following, simplified semantic diagram:

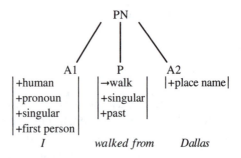

A similar representation can be made for the three other formulas in couplet 1: *I walked to Wichita Falls, I lost my sugar,* and *I wasn't going to walk at all.* (I discuss the role of the word *after* and the subordination of the first clause in the second line in chapter 4.)

This arrangement of the formulas in the lines automatically separates the types of blues formulas into two positional categories: those that contain a rhyme word and those that don't. These types of formulas might be labeled "r-formulas" for those that carry the rhyme and "x-formulas" for the others. Couplet 1 might thus be represented in the following manner, according to the types of formulas in the stanza:

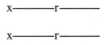

Because rhyme is essential to the blues stanza, it follows that every blues line must contain one r-formula. The x-formula, however, though present in the great majority of blues lines, is optional. Note the following blues couplet:

2 Take one more drink; make me tell it all
   Somebody stole my little all in all
   (Mississippi Bracey, 1930)

Although the second line of this example exhibits the usual half-line caesura (after the word *Somebody*), there is present only one predication and thus only one formula, an r-formula:

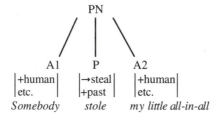

The formula positions in couplet 2 might be represented as follows:

Blues couplets composed of only two formulas also occur, although they are not as plentiful as the kinds of couplets described previously. Note the following example:

3   And when I'm feeling lonesome and blue
    My baby know just what to do
    (Papa Charlie Jackson, 1926b)

Couplet 3 contains the minimum two r-formulas necessary for a well-formed blues couplet.

These three examples describe most blues couplets. Two other categories of formula placement also exist, although their occurrence is rare. One category is the blues couplet in which one of the lines is nothing more than a moan or hum, devoid of linguistic structure (although certainly not meaning):

4   Mmmmm mmmmm
    Lord I walked all last night, and all last night before
    (Texas Alexander, 1928a)

The line carrying linguistic information may be composed of either an x-formula and r-formula, as in couplet 4, or simply an r-formula.

The other category consists of blues lines that contain more than one x-formula before the r-formula. Because of the complexity involved in fitting three or more formulas, and therefore three or more complete thoughts, within the short space of a blues line, this "crowding" is quite rare:

5 When I start drinking, I'm mean and hateful; and I won't treat nobody right
I just keeps on walking; looking for places, where they fuss and fight
(J.T. Funny Paper Smith, 1931a)

Couplet 5 can be divided into at least six predications: *I start drinking, I'm mean and hateful, I won't treat nobody right, I just keeps on walking,* [I'm] *looking for places,* and *where they fuss and fight.* In terms of formula placement, the couplet looks like this:

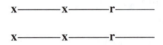

In some ways, this couplet is like the hypometric (or metrically crowded) lines in Old English poetry, which Nicholson similarly described as being overstocked with formulas (1963). The lax metric rules of blues verse, however, allow such crowding to occur without any damage to normal poetic scansion.

How does one know whether two phrases are members of the same or different formulas? As I will show, the exact boundaries of any given formula are fluid, but one criterion for distinguishing between one formula and the next is the placement of predications within the couplet. It is not enough that the same or similar groups of words be "regularly employed" or "appear three or more times" to qualify as being members of the same formula. They must also fulfill the same function within the overall poetic structure of the song. Note the following two couplets:

6 *I walked away,* and I wrang my hands and cried
Didn't have no blues; I couldn't be satisfied
(Edward Thompson, 1929a)

7 Mmm I fold my arms, and *I walked away*
That's all right mama; your troubles will come some day
(Son House, 1930a)

Both couplets include the predication *I walked away*, but these two phrases cannot be classified as members of the same formula. Although their semantic, syntactic, and lexical structures are virtually identical, they fulfill different functions within their respective couplets: in couplet 6 the phrase is an x-formula, while in couplet 7 the phrase is an r-formula.

The phrase is couplet 7 carries the rhyme of the stanza, whereas the same phrase in couplet 6 is free of this function. Just as metrical and alliterative constraints determine the definition and boundaries of formulas in Old English poetry and Homeric epics, the factor of rhyme is of prime importance in placing phrases within the same formula in the blues. An x-formula may undergo certain syntactic transformations (to be discussed later) that would be impossible for an r-formula, because the r-formula must always retain its rhyme word in its final position. Put in another way, the blues singer was confronted with different choices and possibilities when composing the first half of a line than when composing the second half. For two phrases to be members of the same formula, they must be mutually replaceable, and an x-formula cannot replace an r-formula.

For much the same reasons, two phrases in the r-formula position might not be members of the same formula, even if they are synonymous. Note the following two couplets:

8   The woman I love, she must be out of town
     She left me this morning *with a face that's full of frowns*
     (Blind Lemon Jefferson, 1927c)

9   She carried a razor in her pocket *with them frowns all in her face*
     Lord I believe some other good joker trying to root me out of my
     place
     (Walter Davis, 1935d)

The italicized phrases in these two couplets are virtually synonymous, with the only major difference being syntactic reordering. This reordering, however, places different rhyme words at the ends of these two phrases: *frowns* in couplet 8 and *face* in couplet 9. This difference, in turn, means that these two phrases require different rhyme sounds in their respective accompanying lines in the couplet: *town* in couplet 8 and *place* in couplet 9. Because of this rhyme difference, these two phrases are not mutually replaceable, and therefore they are not members of the same formula. Once blues singers chose a particular rhyme sound in the first line in the couplet, their options in the second line became channeled toward a particular subset of r-formulas in the matching line.

Note that in couplets 8 and 9, aside from everything else, the italicized phrases occur in two different r-positions: the second line in couplet 8 and the first line in couplet 9. This difference by itself, however, would not disqualify the two phrases from belonging to the same formula. I discuss the differences between the two lines of a couplet in chapter 4, but suffice it to say that any given x-formula will function equally well in either x-position, and that any given r-formula will function equally well in either r-position. The italicized phrases in the following two couplets are both members of the same formula:

10   Well poor Joe leaving this morning; *my face is full of frowns*
     I got a mean stepfather, and my dear mother she don't allow me
     around
     (Big Joe Williams, 1935e)

11   Oh well where were you now, baby, Clarksdale mill burned
     down
     I was way down Sunflower *with my face all full of frowns*
     (Charley Patton, 1930b)

A more difficult problem in identifying the boundaries of a formula occurs when examining the internal structure of phrases. No modern scholar conceives of formulas as exact, word-for-word repetitions; rather it is commonly assumed that individual manifestations of a formula might vary slightly in word order, tense, modification, and lexis. The problem lies in determining how much variation can occur between one phrase and another before they can no longer be called members of the same formula.

With every change in the semantic, syntactic, or lexical structure of a phrase, no matter how slight, there is a change in meaning. The formula, therefore, must be perceived not as having one exact meaning but as having a more general meaning that can be modified, embellished, or otherwise altered. What must remain is the essence of the formula—Parry's "essential idea"—however that is to be defined. As Diamond put it, "Any word added [to a formula] must alter the meaning as little as possible" (1963, p. 7), but how little is "little"?

Parry, as previously noted, was aware that certain parts of a phrase are more essential to its overall meaning than are others. The "stylistic superfluity" that he described is made up of the conjunctions, adverbs, adjectives, and other "small" modifiers that usually add little to the essential meaning of a phrase (see as well Parry, 1930, p. 272). In poetry that is metrically constrained, these modifiers tend to be unstressed or unimportant to the metric structure, as Cassidy ably showed for Old English verse (1965, p. 76). Like Cassidy, several scholars have tried to deal with the problem of how little is little by establishing a hierarchy of formulas, formula systems, formulaic themes, and type scenes in an attempt to order these phrase variations on a scale of "slight" to "major" (see especially Parry, 1932, p. 329; Lord, 1938, 1951; Fry, 1967, 1968). I discuss the drawbacks to these hierarchies later, but first it is important to describe some of the typical variations that occur within a blues formula.

Among the most common variations within a formula are changes in inflection. The tense and modification of verbs within a formula are quite variable; in fact, there seem to be no special stylistic rules governing which verb inflections are permitted in the blues. Note the treatment of the verb change in these examples of the formula *I change my mind:*

12 Baby, fix me one more drink, and hug your daddy one more time
    Keep on spilling my malted milk, mama, until *I change my mind*
    (Robert Johnson, 1937d)

13 I started to Heaven, but *I changed my mind*
    But I'm going to Little Rock, where I can have a better time
    (Pearl Dickson, 1927)

14 Now you don't want me, when I was treating you nice and kind
    Now it's too late, baby; *I have changed my mind*
    (Bill Jazz Gillum, 1941a)

15 I used to try to love you, baby; a loving you *in crime*
    Some day you going to want to love the poor boy, and *I'll be done
    changed my mind*
    (Willie Lofton, 1934)

16 Well but some day, some day, people, *I'm going to change my
    mind*
    Well now I'm going to stop running at women, and staying drunk
    all the time
    (Sonny Boy Williamson, 1938h)

It seems that any tense or form of verb is acceptable in blues formulas, including dialectical constructions such as "will be done changed."

Similarly, nouns may be singular or plural within a formula without changing the essential meaning of that formula, even if those words are rhyme words, because pluralizing does not generally alter rhyme in the blues (Taft, 1978, p. 59). Note the word *dress* in the following two couplets:

17 She pulls her *dress* up above her knees
    She shakes her shimmy to who she please
    (Sam Collins, 1931a)

18 Pull your *dresses* above your knees
    Sell your stuff to who you please
    (Joe McCoy, 1936b)

Note the word *knee* in the following couplets:

19 Mmmmm hear my lonesome plea
    I'm worried about my baby; down on my bended *knee*
    (King Solomon Hill, 1932c)

20 Oh babe, oh baby, down on my bended *knees*
    Begging you now, baby; don't leave me please
    (Walter Davis, 1941)

And note the word *ring* in these couplets:

21 I bought all her clothes; I bought her a diamond *ring*
    Then along come a fat mouth; keep me shaking that thing
    (Charlie Jackson, 1927a)

22 I ain't going to buy you no more pretty dresses; I ain't going to
    even buy you no diamond *rings*
    And I'm going to sell my V-Eight Ford, because I don't want a
    doggone thing
    (Sonny Boy Williamson, 1939)

(I discuss later the negative inserted in couplet 22.)

As stated earlier, formulas may undergo changes in word order, especially x-formulas, where there is no need to keep a specific rhyme word at the end of the phrase. These syntactic changes follow the usual transformational rules of linguistics, which generate surface-level sentences from deeper syntactic structures; thus, the following italicized phrases are all surface structures generated from a deep syntactic structure that might be represented as *time come*:

23 *And the time coming;* it's going to be so
    You can't make the winter, babe, just dry long so
    (Robert Johnson, 1936c)

24 *There come a time;* I can't say no more
    I'll be a hearsing out my door
    (Joe McCoy, 1934a)

25 I love my man; tell the cockeyed world I do
    It's coming a time, that he'll sure love me too
    (Minnie Wallace, 1935)

Syntactic reordering can also occur in r-formulas, however, as long as the rhyme word maintains its final position:

26 And I stay at home, baby; *you don't treat me right*
    The best time I have, girl, when you's out of my sight
    (Gus Cannon, 1928)

27 Tell my dad I won't be home tonight
    My heart aches; said *I'm not treated right*
    (Gertrude Ma Rainey, 1926b)

The highlighted formula in couplet 27 exhibits syntactic reordering after undergoing a passive transformation, yet the rhyme word *right* remains at the end of the phrase.

Further variations occur in the type of sentence generated from the deep structure formula; that is, the same formula might be expressed as a declarative, interrogative, or imperative sentence:

28 I wring my hands, baby, and I want to scream
    And I woke up; I found it was all a dream
    (Skip James, 1931f)

29 *Did you ever wake up,* twixt night and day
    Had your arm around your pillow, where your good gal used to lay
    (Charley Lincoln, 1927c)

30   *Wake up, baby;* please don't be so still
      Unless you fixing a good way to get your daddy killed
      (Clifford Gibson, 1929e)

I previously noted that the predications that underlie formulas should not be thought of as simple sentences. A further kind of formulaic variation illustrates this point: a formula might generate a complete sentence or only a part of a more complex sentence. Note the following two couplets:

31   You know the baby kitten jumped up, oh and began to whine
      You know he didn't know the racket, but *he had the same thing on his mind*
      (Charlie Burse, 1934)

32   Got up this morning with *the same thing on my mind*
      And the girl I'm loving, but she don't pay me no mind
      (Big Bill Broonzy, 1930a)

These couplets show the use of the same formula as a sentence or at least an independent clause complete with subject and predicate (couplet 31) and as a complex prepositional phrase within the predicate of another sentence (couplet 32). This kind of formulaic variation is often a function of how the singer joins two half lines, which I discuss in greater detail later.

Up to this point I have described only slight variations in a formula. Changes in inflection, syntax, or sentence type have little effect on the essential meaning of a phrase. More profound changes occur, however, when one word is substituted for another in the same formula. Other formula scholars have recognized this type of substitution, but such variations have been the source of most of their disagreements over the boundaries and definitions of the formula.

In general, these word substitutions might be termed "slot fillers," in which a "slot" in the formula can be filled by a number of different, but related, words. These words must have certain semantic features in common, but what these features are has been open to considerable argument. Parry, as usual, the pioneer in formulaic theory, recognized these slot fillers as early as 1928, when he described formulas such as "and X replied" and "X answered him" (1928, pp. 10, 14). The "X" was a slot to be filled by the appropriate proper name. Magoun, following Parry's lead, applied the same slot-filling theory to Old English (1953, p. 450), and Magoun's student, Creed, expanded on the Old English slot-filling system by showing how different human subjects could fit the "x *answarode*" formula (1957). Similarly, Lord described slot filling in Yugoslavian epics (1960, p. 35), while Rosenberg described the same phenomenon in American folk sermons (1970a, pp. 49–50), and McCulloh applied slot-filling theory to American lyric folk-song clusters (1970, p. 73).

In the blues, slot filling acts in much the same way as it does in other formulaic poetries. The parts of the formulaic predication most open to slot filling are arguments, especially those arguments that regularly generate nouns in the surface structure of the formula. Note the italicized formula in the following two couplets sung by Blind Lemon Jefferson:

33 Mmmmm *Papa Lemon's feeling so blue*
   Eagle eyed mama's worrying me; what am I going to do
   (Blind Lemon Jefferson, 1929a)

34 Sometime I feel disgusted, and *I feel so blue*
   I hardly know what in this world, baby, a good man can do
   (Blind Lemon Jefferson, 1928f)

The persona in couplet 33 is Papa Lemon, which is most likely equivalent to the "I" in couplet 34; the singer merely chose to fill the argument slot in X—"feel so blue"—with a pronoun in the second couplet.

The italicized formula in the following example is almost always filled by the pronoun in its surface manifestations:

35 I'm going away; *it won't be long*
   I know you'll miss me from singing this lonesome song
   (Lottie Beaman, 1928)

The *it* stands for *time* in this formula, and though *time* rarely fills the slot in surface manifestations, such a choice was always open to the singer:

36 Well I'm going away; swear *the time ain't long*
   If you don't believe I'm leaving, daddy, count them days I'm gone
   (Louise Johnson, 1930a)

It might be argued that pronominalization is not true slot filling, because the replacement of a noun by its pronoun is more a syntactic transformation than a clear lexical variation (see Ross, 1967). In fact, Postal (1966) believed that pronouns are generated only at an intermediate syntactic level and are really articles, which brings into question the notion that pronouns are "substitutes" at all. These linguistic niceties, however, mattered little to the singer who clearly had a choice between a noun and its pronoun, no matter how or where the pronoun emerged from the deep structure of the formula.

Of course, the lexical choice in the argument of a formulaic predication can go well beyond simple pronominalization. Note the following two italicized phrases:

37   *I went to the station;* I looked up on the board
     Well my train ain't here, but it's somewhere on the go
     (Tom Dickson, 1928b)

38   *I went to the depot;* I looked up on the board
     And the train had left; went steaming up the road
     (Charley Patton, 1929g)

It seems, from these two examples, that a formula exists that might be represented as *I went to X,* where *X* is defined as "a place where trains stop." The words *station* and *depot* both qualify to fill this slot, and the singer had to make a lexical choice as to which word to use. The choice may have been based on the singer's idiolect or local dialect or on the singer's aesthetic criteria, but whatever the reason, the option was there.

In couplets 37 and 38, the choice is limited to those words that mean "a place where trains stop," but some slots are open to a much wider range of lexical items. For the most part, these slots appear as subjects of surface-level sentences. Note how different singers filled the subject slot in the following examples of *X getting the blues:*

39   *I* got the blues; blue as I can be
     Because these no good gals trying to back bite me
     (Maggie Jones, 1924a)

40   I cut that joker so long, deep and wide
     You got the blues, and still ain't satisfied
     (Mississippi John Hurt, 1928c)

41   When a *woman* gets the blues, she goes to her room and hides
     When a *man* gets the blues, he catches a freight train and rides
     (Clara Smith, 1924e)

The singer could fill the X slot with anything "capable of having the blues," whether it be a human, an animal, or perhaps, in more a figurative sense, an inanimate object. Proper names, pronouns, and many nouns could all fit in the slot without destroying the logic of the phrase. In fact, in couplet 41, it is essential that the X slot be filled by a different lexical item in the two lines, if the stanza is to make sense.

Slot filling might also occur in the predicate of a formula, and indeed in the surface verb. But the verb is the least changeable part of the formula, because it usually carries the bulk of the meaning of the formula. Finlayson pointed out the importance of the verb in Middle English formulaic verse (1963, pp. 379–83); Propp, in discussing the basic structural units of the Russian fairy tale, also recognized that action, rather than personae, was of prime importance (1928, p. 21).

Within limits, however, the singer did have some lexical choice in the verb slot in a formulaic sentence. Note the following couplets:

42 *I woke up this morning;* my good gal was gone
Stood by my bedside, and I hung my head and, hung my head and moaned
(Willie Baker, 1929b)

43 *I got up this morning;* said my morning prayers
Didn't have nobody to speak on my behalf
(Joe McCoy, 1929a)

The two italicized phrases are fairly synonymous, even though the verb is different in each case. The verb *got up* does imply a bit more activity than *woke up;* one might wake up but not necessarily get up out of bed. But in actual usage in the blues, little distinction was made between these two verbs, and both were used in the same stanzaic contexts and by the same singers.

Similar lexical choices appear in the following couplets:

44 *I got the blues so bad,* it hurts my feet to walk
I wouldn't hurt so bad, but it hurt my tongue to talk
(Furry Lewis, 1927d)

45 Lord I woke up this morning; blues all around my bed
Had the blues so bad, mama, till I couldn't raise my head
(Tommy Johnson, 1929a)

They appear as well as in the following two phrases:

46 *My man left me;* he left me feeling bad
He's the best *kind fellow* that I ever had
(Mae Glover, 1929b)

47 *My woman quit me;* got her another man
And the way she had that thing on me, I couldn't raise my hand
(Clifford Gibson, 1929c)

In each of these examples, slight semantic differences might be attached to the individual verbs, but in practice these slot fillers were usually interchangeable.

Given the possibility of slot filling throughout the formulaic predication, it is best to represent the semantic structure of formulas without surface-structure lexical items. Thus, the phrase *I went to the station* might be part of a formula represented by the following generalized predication:

PN

A1   P   A2

|+human||movement→||+place where trains stop|

The A1 argument is a slot that might be filled by any *+human* lexical item: *I, You, My woman, The ticket agent,* and so on. The predicate, P, could conceivably be satisfied by such verbs as *go to, walk to, make for,* or *run to,* among others. The A2 argument, as noted earlier, might generate *station* or *depot.*

If formulas, then, are not bound by specific lexical items, the problem becomes which semantic features in which part of the predication define the limits of variation of any given formula. For example, the phrase *I went to the station* also can be shown to be a part of a more generalized predication:

PN

A1   P   A2

|+human| |movement →| |+place built by humans|

The A2 argument may now generate not only *station* and *depot* but also *house, jail, store,* or any number of other places built by humans. The A2 semantic features might be still further generalized to simply "+place," which would generate everything from buildings to cities to natural geographical locations in the lexical slot. Given such a generalized predication, all of the following phrases might be considered members of the same formula:

48 You press my jumper, my overalls
    Went to the station; meet the Cannonball
    (Sam Collins, 1931c)

49 *I'm going to Tishamingo* to have my hambone boiled
    These Atlanta women done let my hambone spoil
    (Peg Leg Howell, 1926b)

50 He stays out late every night
    Comes back home, and want to fight
    (Maggie Jones, 1924b)

51 *Went up on Kinnesaw Mountain;* gave my horn a blow
    Prettiest girl in Atlanta come stepping up to my door
    (Blind Willie McTell, 1929a)

52 Now what you going to do, babe, your dough roller gone
    Go in your kitchen, Lord, and cook until she come home
    (John Estes, 1929a)

The more generalized the features of the components of a predication, the more inclusive will be the boundaries of the formula. Predications with more specific semantic features telescope into predications with more general semantic features to form a continuum on which formulaic boundaries might be determined. This telescoping phenomenon is what semanticists call "entailment": "A relationship of entailment arises between two assertions whenever (the assertions being otherwise identical) an argument or predicate in one assertion is hyponymous [i.e., included in the meaning of] an argument or predicate in the other" (Leech, 1974, p. 137).

Thus, the clause *I went to the station* might be seen as the initial assertion in a series of entailments:

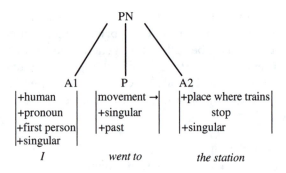

Entails:

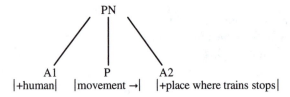

Entails:

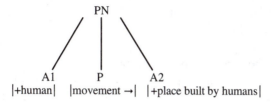

$$\text{A1} \quad \text{P} \quad \text{A2}$$
|+human| |movement →| |+place built by humans|

Entails:

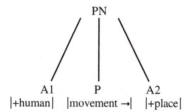

$$\text{A1} \quad \text{P} \quad \text{A2}$$
|+human| |movement →| |+place|

There is no simple answer as to whether these examples are all a part of the same formula. In the sense that they all stem from the same generalized, deep-structure predication, they are all related formulaically, but their differences from one another are also quite obvious. If the analyst is looking at deep-structure semantic similarities, then these examples are all manifestations of one formula; if the analyst is interested in surface-structure similarities, then these examples belong to related but different formulas. This is why the formula is a theoretical construction rather than a well-defined, predetermined structural entity. As Rosenberg wrote, concerning formulas in folk sermons,

> With a fixed text in front of us we can define formulas as precisely or as liberally as we choose, but the singers are not thinking in terms of formulas or systems. One of the problems in defining these terms comes about because they are the scholar's attempts to impose a logical precision, a rationale, and a method where no such logical, rational method exists in the field—the singer's mind. (1975, p. 98)

I am not convinced that there was no method at all behind the composition of the blues. I doubt that there is any "methodless" poetry.

Yet Rosenberg is correct in implying that while scholars have turned themselves inside out trying to define the boundaries of the formula, the singers had no such problems. The blues singers had no need to explain the way they conceived of the formula or what personal rules of composition they used. The difficulty that scholars have faced, however, comes from the fact that they have had to try to generalize from what they have observed in the performances of the individual singers. In effect, scholars have tried to discover the compositional "competence" of the singers, based on blues "performance," to borrow Chomsky's terminology (1965). Yet while linguists have been free to construct hypothetical examples in exploring language competence, blues scholars, in their analyses, have not had the luxury of going beyond the collected performances of blues singers. To begin constructing hypothetical blues songs to explore the formulaic structure of this song form would negate the whole purpose of the endeavor.

There are, however, some clues in blues performances as to how the singers conceived of the boundaries of the formulas they used. For example, the sung repetitions of lines in blues stanzas sometimes exhibit variations that indicate that the singers made certain conscious lexical choices in repeating formulas:

53   Dumb man asked her, *who your man can be*
      Dumb man asked her, *who your regular can be*
      (Ed Bell, 1927a)

54   And that good looking meat *going to carry me to my grave*
      And that good looking meat *going to take me to my grave*
      (Lucille Bogan, 1935a)

55   A look a here, baby, *you going too fast*
      A look a here, baby, *you traveling too fast*
      (Bo Chatman, 1931)

56   If you ever been down, mama, *you know just how I feel*
      If you ever been down, mama, *you know just how a prisoner feel*
      (Bob Coleman, 1929)

57   *When your brown gets funny,* everything you do she gets off
      When your brown acts funny, everything you do she gets off
      (Robert Hicks, 1927b)

58   *I begun to walk;* walked till my feet got soaking wet
     I commenced to walking; walked till my feet got soaking wet
     (Blind Lemon Jefferson, 1927k)

59   *Mozelle you know you like your whisky; don't forget I likes mine*
     too
     Mozelle you know you love your whisky; don't forget I love mine
     too
     (Tommy McClennan, 1942a)

60   *Don't fret and worry; and don't grieve after me*
     Don't grieve and worry; and don't fret after me
     (Blind Willie McTell, 1929e)

61   Now old Bunker Hill, *place that I long to stay*
     Now old Bunker Hill, *place that I wants to stay*
     (Frank Stokes, 1929c)

62   Singing now hey how long *is you going to still do me wrong*
     Singing now hey how long *is you going to still treat me wrong*
     (George Torey, 1937b)

63   I mean now some pretty mama *done run my black snake home*
     I mean now some pretty mama *done drove my black snake home*
     (Louis Washington, 1934b)

64   But some old day, *some old rainy day*
     But some old day, *some old sunny day*
     (Nolan Welsh, 1926b)

65   *I'm going to wake up in the morning;* I believe I'll dust my bed
     Well I'm going to get up in the morning; I believe I'll dust my bed
     (Big Joe Williams, 1941c)

Most of these examples show strong semantic and syntactic similarities between their italicized pairs, and one might assume that the singers conceived of these pairs as being variant manifestations of the same formulas. But again, that is only an assumption. Although it was unusual, singers did alter the repeated line by substituting one formula for another:

66 *Now it's listen here, pretty mama,* a-what is on your mind
    And it's tell me, pretty mama, a-baby, what is on your mind
    Says it looks like you're worried and bothered; grieving, baby, all
    the time
    (Kid Cole, 1928b)

67 Now you men got these women; *oh treat them nice and kind*
    Say you men got these sweet women; *how come you don't be nice
    and kind*
    Because don't you know Little Hat got something; going to change
    your sweet woman's mind
    (Little Hat Jones, 1930c)

The semantic deep structures of these italicized pairs seem quite different, and formula substitution has probably taken place. It is impossible,
therefore, to state categorically that a variation in a repeated phrase in a
blues stanza is caused by slot filling and not formula substitution.

Ultimately, the boundaries of a formula must be determined according to the questions that the analyst wishes to answer. Whether *got
up this morning* and *woke up this morning* are manifestations of the same
formula depends on such questions as the following: How was the concept of "emergence from sleep" expressed in the x-position in the blues?
How did blues singers distinguish between verbs of greater or lesser
action? How did variations in the lexical choice of a surface-structure
verb affect the overall meaning and structure of the blues line, stanza, or
song? Did some individual singers distinguish between *got up* and *woke
up* as these verbs were used in their songs, while others did not?

With each of these questions, it might be necessary for the analyst to
see the two phrases either as members of separate formulas or as manifestations of the same formula. In fact, even slight variations, such as *I
woke up* and *I wake up,* might be seen as two different formulas, if the
analyst wishes to investigate the use of different verb tenses in the blues.
That the formula is flexible and that it is a theoretical construction, however, does not mean that formula study is nothing more than intellectual
game playing. If one has a clear idea of the aspect of blues lyrics that one
wishes to investigate, the boundaries of the blues formula become clear
and the formula becomes a useful analytical tool. For the same reasons,
however, an inflexible hierarchy of formulas, systems, themes, and type
scenes as proposed by some scholars cannot be established. Only a specific analytical focus can determine where to place formula boundaries
on the continuum of a generalized predication.

This explanation of the blues formula has, of necessity, described blues compositional competence. Even though I chose examples from actual performances, I have established general rules for describing an entire corpus of the blues, and such a general description is a description of competence. But as the analysis of blues structure moves from questions of a general nature to questions of a specific nature, compositional performance becomes more important than compositional competence.

Correspondingly, as analytic questions become more clearly and specifically focused, the boundaries of individual formulas become more tangible. At the level of compositional competence, a formula may move freely on a continuum of meaning and may have many different surface manifestations. But at the level of performance, singers chose a finite number of positions on this continuum for their own manifestations of the formula, and thus the boundaries of the formula become quite apparent. Indeed, in the study of blues performance, one finds that one singer made certain formulaic distinctions while another did not.

It is a paradox that the blues formula can be both a theoretical construction and a concrete reality of poetic structure. Its boundaries exist in the mind of the analyst, yet its manifestations appear, quite clearly, in the poetic language of the singer. The more general and unfocused one's research, the more elusive is the blues formula. For this reason, studies of specific singers or specific repertoires make the best use of formulaic theory and show more clearly the nature of formulaic systems than do large-scale overviews of the entire poetic corpus of the blues. In chapter 6, I show how clearly the boundaries of formulas reveal themselves in the recorded repertoire of a specific singer, Garfield Akers. For the moment, however, the reader must be content with the general operational definition outlined previously.

CHAPTER 3

Fine Adjustments: Extraformulaic Elements in the Blues

The blues is not made up entirely of unembellished formulas. The "building block" metaphor that recurs so often in the scholarship is a distorted image of the poetic formula. There are no sharp corners or hard surfaces to formulas, and they do not fit together in neat patterns.

The elements in the blues that "soften," or make more flexible, the structure of the lyric are extraformulaic elements. Because the words that I use to describe these elements are often longer than the actual elements, I have found it convenient to use the following abbreviations:

Para = paralinguistic element
Ex = exclamatory element
Voc = vocatory element
Loc = locutionary element
Aux = auxiliary element
Emb = embedding element
Adj = adjectival element
Adv = adverbial element
Neg = negation element

In the preceding chapter, I showed that blues singers had a considerable choice as to the surface manifestations of a formula. Lexis and syntax were often variable, and semantic features might be adjusted to a great extent to place the formula at different positions on a continuum of meaning. The singers' options, however, were not limited to the internal structure of the formulaic predication. The predication might be modified or embellished in a number of ways by words and phrases external to its structure.

When Parry wrote of the "stylistic superfluity" that was not a part of the "essential idea" of the formula (1928, p. 11), he was describing the kinds of external modifications of the formulaic predication with which this chapter is concerned. Because these stylistic superfluities are external to the structure of the formulaic predication, I have labeled them "extraformulaic elements."

As indicated earlier, these elements take a number of different forms, ranging from paralinguistic utterances to complex predications in their own right. To call these elements stylistic superfluities, however, is a misnomer, because the individualistic style of a blues singer's lyrics often depended on his or her use of extraformulaic elements. The embellishment of the basic formula, whether internal or external to the predication, is fundamental to blues style.

The Paralinguistic Element (Para)

Perhaps the simplest kind of extraformulaic element is the paralinguistic element (Para)—the moan, hum, or cry. These utterances usually function as emotive adjuncts to formulas. The nasal moan, which might be represented as *mmmmm*, is probably the most common Para in the blues, and it often occurs at the beginning of the line. Indeed it sometimes fills the entire first half line as a kind of emotional preparation for the r-formula:

1 *Mmmmm* corn liquor on my mind
   If you catch me out drinking, I'm not drinking just to keep from crying
   (Lewis Black, 1927c)

The nasal moan also prefaces x-formulas, as in the following couplet:

2   *Mmm* I've been asking for a favor; even I ask the good Lord
above
I cried, oh Lord listen; please send back the woman I love
(Henry Townsend, 1929)

Or it might preface an r-formula:

3   You can't give your sweet woman everything she want in one
time
Well boys, she get rambling in her brain; *mmm* some other man
on her mind
(Robert Johnson, 1937b)

More rarely, this Para might occur within the phrase:

4   Up a-yonder she goes, friend; please run try to call her back
Because that sure was one woman I did *mmm* love and like
(Robert Wilkins, 1930)

Other Paras act in much the same way as does the nasal moan:

5   *Ohhhh* I ain't got no mama now
Going to be another *war*; don't need no mama nohow
(Papa Harvey Hull, 1927b)

6   *Oh* he took me to the judge with my head hanging low
And the judge said hold you head up, for you are bound to go
(Alice Moore, 1929c)

7   The man I love is *oh* so good to me
I'm just crazy; want the world to see
(Maggie Jones, 1926)

8   When I get you, mama, we going to move on the outskirts of
town
Because I don't want nobody *ooo* always hanging around
(Washboard Sam, 1937b)

9   Lord she treat me like a hog; treated me like a dog
She treated me like a bear one morning, and then *ah* just like a
log
(George Noble, 1935)

10   *Ah* wake up, mama; wake up and don't sleep so sound
      Give me what you promised me before you lay down
      (Jesse James, 1936a)

The Exclamatory Element (Ex)

Similar to the Para are words and phrases of exclamation—exclamatory elements (Exs). Although these utterances contain meaning as lexical items within the blues singer's vocabulary, their main function is emotive and their semantic structure is not integrated with that of the formulaic predication. Such words as *well, now, Lord,* and *yeah* are common Exs in this category.

As with Paras, these exclamations might occur at the beginning, at the end, or in the midst of a phrase, as well as filling an entire x-position:

11   *Lord Lord now,* I ain't got a friend
      Now one gal is in jail, and the other one is in the pen
      (Eurreal Little Brother Montgomery, 1935a)

12   *Now* if I had just a-listened, what my mama said
      I would have been at home, *Lord,* in my faro's bed
      (John Estes, 1930c)

13   I'm going to sing this verse, and I ain't going to sing no more
      I got them blues, and I'm sure, *Lord,* got to go
      (Robert Hicks, 1927e)

14   *Now* don't you think I know my baby love me so
      She make five dollars and she give me four
      (Frank Stokes, 1927c)

15   *Now* you can't have me, Elsie, *now now* and my partner too
      Because your no-good way, baby, oh baby that won't do
      (Tommy McClennan, 1940g)

16   *Well* what evil have I done
      Well it must be something my man have heard before he gone
      (Louise Johnson, 1930a)

17 *Well now* I have a woman; I try to treat her right
    Well now she will get drunk, ooo *well well* and fuss and fight all
    night
    (Andrew Hogg, 1937)

18 *Well* I went down *yeah* to the churchhouse; *yes well* they called on
    me to pray
    Got on my knees *now* mama; I didn't know not, not a word to
    say
    (Robert Petway, 1941)

19 *Yeah* I don't believe no woman in the whole round world do
    right
    She act like an angel in the daytime; crooked as the devil at
    night
    (Blind Boy Fuller, 1940d)

The Vocatory Element (Voc)

Neither the Para nor the Ex bear any direct semantic or syntactic relationship to the formulas they modify. There is another type of extraformulaic element, however, though similar to the two elements already
described, that does relate more directly to the formula to which it is
attached: the extraformulaic vocatory element (Voc), which calls attention to the one whom the singer is addressing. Among the most common Vocs are *baby, gal, woman, mama,* or other terms for female; or,
conversely, *daddy* or *papa* for male addressees; or *Lord* for invocations
to the deity.

The varied positions of the Vocs are the same as those of Paras and
Exs. They tend to float quite freely within the structure of the blues
line:

20 There's no use a-worrying, *baby,* about the days being long
    The black snake is got the dough; you can't roll him from home
    (Lonnie Johnson, 1928)

21 I helped you, *baby,* when your kinfolks turned you down
    Now you loving someone else, *baby,* and you done left this town
    (Blind Darby, 1929)

22   When you have a feeling that I sure, *gal*, don't want no more
     You just might as well leave her; even if it hurts you so
     (Bobby Grant, 1927b)

23   You going to wake up one of these mornings, *mama baby*, and I'll
     be gone
     And you may not never, *mama*, see me in your town no more
     (Walter Buddy Boy Hawkins, 1927b)

24   You know I done, *woman*, all in this world I could
     But I found out, *baby*, you didn't mean no good
     (Peter Chatman, 1941)

25   Ohhhh, *baby*, why don't you let me go
     Daddy, if you don't want me, had a-plenty more
     (Victoria Spivey, 1927)

26   I been your dog, ever since I been your gal
     You know I love you, *pretty papa;* love you each and everywhere
     (Ollie Rupert, 1927b)

27   *Good Lord good Lord*, send me an angel down
     Can't spare you no angel, but I'll swear I'll send you a teasing
     brown
     (Blind Willie McTell, 1930)

Note that the word *Lord* can be used either as an Ex or a Voc, depending on whether the singer is actually addressing the deity.

   The relationship between a Voc and a formula might take at least two forms. It might correlate directly with an argument in the formulaic predication, or it might refer only to the one addressed without having any direct correlation to any specific part of the predication. In couplet 21, for example, the word *baby* is directly associated with the A2 argument *you* in the formula *I helped you* and may be represented as part of the surface predication of this formula, as follows:

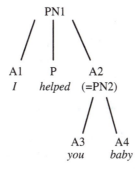

The correlation between *you* and *baby* is, in fact, an "embedded predication" within the formulaic predication (PN1). This embedded predication (PN2) is an equative predication, best represented by two opposable arguments without a predicate (see Leech, 1974, pp. 268–69). The embedded predication might be read as *you is baby,* because *baby* refers directly to the *you* of the formula.

In the case of couplet 21, the Voc has attached itself to the internal structure of the formula; that is, the PN2 *you is baby* attached itself to the A2 argument of the formulaic predication, PN1, forming a deep structure that is something like *I helped you you is baby.* With the redundant features of this deep-level sentence eliminated, the phrase *I helped you, baby* emerges. In couplet 24, however, there is no such semantic correlation between the word *woman* and the formula in which it is found; rather it might be assumed that the one whom Chatman is addressing when he sang *You know I done all in this world I could* is synonymous with the invocation *woman.*

The Locutionary Element (Loc)

The explanation of how such simple Vocs as *baby* or *woman* fit into the structure of the formula may seem overly complex—even unnecessary to an understanding of their function—but a knowledge of this process becomes increasingly necessary as one progresses to more complicated kinds of extraformulaic elements. In general, the more complicated elements might be seen as predications that, in one way or another, impose themselves on the structure of the formulaic predication. Thus, given a formulaic predication, PNf, and an extraformulaic predication, PNe, the resultant phrase in the blues line will be a combined predication, PNf+e.

This combination of a formula and an extraformulaic element might take a number of different forms. In couplet 21, the extraformulaic element became an embedded predication within the formulaic predication, but the reverse process also occurs. One example is the locutionary element (Loc), which embeds the formulaic predication within the extraformulaic predication. This element includes such phrases as *I said, I cried*, and *tell me*, which preface an assertion:

28 Mama, here I am, right out in the cold again
   Says the woman that I'm loving got brains just like a turkey hen
   (Kokomo Arnold, 1935c)

29 Women and children were screaming; *saying* mama, where must we go
   The flood water have broke the levee, and we ain't safe here no more
   (Lonnie Johnson, 1937a)

30 Now my little woman, *I said* she's sweet as she can be
   Every time I kiss her, send a cold chill run over me
   (Blind Boy Fuller, 1940e)

31 *Crying* mama, mama, mama, you know canned heat killing me
   Canned heat don't kill me, *crying* babe I'll never die
   (Tommy Johnson, 1928d)

32 Mmmmm what's the matter now
   Tell me what's the matter, baby; I don't like no black snake no-how
   (Blind Lemon Jefferson, 1927a)

33 Eat my breakfast here; my dinner in Tennessee
   I told you I was coming; baby won't you look for me
   (Mississippi John Hurt, 1928a)

34 I feel like falling down on bended knees
   Cried Lord have mercy, if you please
   (Joe McCoy, 1931b)

The Loc might be thought of as a predication with an open slot in its A2 argument that must be filled by a formulaic predication: *I said PNf, Tell me PNf, Cried PNf*. Leech's "performative introduction rule" is helpful here (1974, 352–55), although the following semantic tree is rather simplified for the purposes of the present study:

PN(Loc)

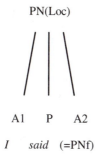

A1   P   A2

I   said   (=PNf)

The Auxiliary Element (Aux)

Similar embedding of the formulaic predication (PNf) occurs in another type of extraformulaic element. Auxiliaries to verbs are also PNf embedders. In the previous chapter, I showed how verbs might undergo tense changes in different manifestations of a formula; many of these changes involve the use of the auxiliary verbs *to have* and *to be*. These verbs, as well as modal auxiliaries such as *will* (*going to*), *must* (*have to*), *may, ought, can, do, shall, dare,* and *need* are, in fact, extraformulaic elements. (I have taken this list from Joos, 1964, p. 76.) As with Locs, auxiliary elements (Auxs) have a slot in their A2 arguments that must be filled by an embedded PNf:

PN(Aux)

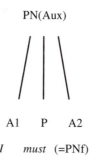

A1   P   A2

I   must   (=PNf)

The following are some examples of Auxs:

35 I'*ll* sing you these verses, and it didn't take long
    If you want to hear any more, you'*ll have to* buy this song
    (Jim Jackson, 1930)

36 Now I *may* miss you, but I *don't* think I will
    I'*m going to* get me a new woman to love me till I get my fill
    (Leroy Carr, 1934d)

37 Oh I *don't* mind drowning, but the water is so cold
    If I *must* leave this good world, I want to leave it brave and bold
    (Clara Smith, 1925)

38 I *can* sit right here, and look on Jackson Avenue
    I *can* see everything that my good woman do
    (Furry Lewis, 1928c)

39 Oh I woke up this morning, honey, about the break of day
    I hugging the pillow, where my fair brown *did* lay
    (Marshall Owens, 1932a)

40 I got a letter, mama; you *ought to* heard it read
    Says you coming back, baby, and I'*ll* be almost dead
    (Ashley Thompson, 1928)

The embedding of the formula *I miss you* in couplet 36 might be represented as follows:

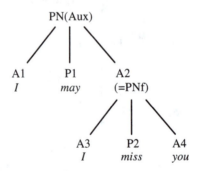

In couplet 35, the clause *you'll have to buy this song* exhibits double embedding: the formula *you buy this song* is embedded in the A2 of the Aux *you have to PNf,* which in turn is embedded in the A2 of another Aux, *you will PN(Aux).*

Other Embedding Elements (Embs)

There are many other verbs that act like these auxiliaries in that they embed predications within their A2 arguments. Verbs such as *begin to, hear, want to, make, see,* and many others act in this manner, and blues singers used them extensively to modify their formulas:

41 I *began to* moan, and I *began to* cry
   My sweet man went away; you know the reason why
   (Lil Johnson, 1929)

42 Down in the levee, camp number nine
   You can pass my house; honey, you can *hear* me cry
   (Lucille Bogan, 1927a)

43 Now Mr. depot agent, don't you *make* me cry
   Did my baby stop here; did she keep on by
   (Sonny Boy Williamson, 1938b)

44 Once I couldn't *stand to see* you cry
   But I feel all the same, mama, if you die
   (Charlie Spand, 1929a)

How these verbs affect the meaning or essence of the formulaic predication is a difficult linguistic problem, but many of them describe how the persona relates to the embedded predication; for example, how he or she perceives it, feels it, starts it, stops it, and so on. Austin probably came closest to describing how these verbs are used in formulaic predications:

> It has come to be seen that many specially perplexing words embedded in apparently descriptive statements do not serve to indicate some specially odd additional feature in the reality reported, but to indicate (not to report) the circumstances in which the statement is made or reservations to which it is subject or the way in which it is to be taken and the like. (1975, p. 3)

Thus, the statement *I cry* in couplets 41 to 43 is prefaced by Embs that indicate the circumstances in which we are to understand the situation: *I cry.* Couplet 44 shows the statement *I cry* prefaced by two Embs: *I stand* and *I see.*

Unlike Auxs, some of these Embs do not have to contain the same subjects as those of the phrases they preface. Auxs must always show complete synonymy between their subjects and those of the phrases they preface. The diagram for the phrase *I may miss you* given previously illustrates this point: the *I* of A1 must be synonymous with the *I* of A3. If this was not the case, then such strange and ungrammatical constructions as *I may she miss you* would occur. The subjects of some Embs, of course, must be synonymous with those of the phrases they preface— the verb *began* in couplet 41, for example—which indicates that further classification of these Embs might be necessary. But for the purposes of this study, such fine distinctions are not important.

A diagram showing the embedding of a formula within the predication of an Emb is similar to that of Auxs and Locs:

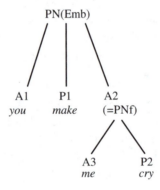

Note that the embedding of the formula *I cry* within the Emb *you make* transforms its subject from the word *I* to the word *me*. This occurs because a deeper structure predication of the formula is (+*human*, +*pronoun*, +*singular*, +*first person*) *cry*, which can generate either the subject *I* or *me*, depending on the constraints of the surface manifestation of the formula.

There are hundreds of possible Embs in English, but only a small number of them were used with any regularity by blues singers. Verbs such as *make, want to, see, know, hear, try to,* and *hate to* are quite common Embs, and they may well be thought of as a formulaic substructure within the greater structure of the lyric. In fact, the Embs, more than any other extraformulaic elements, test the outer limits of the meaning of a given formula, but, as I stated in the previous chapter, whether *I cry* and *you make me cry* should be considered members of the same formula is dependent on the direction and scope of one's analysis. What can be affirmed, however, is that *I cry* and *you make me cry* both include the same underlying, generalized predication within their structures.

The Adjectival Element (Adj) and Adverbial Element (Adv)

The Locs, Auxs, and Embs all share the common feature of embedding the formulaic predication (PNf) within their A2 arguments. Two further types of extraformulaic elements undergo a different kind of attachment to the PNf. These are the adjectival element (Adj) and adverbial element (Adv), and they closely correspond to adjectives and adverbs in the surface-level sentences of formulas. When either of these elements is used, it describes or embellishes an argument or a predicate; it attaches itself to arguments and predicates as semantic features within a formulaic predication. Instead of embedding themselves within a slot in the formulaic predication (as is the case with Vocs), these elements embed themselves in the very list of features of an argument or predicate.

This phenomenon is called "downgrading" (Leech, 1974, pp. 149–54), wherein an entire predication is downgraded to a semantic feature. The following examples illustrate the use of the Adj:

45   I got a girl *across town;* she crochets all the time
     Mama, if you don't quit crocheting, you going to lose your mind
     (Blind Lemon Jefferson, 1927e)

46   Just as sure as a sparrow, mama, babe, flying in the air
     I got a *sweet loving* mama in this world somewhere.
     (Charley Lincoln, 1927a)

47   Highway Fifty runs right by my baby's door
     Now if I don't get the girl *I'm loving,* ain't going down Highway Fifty-One no more
     (Tommy McClennan, 1940a)

In each of these cases, the words *girl* and *mama,* which are both generated from semantic features such as +human, +female, +singular, +(potential) lover, are qualified by Adjs: a prepositional phrase, adjectives, and a relative clause, respectively.

The phrase *I got a girl across town* might be represented in the following way:

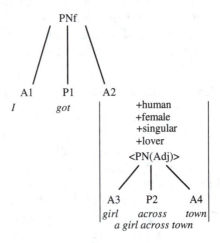

Note that the entire Adj is downgraded to a semantic feature of the A2 argument of the formulaic predication. In couplet 46, the A2 of the formulaic predication contains two Adjs within its semantic features: the adjectives *loving* and *sweet*.

In similar fashion, Advs act on predicates within the formulaic predication:

48 Have you *ever* woke up with them bullfrogs on your mind
    (William Harris, 1928)

49 I woke up *weak and dizzy;* he told me that I would
    But all my pain had left me; he really done me good
    (Laura Bryant, 1929)

50 Mama, I woke up *this morning;* mama, had the sundown blues
    And my fair brown told me I refuse to go
    (Daddy Stovepipe, 1924)

Just as Adjs become attached to the semantic features of arguments, Advs embed themselves in the semantic features of predicates:

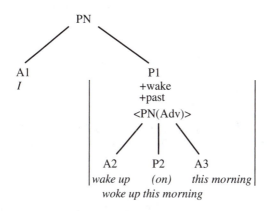

Note in this diagram that the predicate, P2, of the Adv is deleted in the surface-structure manifestation of this formula. It does appear as *in* or *on* in such sentences as *I woke up on Monday morning* or *I woke up in the morning*.

One of the more interesting features of the complex extraformulaic elements (Loc, Aux, Emb, Adj, and Adv) is that because they are well-formed predications in themselves, they might also function as formulas. This happens when these elements are used without being attached to a PNf. In theory, one might say that when a PNe is attached to a PNf that is devoid of semantic features, then the PNe is equivalent to a PNf.

The following examples illustrate this point:

51 *I say mama told me;* papa told me too
All of these Winston women going to be the ruin of you
(King Solomon Hill, 1932b)

52 *Sometime I believe I will;* sometime I believe I won't
    Sometime I believe I do; sometime I believe I don't
    (Furry Lewis, 1928c)

53 I'm drunk and disorderly; I don't care
    If you want to, you can pull off your underwear
    (Thomas A. Dorsey, 1931)

54 Woke up this morning; get my shoes
    I love a woman, that I can't give it to
    (Marshall Owens, 1932b)

55 *It was early this morning;* I was laying out on my floor
    I was keeping daily watch on my wall, so that granddaddy won't
    crawl in my house no more
    (Jaydee Short, 1932c)

In couplet 51, the Loc *mama told me* stands alone without prefacing another assertion in the line; in couplet 52, the Aux *I will* refers to some action that is not explicit in the line; in couplet 53, the Emb *you want to* indirectly prefaces the statement *you can pull off your underwear* in the r-formula, but it stands alone as an x-formula in the line; in couplet 54, the common formula *I love a woman* also quite often manifests itself as an Adj, as in couplet 47; and in couplet 55, the Adv *this morning* modifies no particular predicate and therefore appears as a formula, modifying the word *it,* which is empty of meaning and indicates an empty semantic set. Note also that several of these examples include extraformulaic elements attached to these "upgraded" extraformulaic elements: a Loc in couplet 51, an Adv and an Emb in couplet 52, and an Adv in couplet 55. In fact, it is quite common for extraformulaic predications to be embellished by other extraformulaic elements.

The Adv is more likely to be upgraded to a formulaic predication than any of the other elements. This is especially true of adverbials that place an action within a time period. For example, the Adv *this morning* almost always appears with the formula *I woke up* (as in couplet 50) but may also appear as a formula in its own right, as in couplet 55.

It is rather difficult, therefore, to know whether to label certain time-adverbials as formulas or as Advs. Note the following couplet:

56 I got up this morning *just about the break of day*
    I could hear *a bunch of* bloodhounds a-coming down my way
    (Sam Collins, 1931d)

The first line in this couplet might be described as a single r-formula with two final Advs: *this morning* and *just at the break of day*. It is also clear, however, that the phrase *I got up this morning* is one of the most frequent x-formulas in the blues (to be discussed later) and that it is combined with many different r-formulas. Similarly, the time-adverbial *at the break of day* appears independently of the formula *I got up this morning*, as in this example:

57 Captain rung the bell this morning *just at the break of day*
   Said now it's time for you to go rolling; buddy don't you be on
   your way
   (Kokomo Arnold, 1937c)

Bearing this in mind, we might see the first line of couplet 56 as two separate formulas: *I got up this morning* and *it was at the break of day*, where the words *it was* have been deleted in a surface-structure transformation.

There are some time-adverbials, however, that are permanently attached to the PNf of a formula. These adverbials form the final part of an r-formula and thus carry the rhyme of the line. Note the following examples:

58 Now pack up my clothes; shove into your door
   I'm leaving this morning, mama; *I won't be back no more*
   (Big Bill Broonzy, 1935a)

59 I'm going to west Texas; won't be back till fall
   If the blues overtake me, *I won't be back at all*
   (Ramblin' Thomas, 1928d)

60 Pack up my suitcase; give me my hat
   No use asking me, babe, because *I'll never be back*
   (Walter Vincson, 1931b)

All three italicized phrases share the same generalized predication +*human come/be back,* but the first two examples include a final time-adverbial attached to the basic predication, thereby giving the phrases different end rhymes: *more* and *all*. As discussed in the previous chapter, this difference in rhyme marks these phrases as manifestations of different r-formulas rather than as members of the same r-formula.

Because the time-adverbials in couplets 58 and 59 cannot be detached from the predication *I be back,* they cannot rightly be called extraformulaic elements. Extraformulaic elements must be free to attach or detach themselves from formulas; that is, the singer had to have the choice of either using such an element or not using it in shaping a particular formula to fit a particular position in a song. As I pointed out earlier, the constraint of rhyme in the blues is one of the fundamental facts of the lyric form, and the "fusing" of a predication and a time-adverbial, as shown here, is a prime example of the power of rhyme in the blues.

The Negation Element (Neg)

There is one final embellishment on the formulaic predication that is similar to those already discussed, but it is also significantly different. This is the negation element (Neg), and it occurs in many blues lyrics. Formulas that are usually expressed in positive terms might also be expressed in negative terms by the application of the Neg. Note these two examples:

61   It's hard to love you, Lilly; *you love somebody else*
     I believe it's going to make me grieve myself to death
     (Sam Townsend, 1930)

62   I says I love my baby better than I do myself
     If she don't love me, *she won't love nobody else*
     (Texas Alexander, 1929)

The major difference between these two italicized phrases is one of negation. It is not necessary, for the purposes of this study, to investigate the complex nature of negation in semantics. Leech wrote that for a predication X, one might formulate its negative, *not*-X (1974, p. 165). Similarly, for a given formulaic predication, PNf, a Neg might be attached to it to form *not*-PNf.

Some formulas do not lend themselves as readily to Neg as do others. For example, the common formula *I woke up this morning* might, logically, be negated: *I didn't wake up this morning.* It is hard to conceive of how this sentence could be used in the blues, however, although it is a perfectly well-formed and understandable assertion. In fact, there are no examples of this particular negation in the corpus under analysis. Some formulas, conversely, appear only in the negative; for instance, the r-formula *it won't be long* never occurs in the positive, *it will be long*—at least in the corpus under analysis. Like *I didn't wake up this morning*, the phrase *it (time) will be long* is an absurd—perhaps nonidiomatic—concept that is not likely to be found in blues lyrics.

Negation is, in many ways, a much more fundamental alteration in the meaning of a predication than any of the other elements. To understand this, one must again look at how entailment applies in blues formulas. In all the previous types of extraformulaic elements, the embellished formula entailed the unembellished formula: *Mm I woke up* entails *I woke up; Lord, I woke up* entails *I woke up; I said I woke up* entails *I woke up; I woke up this morning* entails *I woke up;* and so on. The Neg of a predication, however, does not entail the positive of the same predication: *I didn't wake up* does not entail *I woke up.*

This peculiarity of logic places Neg apart from the other elements discussed in this chapter. One might argue, with some justification, that the negative and the positive of the same predication are not members of the same formula because they lack entailment. Conversely, one might argue that, philosophically, a negative and a positive are mirror images of each other—they imply each other—and that, therefore, they deserve to be placed within the confines of the same formulaic boundaries. Again, the choice comes down to the analyst's own perceptions and the requirements of the analysis—in the same way that the singer had a choice between accepting or rejecting a Neg as an embellishment on a formula.

* * *

The blues singers' choice of adding one or more extraformulaic elements to a formula allowed them to expand the formula considerably. Earlier I stated that there is no metrical demand on the blues formula; it is largely because of the extraformulaic elements that the formula is free of such demands. Depending on the metrical structure of the tunes that singers chose, they could expand or contract any given formula by using these elements. Perhaps this ability relates to Nagy's (1976) observation about Homeric verse: Homeric formulas were flexible and that, indeed, the formula determines the metrics rather than metrics determining the formula.

Note these two manifestations of the same formula:

63   Beef to me, baby; me and pork chops do not agree
     I love you, but I don't like the way that you are jiving me
     (Blind Darby, 1931a)

64   Don't believe I'm sinking, believe what a hole I'm in
     You don't believe I love you, Lord, think what a fool I been
     (Ishman Bracey, 1928d)

In couplet 63, the formula *I love you* is unadorned, whereas in couplet 64 the same formula includes Neg, Emb, and Ex. It would be difficult, if not impossible, for the two italicized phrases to fill the same metrical demand, yet by the definition of the blues formula adopted in this study, the two phrases are clearly manifestations of the same formula.

Para, Ex, and Voc function more readily in filling metrical gaps than do the other elements. They alter the semantic message of the formula very little, and they are not highly integrated in the predications they embellish. These factors make such elements much easier to insert in a formula without regard to the specific context in which the formula is being used.

These same noncomplex elements (Para, Ex, and Voc), besides having an emotive and metrical function, were also used by many singers to make their lyrics stylistically distinctive. Tommy McClennan punctuated his lyrics with the continual use of the Ex *now:*

65 *Now* I told you once *now,* baby, *now;* ain't going to tell you no more
   (Tommy McClennan, 1939)

Peetie Wheatstraw became famous for his Para and Ex *ooo well well,* which prefaced most of his r-formulas in the second line of his couplets:

66 When she says she want loving, don't tell her that you too tired
   Some other man might flag her train, *ooo well well* and she might let him ride
   (Peetie Wheatstraw, 1936h)

Even the Loc was used to create a distinctive style. Tommy Johnson's individualistic style was partly due to the Loc *crying,* which prefaced many of his formulas:

67 *Crying* mama, mama, mama, *crying* canned heat killing me
   (Tommy Johnson, 1928d)

These "stylistic superfluities" are far from superfluous. There is not a singer who did not make use of extraformulaic elements and not a single blues song in which these elements do not play a part. As much as anything else, these elements allowed singers to be creative and individualistic within the confines of a traditional, formulaic system. These elements also allowed singers to expand and alter the meaning of formulas, giving them more flexibility in the composition of their blues.

As a final illustration of the importance of extraformulaic elements, observe the following song, in which the extraformulaic elements are marked. Each element is italicized, and below the word or phrase appears the appropriate extraformulaic symbol.

68 I've got your picture, and I'm going to put it in a frame
   Aux   Aux
   And then if you leave town, we can find you just the same
                                      Aux
   Now if you don't love me, please don't dog me around
   Ex   Neg+Aux   Ex   Neg+Aux
   If you dog me around, I know you put me down
                      Emb

   I know my baby thinks the world and all of me
   Emb   Adv
   Every time she smiles, she shines her light on me
   Emb

   Oh I said fair brown something's going on wrong
   Para Loc Adj Voc
   This here woman I love, she's done been here and gone
                  Adj   Aux

   Oh listen, fair brown; don't you want to go
   Para   Adj Voc Neg+Aux Emb
   Going to take you across the water, where that brownskin man can't go
   Aux   Adv   Adj   Neg+Aux

   Lord, I'm worried here; worried everywhere
   Ex   Aux   Adv
   Now I just started home, and I'll not be worried there
   Ex   Adv   Aux Neg

   Lord, I'm tired of being married; tired of this settling down
   Ex   Aux Emb   Emb
   I only want to stay like I am, and slip from town to town
   Adv Emb
   (Blind Lemon Jefferson, 1926j)

Note that some superfluous words remain unmarked. Words such as *and*, *then*, and *if*, though certainly extraformulaic in the sense that they are external to the formulaic predication, have a different function from the words and phrases discussed here. I explain these superfluities in the next chapter.

CHAPTER 4

The Ties That Bind: Formulas to Lines, Lines to Stanzas, Stanzas to Songs

Through extraformulaic embellishment, singers had considerable freedom to be innovative within the formulaic structure of the blues. The singers' choices, however, extended beyond the internal structure of the formula. In combining formulas to make lines, lines to make stanzas, and stanzas to make songs, singers were again confronted with both options and limitations.

In this chapter, I describe the nature of the superorganic structures that bind formulas together into a song: how formulas are juxtaposed to form the larger units of lines, stanzas, and songs. As the focus of this chapter moves from smaller poetic units to larger ones, however, it will become increasingly difficult to discover clear and consistent structural patterns. This phenomenon is perhaps further indication that the fundamental unit of blues composition is the formula and that other, larger units grow out of this elemental structure.

Formulas to Lines

The joining of an x-formula and an r-formula to make a line is a complex procedure. Because each formula is a predication—a complete thought—singers had to decide which thoughts to juxtapose within a line and in which of several ways to juxtapose them. The basic criterion singers used in these juxtapositions was logic; the linked formulas had to be logical in terms of the two complete thoughts expressed and also had to be logical in terms of how the two complete thoughts related to each other within the line.

When an x-formula and an r-formula were linked in a line, they could not create an overall thought or image that was ambiguous, meaningless, or absurd in terms of what was expected of blues lyrics. Of course, logic is subjective, especially within a rich, metaphorical, poetic tradition such as the blues, and what was absurd or meaningless to one singer might have made perfect sense to another. There are, however, some general observations that can be made about the logic of linked formulas in a line.

There had to be certain agreements in terms of number, person, and tense between one formula and the next in a line. For example, note the following line:

1   I woke up this morning; I had the blues three different ways
     (Ramblin' Thomas, 1928h)

The two formulas in this line, *I woke up this morning* and *I had the blues three different ways,* agree in that both contain the semantic features for a first-person, singular pronoun in their A1 arguments; in fact, the two A1 arguments must refer to the same persona and not to two different *I*'s. Both predicates, *wake up* and *have,* also agree in terms of their tenses. Ignoring the adverbial modifiers in the two formulas, we see that the agreement of their arguments and predicates might be represented by the following diagram:

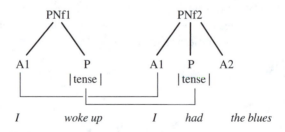

If either of the agreements in example 1 is broken, the resulting formula juxtapositions become illogical:

2 I woke up this morning; they had the blues three different ways

3 I woke up this morning; I will have the blues three different ways

In example 2, the lack of agreement between the two A1 arguments results in a rather peculiar construction: a non sequitur because the first assertion does not bear any overt relationship to the second. Such a construction is not found in the corpus under analysis. Example 3 is also clearly a non sequitur, because the past action of the x-formula bears no overt relationship to the future action of the r-formula. This type of line is also absent from the corpus. In their separate ways, both lines defy the logic expected of blues poetry.

Argument and predicate agreement in linked formulas is a relatively simple example of logical juxtaposition. Of more complexity, however, is the matching up of two formulas so that the overall message is logical. There might be complete agreement between corresponding arguments and predicates in two linked formulas, but the message or image of the x-formula might conflict with that of the r-formula. If, for example, the singer begins a line with the x-formula *I woke up this morning,* he or she must choose an r-formula that completes the line in a logical or meaningful way; example 1 illustrates one logical r-formula that might be linked with *I woke up this morning* to form a perfectly acceptable blues line.

Indeed, *I woke up this morning* is open to many different kinds of r-formula links, because it seems to put few restrictions on the type of action or situation to be described in its accompanying r-formula. The choice, however, is not completely unlimited. Note the following hypothetical line:

4 I woke up this morning; I lay down to take my rest

Both half-line formulas appear, separately, in the corpus, but when placed together in the fashion mentioned earlier, they seem to be out of sequence. Certainly, waking up conflicts with lying down, when juxtaposed in this way, and the illogical nature of such an assertion would probably have prevented it from appearing in blues compositions.

Other formulas are much more restrictive in terms of the kinds of juxtapositions they allow. Take, for example, the formula with the usual surface manifestation, *I ain't going to marry*. This x-formula presents a very specific image, and its accompanying r-formula must, in some way, relate to the image of marriage, or at least modify and agree with the statement already asserted by the x-formula. For this reason, we do not find this formula linked with the r-formula in example 1:

5 I ain't going to marry; I had the blues three different ways

In every case in the corpus, this manifestation of the x-formula is linked with the following r-formula:

6 I ain't going to marry; ain't going to settle down
   (Bessie Smith, 1925b; see also Kid Bailey, 1929; Carl Davis, 1935;
   Bertha Chippie Hill, 1925a; Blind Lemon Jefferson, 1926f; James
   Stump Johnson, 1932; Willie Lofton, 1935; Sara Martin, 1923;
   and unknown artist, 1926)

The same formula with the attached Emb *want to* (see chapter 3 for explanation of abbreviations) is linked with another formula:

7 I don't want to marry; just want to be your man
   (Charley Patton, 1929c; see also Big Joe Williams, 1935d)

In examples 6 and 7, the linked r-formulas collocate with the idea of marriage: *settle down* in example 6 and *be your man* in example 7. The lines are both logical and meaningful in the context of blues lyrics. The following examples, although they do not occur in the corpus, probably were also acceptable to the singer:

8 I ain't going to marry; I'm going to leave your town

9 I ain't going to marry; I ain't going to be your dog

10 I ain't going to marry, until this time another year

11 I ain't going to marry with that no-good gal of mine

The r-formulas in these examples all occur in the corpus, attached to other x-formulas. Their hypothetical acceptability is based on the overall logic of the lines that they form.

Some formulas are severely restrictive because their images are only a part of an accepted idiomatic expression or proverb. Thus, the x-formula *a nickel is a nickel* is part of a proverb expressed as a complete line in the blues:

12   A nickel is a nickel; a dime is a dime
     (Walter Buddy Boy Hawkins, 1929a; see also King Solomon Hill, 1932d; unknown artist, 1930d; Washboard Sam, 1941a; and Bill Wilber, 1935)

Because of the strong proverbial link between these two formulas, it is not likely that either formula would occur in any context other than that of example 12.

But there are means by which two disparate thoughts might be linked to form a logical and meaningful line. In most of the examples given earlier, the formulas are linked in a very simple fashion: two independent clauses that follow in a sequence from x-formula to r-formula without any overt syntactical relationship between them. In other words, the two formulas appear as two independent sentences. Note once again example 1:

1   I woke up this morning; I had the blues three different ways
    (Ramblin' Thomas, 1928h)

This juxtaposition, however, is by no means the only way that singers linked their formulas. As in regular language usage, two formulaic predications can be linked in various logical (and syntactical) relationships.

The insertion of a conjunction between two formulas establishes certain logical links between the predications that may alter, considerably, the overall meaning of the line. Note how the formula +*human be satisfied* is used in the following two examples:

13   He is a rambler, he is a rambler, *and* he is never satisfied
     (Lucille Bogan, 1934c)

14   I did not have the blues, *but,* little mama, just wasn't satisfied
     (Bob Coleman, 1929)

In example 13, two statements are made about a man, both of which are independent of each other (though it may be assumed that dissatisfaction and rambling are two symptoms of some deeper trouble). The logical link between the two assertions in example 13 is symmetrical, and neither statement is dependent on the other for truth-value. (For a detailed examination of conjunction, see Lakoff, 1971.)

In example 14, however, the insertion of the conjunction *but* before the formula *(I) wasn't satisfied* makes this predication logically dependent on the x-formula *I did not have the blues*. The *but* in this line denies the expectation that the lack of blues leads to satisfaction; if the conjunction were symmetric, the sense of the line would be rather strained:

15　I did not have the blues, *and* I wasn't satisfied

In normal blues contexts, such a statement would be contradictory, absurd, and illogical if left unexplained. The insertion of the word *but* between the two formulas makes clear the meaning of the line, which might be paraphrased as "even though I didn't have the blues, and thus one would expect that I would be satisfied, I was, in fact, not satisfied."

Other logical relationships are also possible between two formulas. Note the following examples:

16　I lose all my clothes, baby; believe I'm going to lose my mind
　　(Aaron T-Bone Walker, 1929)

17　You will either run me crazy, *or* I will lose my mind
　　(Lonnie Johnson, 1927a)

In example 16, the formula *I will lose my mind* neither denies nor confirms the truth of its paired x-formula. In example 17, however, the insertion of the conjunction *or* establishes a logical relationship wherein, if the x-formula is true, then the r-formula is false (and vice versa).

The relationship of causality is also common between the two formulas—the x-formula will result if the r-formula is true:

18　Now I'm leaving town, baby, *because* you know you treated me wrong
　　(Eurreal Little Brother Montgomery, 1936b)

In another type of logical relationship, the two formulas are placed within an *if ... then* equation:

19 Then *if* you love me now, woman, *then* you won't do nothing
    wrong
    (Blind Boy Fuller, 1940e)

Further logical relationships between two formulas involve a time
factor: the truth of one assertion being dependent on the prior estab-
lishment of the truth of the other assertion. Note the way the following
formulas are linked:

20 Now mama, *when* I die, I want you to bury me deep
    (Lewis Black, 1927c)

21 Remember me, *after* the days I'm gone
    (Lonnie Johnson, 1925)

22 I'm going to roam this highway, *until* the day I die
    (Bill Jazz Gillum, 1940)

23 The first shot I fired, *then* the man fell dead
    (Blind Willie McTell, 1935a)

24 So you well as to give me some of your loving, *before* you pass
    away
    (Big Bill Broonzy, 1932b)

25 I stood there laughing over him, *while* he wobbled around and
    died
    (Bessie Smith, 1927b)

In all of these lines, a formula that asserts the death of some person is
prefaced by a conjunction that places the death in a temporal relationship with some other assertion. In example 24, the action of the x-formula occurs prior to that of the "death" formula; in example 25, both
actions occur at the same time; in example 20, the action of the "death"
formula occurs before that of the r-formula. Other time conjunctions
found in the blues are *during* and *as soon as*.

The logical relationships expressed by all of these conjunctions
may be represented semantically in the following manner: the x-formula predication (PNfx) and the r-formula predication (PNfr) are both

embedded within a linking predication (PNlink), such that the two arguments of the linking predication equal the two formulas of the line:

PNlink

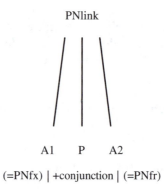

A1   P   A2

(=PNfx) | +conjunction | (=PNfr)

The semantic feature *+conjunction* in the predicate of PNlink could generate *and, but, or, because, if … then, when, after, until, then, before, while, during,* or *as soon as,* depending on the type of logical relationship the singer wished to establish between the two formulas in the blues line.

One final way in which two formulas were linked was through the downgrading of one formula within the structure of the other. I have already demonstrated, in the preceding chapter, that one formula could act as an adverbial modifier to another:

26   I got up this morning *just about the break of day*
     (Sam Collins, 1931d)

This is an example of semantic downgrading as a way of linking two formulas. Time-adverbials that are r-formulas usually link two x-formulas in this manner. When the time-adverbial appears as an x-formula, however, the singer might choose between separating the formulas into two distinct sentences or embedding the r-formula within the x-formula adverbial phrase:

27   *It was soon this morning;* I heard my doorbell ring
     (Hattie Hart, 1934)

28   *Early this morning* you wanted to fight
     (Ethel Waters, 1923a)

Not only time-adverbial formulas act in this manner; earlier (pp. 39–40), I showed how the formula *my face is full of frowns* has at least two surface manifestations:

29 Well poor Joe leaving this morning; *my face is full of frowns*
    (Big Joe Williams, 1935e)

30 I was way down in Sunflower *with my face all full of frowns*
    (Charley Patton, 1930b)

In example 29, the formula is an independent sentence, whereas in example 30, it is linked to the x-formula as a prepositional phrase.

Further examples of this type of linkage are affected by the words *who, that, which,* and *where,* all of which subordinate one formula to another. Note the following paired examples:

31a Now if it's starting a-raining, *I'm going to drive my blues away*
     (Robert Johnson, 1936g)

31b I'm going to get someone, *who can drive my blues away*
     (Ed Bell, 1929b)

32a Well I tried to love a sweet mama, *but she couldn't understand*
     (Little Hat Jones, 1930a)

32b I say you got a sweet woman, *man, which you just don't understand*
     (Little Hat Jones, 1930b)

33a You want your ashes hauled, you want your ashes hauled, *and ain't got no man, ain't got no man*
     (Kokomo Arnold, 1935f)

33b I am looking for a woman *that ain't got no man*
     (Will Shade, 1929b)

34a I started blowing my gauge, *and I was having my fun*
     (Lil Green, 1941a)

34b I'm going to Florida, *where I can have my fun*
     (Edward Thompson, 1929b)

All of these formulaic linkages represent a superstructure into which singers fit their formulas. This superstructure is a logical equation, and the formulas are the assertions within this equation. The varied equations that were available to singers opened up further choices and gave blues compositional structure further flexibility. By the insertion of *and, but, because, if ... then,* or some other conjunction between two formulas, or by the subordination of one formula to another, singers were able to change the equation of the blues line and thus change the logical juxtaposition of the formulas.

Obviously, not all formulas will fit all possible equations. The two formulas in example 1 might be placed in the following equations:

35   I woke up this morning *and* I had the blues three different ways

36   *When* I woke up this morning, I had the blues three different ways

37   I woke up this morning *with* the blues three different ways

But the same two formulas do not permit the logical and meaningful use of the following equations:

38   I woke up this morning *or* I had the blues three different ways

39   I woke up this morning *until* I had the blues three different ways

40   I woke up this morning *which* had the blues three different ways

Note that example 39 becomes logical if its assertions are reversed in the equation:

41   *Until* I woke up this morning, I had the blues three different ways

Once singers placed the two formulas within an equation, they again had certain options. As I stated earlier, argument and predicate agreement was often necessary when two formulas were linked. This agreement, however, might lead to redundancy in the line, especially if the A1 arguments of the two linked formulas referred to the same persona. Note the following example:

42 I woke up this morning; I couldn't even get out of my door
    (Kokomo Arnold, 1937a)

The two *I*s in this line refer to the same persona and are in a sense redundant. This being the case, the singer could have chosen to delete the
repetition of the *I,* as seen in the following example:

43 I woke up this morning; couldn't even get out my door
    (Lonnie Johnson, 1938b)

   The deletion of arguments in two linked formulas is almost always
optional, and whether singers chose deletion depended on their sense of
style and on the metric demands of the tune for a specific blues song. In
fast-paced blues, singers might have taken advantage of every possible
deletion to fit the lines to the meter; in slow-paced blues, singers might
have included as many redundant features as possible to elongate the
blues line.
   Predications could also be deleted, if they were synonymous. Note
the following line:

44 Some of these days *she going to love me too*
    (Edward Thompson, 1929a)

The italicized formula is one manifestation of +*human love +human too.*
If the same formula is preceded by another formula in which the predicate has the feature +*love,* the r-formula predicate could be deleted:

45 I believe trying to love me, Black Minnie, *and my partner too*
    (Tommy McClennan, 1940f)

The italicized formula in example 45 might be represented at a deeper
syntactic level as *you are trying to love my partner too,* but surface-structure deletions have eliminated *are trying to love* from the phrase. Again,
such a deletion was optional, and singers could just as easily have included the redundant predicate:

46 You can't love me, baby *and love my brother too*
    (Robert Hicks, 1929c)

   It should be noted that some of these examples are hypothetical
and do not occur in the corpus. Again, this points to the difference between blues competence and blues performance. According to blues

competence, there is no reason why such a line as example 41 could not occur. Though the combinations and permutations of formulas and their linkages are virtually infinite, singers, of necessity, could make only a limited selection from this infinite corpus of possible lines.

Lines to Stanzas

The options that singers had in juxtaposing two formulas depended very much on semantic and syntactic rules. The lines had to follow the demands that govern the generating of compound and complex sentences within the dialects of African American English, because the blues line is usually a sentence. In fitting two lines together to form a blues stanza, however, different considerations applied.

As I noted earlier, the blues couplet exhibits no enjambment from one line to the next, which means that every line contains at least one complete thought. The two thoughts or complex assertions that make up the blues couplet are much more independent of each other, in syntactical terms, than are the two simpler thoughts that usually make up the blues line. The various choices of conjunction and subordination open to the singer in linking two formulas were severely limited when two lines were juxtaposed. Indeed, in the great majority of cases, there is no syntactical link at all between one line and another in the blues couplet.

Where such a link does exist, however, it usually involves the conjuction *and* rather than linkages in a more complex logical equation:

47 Now I never felt so sorry, 'til the people walked down the lane
And my heart struck sorrow, when they called my good gal's name
(Leroy Carr, 1934h)

The conjunction *but,* which involves a slightly more complex equation, could also, on rare occasions, attach one line to another:

48 I regarded you like I were your baby child
But when it comes to find out you was misusing me all the while
(Blind Darby, 1931a)

These syntactically linked lines, however, compose such a small percentage of all the couplets in the corpus that even citing them gives them more importance than they deserve. Neither syntax nor semantics will explain the juxtaposition of one line with another. The most important link between the two lines of a couplet is rhyme. As I noted earlier, rhyme is one of the major textural features of the blues lyric, and it is the singer's first consideration in linking two lines to form a stanza.

The nature of blues rhyme is complex, and I do not intend to explore the subject in great detail here (as I did in Taft, 1978). Singers had a hierarchical concept of rhyme, wherein some rhymes were more acceptable than others. The most acceptable type of rhyme was one in which the final vowel and consonant sounds of the two words to be rhymed were identical. This "level 1" rhyme is similar to standard masculine rhyme, as it is used in most poetry in the English language. Blues singers might also, however, rhyme words that do not conform to level 1 specifications. Different singers had different concepts of "level 2" rhymes; that is, some made distinctions that others did not. In general, however, three level 2 rules might be postulated:

1. Two words rhyme at level 2 if their vowel sounds are identical and their final consonant sounds include complete oral closure.
2. Two words rhyme at level 2 if their vowel sounds are identical and their final consonant sounds involve complete oral closure plus nasality.
3. Two words rhyme at level 2 if their vowel sounds are identical and one word has incomplete oral closure as its final sound, while the other word has any final sound.

There is a third level of rhyme, the least acceptable, in which the final vowel sound of the two rhymed words varies. For the purposes of this study, however, it is not so important to know the nature of blues rhyme as it is to realize that rhyme is one of the major links between two lines in a couplet. Just as the juxtaposition of two formulas in a line depends on semantics and syntax, the linkage of two lines in a stanza depends on phonology.

These phonological considerations limited a singer's compositional flexibility more than any other feature in the blues lyric. As I previously noted, the r-formula is less variable, syntactically, than the x-formula because of the necessity of keeping the rhyme word at the end of the line. Furthermore, the choice of the second r-formula in a couplet becomes severely reduced, once a rhyme has been established by the first r-formula. For example, if a singer chose the following first line,

49   Lord, I woke up this morning; blues all around my bed
     (Louise Johnson, 1930b)

the singer must complete the couplet with another line which rhymes
with *bed:*

50   I never had no good man, I mean to ease my worried head
     (Louise Johnson, 1930b)

51   Well I had a high fever going up to my head
     (Wiley Barner, 1927)

52   I couldn't help but think about what my good gal said
     (Ishman Bracey, 1930b)

53   I turned back to my *chivver*; blues all in my bed
     (John Estes, 1930c)

54   Thinking about the kind words that my mama said
     (Bo Weavil Jackson, 1926a)

55   Thinking about that wire that my brown had sent
     (Bo Weavil Jackson, 1926b)

56   Went to eat my breakfast, and the blues all in my bread
     (Blind Lemon Jefferson, 1926a)

57   Had the blues so bad, mama, till I couldn't raise up my head
     (Tommy Johnson, 1928a)

58   I didn't have my daddy to hold my aching head
     (Anna Jones, 1923)

59   And the ??? running everywhere
     (Vol Stevens, 1927a)

60   And the blues, they tell me, crying man oh man
     (Vol Stevens, 1928a)

61   And the blues ain't here; they easing everywhere
     (Vol Stevens, 1928b)

62 I turned my face to the wall; baby, these are the words I said
    (Frank Stokes, 1927a)

In these examples, the first lines of the couplets are all the same as in example 49 (not counting extraformulaic elements), and, as shown, the second line, though it might vary in the formulas it contains, must end with an appropriately rhyming word. In examples 59, 60, and 61, Vol Stevens stretched the limits of choice by using level 2 (*everywhere*) and level 3 (*man*) rhymes, as did Jackson in example 55 (*sent*), but these lines still fall within the boundaries of acceptable line juxtaposition. Within the blues corpus, however, there are many different lines that would have been perfectly acceptable—from a logical or thematic point of view—but that could not be used in conjunction with example 49. In the following example, the first line is thematically close to that of example 49, but its different rhyming word requires a different set of linked lines:

63 I woke up this morning; those blues were on my mind
    I was so downhearted, I couldn't do nothing but cry
    (Charlie Kyle, 1928)

Thematic considerations, if secondary to those of rhyme, are still quite important; indeed, this is the other major factor of line juxtaposition. The rules of thematic relationships between lines are not nearly as clear-cut as the rules of rhyme, however. Niles was probably the first to discuss the thematic linkages between lines in his description of the typical AAB-type stanza:

> There might be and usually was one repetition [of the first line of the stanza], but instead the second line might slightly modify, by way of emphasis, the first, while the third would introduce something new: lines one and two having expressed, say, some grief, wistful reflection, or some unhopeful "if," line three would now supply a reason for the grief, some collateral conclusion, or the course which would be taken should the "if" come true; the third thus became the important line, releasing the tension accumulated during the repetition of the first. (1926b, p. 2)

No one else has stated so clearly and so eloquently the thematic relationship of one line to another (see also Evans, 1982, p. 31, on this point), but it is difficult, if not impossible, to determine what is an acceptable, as opposed to an unacceptable, thematic linkage.

Certainly, the B line releases the tension of the stanza. This release, however, might well be a function of the position of the line in the stanza, more than its thematic content. After one or more repetitions of the first line—which very effectively builds up an anticipation and tension within the stanza—any second line might naturally release that tension, regardless of its thematic content. It is also true that the second line often "answers" the thought in the first line, but many instances occur in which the second line is quite independent from the first in this respect.

Examples 49 through 62 illustrate some of the difficulties in establishing thematic rules. Example 50 seems to answer the assertion made in example 49:

64   Lord, I woke up this morning; blues all around my bed
     I never had no good man, I mean to ease my worried head
     (Louise Johnson, 1930b)

One might see the second line as an answer to the question, "Why did she wake up in the morning with the blues around her bed?" But the assumption that the second line answers, or even refers to, the first line is based totally on the juxtaposition of the lines. There is no inherent reason why the second line should be an answer to the first. There is nothing in the internal structure, either semantic or syntactical, that makes the second line an answer to the first. The two lines could as easily be two separate and unrelated assertions by the singer Johnson. It is the position of the lines that determines their thematic relationship, rather than the thematic relationship that determines their position. If the positions in the lines in example 64 are reversed, an appropriate and logical stanza also results:

65   I never had no good man, I mean to ease my worried head
     Lord, I woke up this morning; blues all around my bed

In the hypothetical stanza in example 65, the result of the "grief" of the first line is given: "Not having a good man to ease my worried head caused the blues to be all around my bed when I woke up this morning."

That such a stanza does not occur in the corpus is partly because of the nature of the formula *I woke up this morning*. This formula is an action initiator: it alerts the listener to a new situation. For this reason, the formula usually occurs in the first line of a couplet. It is possible, therefore, to formulate some rule of chronological sequence in relation to the two lines in a couplet. Certainly example 56 shows some sort of sequential relationship: one must wake up before one can have breakfast.

But many couplets exhibit no such chronological relationship. Note the following example:

66 My heart's in trouble; mind's in misery
    Got the blues so bad; I really can't hardly see
    (Will Day, 1928b)

This couplet is a nonchronological list of troubles that presupposes no set sequence. The lack of chronological sequence in some couplets is best illustrated by their ability to reverse their order. For example, within the same song the following two couplets occur:

67 Lord, I tell you, it wasn't no need of mama trying to be so kind
    Ah you know you don't love me; you ain't got me on your mind

    Mmmmm you ain't got me on our mind
    And it's what is the need of baby trying to be so kind
    (Garfield Akers, 1930b)

It seems that there is no universal rule of chronological juxtaposition that can be formulated for the blues stanza. Again, the very position of the lines tends to give a certain sense of chronological or sequential order in the couplet, which is not inherent in the lines. There are, however, certain differences in the surface manifestations between the first and second lines that contribute to a sense of sequence. Often, the first line in a couplet is in the past tense, whereas the second line is in the present tense:

68 I told the judge, I ain't been here before
    If you give me light sentence, I won't come here no more
    (Peg Leg Howell, 1929)

Or the first line is in the present tense while the second line is in the future tense:

69 Oh you got to stop balking, and raising the deuce
    I'll grab you, mama, and turn you every way but loose
    (Blind Willie McTell, 1931a)

Or the couplet might go from present to past in a reverse chronological sequence:

70 I got a mind, never work no more
    I've been badly treated; I've been drove from door to door
    (Carl Martin, 1935a)

This switch in tense from one line to the next gives the couplet a sense of chronological order. The actual content or semantic structure of the formulas and lines has much less to do with this sense of sequence than does the switch in tense. If, however, the content of the individual lines does not determine chronological order, does the content determine which lines might logically be linked into a meaningful stanza? The test of this hypothesis is to find two lines that cannot be linked because of their conflicting logical statements.

For example, can the following two lines be joined into a couplet?

71 You know I love you, and cannot let you be
(Bessie Mae Smith, 1930a)

72 So the fish and the whales make a fuss over me
(Henry Thomas, 1928a)

The result is not too promising:

73 You know I love you, and cannot let you be
So the fish and the whales make a fuss over me

If, however, the surface structures of the two lines are slightly altered, in terms of extraformulaic elements and verb tense, a logical and meaningful couplet might be formed:

74 You know I love you, and cannot let you be
Maybe the fish and the whales will make a fuss over me

The second line of the hypothetical couplet in example 74 answers the first line by stating, "because I love you and give you no peace—and you don't seem to love me—I'll drown myself, ironically receiving no peace from the fish and whales." The second line is, to use Niles's terminology, a collateral conclusion, and thus the couplet is meaningful and logical.

In fact it is difficult to find two lines that cannot be made to fit together logically, given the flexibility of blues compositional structure. Even nonchronological juxtapositions, such as the reversal of examples 56 and 49, might be made logical with the proper alterations:

75 Went to eat my breakfast, and the blues all in my bread
Lord, I woke up this morning; blues all around my bed

76 If I go in to eat my breakfast, and the blues are all in my bread
    Then you know I woke up this morning with the blues all around
    my bed

Even if virtually any two lines can be made into an acceptable couplet (given the same rhyme ending), the fact is that certain line pairs occur with great frequency, while other possible pairs never occur at all in the corpus. Formulas and lines often develop into a loose association with a small group of other formulas and lines. Given any one member of this rather amorphous group, the chances are that singers would choose to link it with other members of the same group. Within the range of possibilities in formula and line juxtaposition, then, there was a more limited range of probabilities. Again, blues performance is a small subset of blues competence.

Of course, the range of possibilities for some lines seems endless. The line *I woke up this morning at the break of day* is used with a wide assortment of different second lines; as a general action initiator, it allows a great many actions or assertions to be described in its juxtaposed line. But in other cases, a definite "family" of lines and formulas accumulate around such lines as the following:

77 Oh tell me, baby, where did you stay last night
    (Charlie Burse, 1934)

The couplets in which the essence of this line is to be found include the following:

78 Oh tell me, baby, where did you stay last night
    For you come in this morning; sun was shining bright
    (Charlie Burse, 1934)

79 Tell me, pretty mama, where did you stay last night
    It ain't none of your business, daddy, since I treat you right
    (Blind Blake, 1926a)

80 Hey tell me, woman, where did you stay last night
    For your shoes unfastened, and your skirt don't fit you right
    (Tom Dickson, 1928c)

81 Tell me, pretty mama, where'd you stay last night
    Shoes ain't buttoned, and you don't smell right
    (Tom Dorsey, 1930b)

82 Oh Black Mattie, where did you stay last night
    With your hair all tangled; clothes ain't fitting you right
    (John Estes, 1929b)

83 Vernita, baby, where did you stay last night
    Now you come home this morning, and your clothes ain't fitting
    you right
    (John Estes, 1935d)

84 Yeah, mean mama, where did you stay last night
    Oh your hair all wrinkled, and your clothes ain't fitting you
    right
    (William Harris, 1927)

85 Tell me, brownskin mama, where did you stay last night
    With your hair all down; your face is never washed
    (Walter Buddy Boy Hawkins, 1927a)

86 Please tell me, pretty mama, honey, where you stayed last night
    You didn't come home, till the sun was shining bright
    (Robert Hicks, 1927d)

87 Said fair brown, where did you stay last night
    You hair's all down, and you know you ain't talking right
    (Blind Lemon Jefferson, 1926g)

88 Ohhhh baby, where did you stay last night
    You got your hair all tangled, and you ain't talking right
    (Robert Johnson, 1936d)

89 Hey, hey, baby, where did you stay last night
    You didn't come home, till the sun was shining bright
    (Robert Johnson, 1936d)

90 Mmm what's the matter, rider; where did you stay last night
    Hair all down, baby, and you don't treat me right
    (Tommy Johnson, 1928g)

91 Now look a-here, mama, tell me where did you stay last night
    She said ain't none of your business; you know you don't treat me
    right
    (Tommy McClennan, 1940c)

92 Now look a-here, mama, you stay last night
    Said ain't none of your business; you don't do me right
    (Tommy McClennan, 1941a)

93 Now tell me, Mary, where did you stay last night
    Come home this morning; the sun was shining bright
    (Joe McCoy, 1930c)

94 Can't you tell me, pretty papa, where did you stay last night
    He said it's none of your business, mama, so I treat you right
    (Rosie Mae Moore, 1928a)

95 Tell me, fair brownie, where did you stay last night
    You hair's all down, and your clothes ain't fitting you right
    (William Moore, 1928b)

96 Now tell me, little black gal, where did you stay last night
    Just the reason I ask you, black gal, you know your clothes ain't
    right
    (Charlie Pickett, 1937)

97 Hey, mama, mama, where you stay last night
    You hair's all wrinkled, that they beating you right
    (Will Shade, 1927c)

98 Lordy, it's sweet to mama; now mama, where you stay last night
    Because your clothes all wrinkled, mama, and your hair sure ain't
    fixed up right
    (Frank Stokes, 1927a)

99 Corrina, Corrina, where's you stay last night
    Come in this morning; the sun was shining bright
    (James Boodle It Wiggins, 1930)

100 Tell me, baby, baby, where did you stay last night
    Now with your hair all tangled, and your clothes ain't fitting you
    right
    (Sonny Boy Williamson, 1938d)

101 Well I asked you, woman, where did you stay last night
    You said it wasn't none of my business, just since you treating me
    right
    (Sonny Boy Williamson, 1941c)

Judging by these examples, three "answers" to the question *where did you stay last night* are probable: "you are in a disheveled condition as to your hair, clothes, or deportment" (examples 80, 81, 82, 83, 84, 85, 87, 88, 90, 95, 96, 97, 98, 100); "you did not come home until a very late hour" (examples 78, 83, 86, 89, 93, 99); or "you have no right to ask me such a question, because you are well-treated by me, or I am ill-treated by you" (examples 79, 90, 91, 92, 94, 101). Example 90 is a combination of two of the probable answers, and example 97 seems also to be some curious combination of the "dishevelment" and "mistreatment" motifs.

Despite the almost endless possibilities given the line *tell me where did you stay last night*, singers followed one of three types of answers; however, the first line, as well as the three probable answers, might all vary the formulas they contain, to some extent:

102a (90) Mmm what's the matter, rider; where did you stay last night
(Tommy Johnson, 1928g)

102b (91) Now look a-here, mama, tell me where you stay last night
(Tommy McClennan, 1940c)

103a (84) Oh your hair all wrinkled, and your clothes ain't fitting you right
(William Harris, 1927)

103b (87) You hair all down, and you know you ain't talking right
(Blind Lemon Jefferson, 1926g)

This group of lines and the many formulas within them constitute a family of images and themes. This family, however, is not a very cohesive and self-contained unit. Many of the individual formulas that make up this family are also found in entirely different stanzaic contexts. The formula *tell me, mama*, for example, is one of the most frequent in the blues and owes no special allegiance to one or another family. Note its use in the following couplet:

104 *Tell me, mama*, what's the matter now
Trying to quit your daddy, Lord, and you don't know how
(Ishman Bracey, 1928c)

Another manifestation of the formula *where did you stay last night* also occurs in a different stanzaic context:

105   I work all day; I wrestle all night
      I did not think my baby would go out and *stay all night*
      (Bill Jazz Gillum, 1939)

The formula *your hair is all wrinkled* acts in the same way:

106   *Your hair all wrinkled;* you full of sweat
      Your underskirt is wringing wet
      (Walter Davis, 1935c)

The formula *you don't treat me right* has many different stanzaic contexts:

107   I dump sugar all day; clean until broad daylight
      I done everything for that woman; *still she don't treat me right*
      (Black Boy Shine, 1936)

There are some formulas within this family that are found in no other contexts in the corpus. The formula *when the sun/moon was shining bright* is found only in conjunction with the r-formula *where did you stay last night* in the first line of a couplet (see examples 78, 86, 89, 93, and 99). Given the structure of blues lyrics, however, there is no reason why such a phrase could not be fitted into another stanzaic context, such as the following hypothetical couplet:

108   Now all you do is love to fuss and fight
      You walk the streets, till the sun shines bright

Because of the flexibility of blues structure, there was always the potential for new combinations of formulas and lines, but this potential was not in most cases explored by singers.

That a number of formulas and lines always seem to be associated with each other, and never appear in other potentially acceptable contexts, has led to the belief that lines or even whole stanzas might be formulas in themselves. Earlier (pp. 27–28), I showed that the concept of the verse-formula was unproductive. Although it is true, for example, that the x-formula *a nickel is a nickel* always appears with the r-formula *a dime is a dime,* and that together they form a proverbial phrase, there was always the potential of adjoining either of these formulas to some third formula. This potential is part of the compositional competence of the blues but not, perhaps, part of its compositional performance.

One might say that, in blues performance, these two formulas have "ossified" into an indivisible line. Barnie has discussed this process of ossification, but, as he realized, there was always the potential for change (1978a). To see that ossification is never absolute or irrevocable, note the following line:

109   Ashes to ashes; dust to dust
      (Clara Smith, 1924b)

This line, like *a nickel is a nickel; a dime is a dime,* is proverbial; in fact, its source is liturgical (see "The Order for the Burial of the Dead" in *The Book of Common Prayer*), which seems to ensure that these two half lines would remain inseparable. There exists, however, another combination of formulas that means the same as example 109 but that allows another rhyme:

110   Ashes to ashes, and sand to sand
      (Blind Willie McTell, 1933e)

Thus, even a proverbial, liturgical line might undergo formulaic variation.

Supposedly, ossified couplets were similarly alterable. For example, the following couplet is a strong, unified image that would have a specific meaning to anyone from a "rabbit-hunting" culture:

111   Blues jumped a rabbit; run him one solid mile
      This rabbit sat down; cried like a natural child
      (Blind Lemon Jefferson, 1926k)

There are, however, several variations on this same theme, all involving the substitution of other formulas and lines for those in example 111:

112   Lord, said blues jumped a rabbit; run him for a solid mile
      Lord, that fool couldn't catch him, and he fall right down and
      cried
      (James Yank Rachel, 1930)

113   Blues jumped the monkey and run him for a solid mile
      And the poor fellow lie down; cried like a natural child
      (Joe McCoy, 1936a)

114   Hey my doggie jumped a rabbit and he run him for a solid mile
      When he seen he couldn't catch him, so he cried just like a natu-
      ral child
      (Charley Jordan, 1931)

115 My dog got a rabbit; the rabbit fell down on his knees
   He looked up at the dog; he say won't you have mercy on me
   please
   (Lil Johnson, 1929)

Stanzas to Songs

The juxtapositions of formulas and lines might be placed on a continuum from what was possible to what was probable to what was frequently employed. The potential of new and original combinations was ever present in the blues, being a part of the great structural flexibility of the lyric. But even greater flexibility occurred in the linking of stanzas to form songs. The juxtaposition of one stanza with the next did not depend on semantics, syntax, or phonology. Indeed, even theme and logic seemed to play only a minor role in the linking of stanzas.

I have already described the blues as a nonnarrative and emotive form of song. In general, the blues song followed no chronological sequence from its first stanza to the last. Yet there are a small number of blues that run contrary to this rule and are narrative or sequential in form. Again, there is a continuum on which blues songs lie: from well-ordered narrative lyrics to thematically consistent songs to seemingly random collections of unrelated stanzas.

True narrative, ballad-like songs were rare in the blues (leaving aside "blues ballads" such as "John Henry" or "Stackolee," which fall outside the scope of this study), but they do exist. Some of the more common blues of this type describe floods and other natural disasters—the "Back Water Blues" variants, for example. Songs that are concerned with the central topic of the blues, namely, love, and that also are narrative are rarer still. One of the most common examples of this type of love–narrative blues is the "Death Letter Blues," which was sung in many variants throughout era of commercially recorded blues:

116 I received a letter that my man was dying
   I caught the first train and went back home a-flying

   He wasn't dead, but he was slowly dying
   And just to think of him, I just can't keep from crying

   I followed my daddy to the burying ground
   I watched the pallbearers slowly let him down

   That was the last time I saw my daddy's face
   Mama loves you, sweet papa, but I just can't take your place
   (Clara Smith, 1924f)

This song follows a set chronology that would be difficult to disrupt. As a narrative, it seems to fall into what Spaeth termed "epistolary songs" (1927, p. 37) and is somewhat close to "The Letter Edged in Black" (see Spaeth, 1927, pp. 38–39). Whatever its source or analogues, however, this song shows a clear, chronological sequence from stanza to stanza.

In most blues, however, the reason for the juxtaposition of stanzas is not so easily ascertained. A chronological sequence was rare; singers placed stanzas in almost any order without doing harm to the logic of the song. Closest to narratives on the continuum are those blues in which all stanzas deal with the same particular and specific theme. The theme must be more specific than "love," given that love is the underlying theme of the blues in general. One such song is Son House's "Dry Spell Blues" (parts 1 and 2), in which House concentrated on the themes of drought and poverty from one stanza to the next:

117   The dry spell blues have fallen; drive me from door to door
      The dry spell blues have put everybody on the killing floor

      Now the people down South sure won't have no home
      Because the dry spell have parched all this cotton and corn

      Hard luck's on everybody, and many people are blue
      Now besides the shower, ain't got no help for you

      Lord, I fold my arms, and I walked away
      Just like I tell you, somebody's got to pay

      Pork chops forty-five cents a pound; cotton is only ten
      I can't keep no woman, no no nowhere I been

      So dry, old boll weevil turned up his toes and died
      Now ain't nothing to do, bootleg moonshine and rye
      (Son House, 1930d)

      It have been so dry, you can make a powderhouse out of the
      world
      Then all the moneymen like a rattlesnake in his coil

      I done throwed up my hands, Lord, and solemnly swore
      There ain't no need of me changing towns; it's a drought every-
      where I go

      It's a dry old spell, everywhere I been
      I believe to my soul, this world is about to end

      Well I stood in my backyard; wrung my hands and screamed
      And I couldn't see nothing; couldn't see nothing green

Oh Lord have mercy, if you please
Let your rain come down, and give our poor hearts ease

These blues, these blues is worthwhile to be heard
For it's very likely bound to rain somewhere
(Son House, 1930e)

Few blues songs adhere to one nonlove theme as closely as these two do. But for all its thematic consistency, the individual stanzas seem to have no special order. If one were to take all the stanzas in this song and rearrange them in some random way, the logic of the song would not be impaired.

Songs concerned with the theme of love are similar to House's songs in respect to the juxtaposition of the stanzas. The theme is constant, but the stanzas that express this theme follow no particular chronological order or display any development of the theme. In fact, the love lyrics seem even more nonsequential than songs such as House's because, within this broad theme, the singer rarely isolated one particular aspect of love on which to concentrate. Note the following song:

118.1   I've got your picture, and I'm going to put it in a frame
        And then if you leave town, we can find you just the same

118.2   Now if you don't love me, please don't dog me around
        If you dog me around, I know you put me down

118.3   I know my baby thinks the world and all of me
        Every time she smiles, she shines her light on me

118.4   Oh I said fair brown, something's going on wrong
        This here woman I love, she's done been here and gone

118.5   Oh listen fair brown, don't you want to go
        Going to take you across the water, where that brownskin man
        can't go

118.6   Lord, I'm worried here; worried everywhere
        Now I just started home, and I'll not be worried there

118.7   Lord, I'm tired of being married; tired of this settling down
        I only want to stay like I am, and slip from town to town
        (Blind Lemon Jefferson, 1926j)

If one analyzes this song, stanza by stanza, several seemingly uncon-
nected themes and sentiments emerge: stanza 1 implies mistrust of a
loved one, stanza 2 implies that the persona is being toyed with, stanza 3
brags of the loved one's love for the persona, stanza 4 implies an abandoned lover, stanza 5 is a seduction, stanza 6 speaks of some unnamed
anxiety and homesickness, and stanza 7 disparages married life. The
song is a mixture of different emotional states, different attitudes toward
love, and different kinds of loving relationships. As with House's blues,
the stanzas could be repositioned without doing any seeming damage
to the lyric.

The nonchronological, nonsequential nature of most blues lyrics
does not, however, mean that blues songs grew out of confused minds
or jumbled and unrelated images in the brains of the singers. Even if the
blues song follows no narrative sequence, there is usually a narrative
of sorts implicit in the lyric. This narrative might be no more specific
than "the lover abandoned" or "domestic troubles between husband and
wife," but blues singers, instead of relating the event, expressed their
feelings about the event. Different aspects of this implicit narrative give
rise to different emotions, dreams, and imaginary scenes. Singers were
free to express these perceptions from the mind's eye in any sequence
they chose. In effect, singers began with some implicit narrative and
then made free associations around this event from stanza to stanza.

Thus, it might be possible to devise rules of sequence, or even rules
of theme, for the ordering of stanzas in a blues song, but for every rule
so devised, there would probably be more exceptions than examples.
Blaustein (1971) was one of the few to attempt to find sequential rules in
blues stanzas, in his analysis of Blind Willie McTell's "Statesboro Blues."
But his Levi Straussian approach has not been tested beyond this one
song, and it remains to be seen whether "Statesboro Blues" is typical
or anomalous in respect to the sequence of its stanzas. Evans's (1982,
pp. 144–50) attempt at analyzing two related songs by Charley Patton
benefits from a more subjective, less structured approach.

It is probably more profitable to explore ways in which two or three
stanzas within a song interact, for there is often a short-term logical
consistency within portions of blues lyrics. The following three consec-
utive stanzas from the middle of a song hold together thematically and
even have the makings of a small narrative:

119   Ticket agent, ticket agent, which a-way has my woman gone
      Say describe your woman, and I'll tell you what road she's on

      She's a long tall mama, five and a half from the ground
      She's a tailor-made mama, and she ain't no hand-me-down

Mama, if you ride the Southern, I'll ride the Santa Fe
When you get in Memphis, pretty mama, look around for me
(Blind Willie McTell, 1935b)

As Evans pointed out (1982, p. 153), it sometimes seems that one stanza follows another in the blues because an image in the first stanza triggers a similar image in the next, in a free-association manner. The following example seems to be one such case:

120.1   Let me tell you, mama, like the Dago told the Jew
         If you don't like me, it's a cinch I don't like you

120.2   There's two kind of nations I sure can't understand
         That's a Chinese woman and a doggone Dago man
         (Blind Percy, 1927)

The formulas in these stanzas are widespread, and both couplets contain ethnic slurs. Though the message in stanza 1, wherein the slur is secondary to the main theme of "rejection," and the message of stanza 2, which is more directly an ethnic slur, seem to bear no relation to each other, the image in the first stanza seems to have triggered a similar image in the second. In fact, the more common first line associated with stanza 1 is as follows:

121   I'm going to tell you, daddy, like the Chinaman told the Jew
       (Trixie Smith, 1924)

The singer in example 120 might have known of this variant, which would reinforce an association with an anti-Chinese image in the second stanza.

It is, of course, impossible to trace free association from stanza to stanza; one would have had to psychoanalyze the individual singers. At most, one can speculate on associations or connections between stanzas made by the blues audience, based on their shared understanding of the poetic conventions of blues performance, as well as on their shared understanding of African American culture. Jarrett (1984) is one of the few blues scholars to explore the ability of a "speech community" to see connections among blues stanzas in a given song that might escape outsiders. Yet, this quite speculative approach to the study of stanzaic juxtapositions is a far cry from the more concrete, structural description of formula links.

The imprecision in the preceding discussion of stanza linkages and ordering, when compared with descriptions of formula or line juxtapositions, emphasizes the small-unit structure of the blues. Although the stanza is the textural unit of the blues (and perhaps the entire song is the psychological or social unit), the formula is the structural unit, and it is at the formulaic level that the nature and pattern of blues composition becomes apparent.

CHAPTER 5

Twenty Common Formulas

Ideally, a thorough analysis of the compositional structure of the blues would include a complete survey of all formulas discovered in the corpus. A more limited survey, however, would be less burdensome and certainly more practical. Describing the twenty most frequently employed formulas will show a common thread that links almost all blues songs, because there were few singers who did not employ at least some of these twenty formulas in their compositions.

To say that these formulas are the twenty most frequent in the blues is not quite accurate; they are the twenty most frequent in the corpus under analysis, which represents only a fraction of all the blues that were recorded commercially. I doubt, however, that a larger corpus would have revealed formulas more recurrent than these twenty.

The method I employed in determining which formulas were most frequent involved reading through the computer concordance (Taft, 1984) and looking for those phrases that seemed to occur a fair number of times. In the first search, I noted sixty formulas. I analyzed each of these formulas to determine their possible boundaries; that is, all the possible manifestations that each formula underwent in the corpus. I searched for all these manifestations in the concordance and subsequently selected, from among the sixty, the ten x-formulas and the ten r-formulas that recurred the most times in all their manifestations.

In this chapter, I describe the semantic structure of each formula (with appropriate tree diagrams), the various manifestations of these formulas (with appropriate examples), and any interesting minor variations. I also include a discussion of how various extraformulaic elements affect the essential meaning of these formulas and give a statistical account of the ways these formulas have manifested themselves in the corpus. In the case of two of these formulas—*+human wake up* and *+human leave town*—I expand the analysis by listing all manifestations of these formulas found in the corpus. Finally, I attempt an explanation of why these particular formulas were the most popular with blues singers and how these formulas reflect the meaning of the blues.

+human have the blues (x-formula)

This x-formula defines the form of song: the blues. Its A1 argument is always *+human,* because only humans are capable of having the blues, although singers could personify nonhuman subjects to fit them into the *+human* semantic category. The A2 argument is always *the blues,* though as I show, it may undergo various adjectival modifications. The predicate might be described as "to contract or to come down with, as in the case of a cold or fever," and this predicate usually generates one of two possible surface-level verbs: *have* or *get.* The overall structure of the formula can be represented by the following diagram:

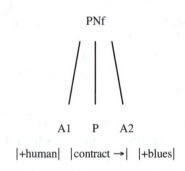

PNf

A1   P   A2

|+human| |contract →| |+blues|

The following two examples demonstrate the two most common manifestations of this formula:

1 *I had the blues* every time I see your face
Well there ain't no other woman, ooo well well, in this world can take your place
(Peetie Wheatstraw, 1936a)

2   I cut that joker so long, deep and wide
    You got the blues, and still ain't satisfied
    (Mississippi John Hurt, 1928c)

The predicate can, however, generate other verbs, although not often. There are only five instances of the verb *take* in this context:

3   Now a colored man go to the river; take him a seat and sit down
    If he takes the blues, he come on back to town
    (Blind Willie McTell, 1933d)

And only two couplets exhibiting the following manifestations:

4   *I keep the blues all night,* and the whole day through
    I'm so full of blues I don't know what to do
    (Leroy Carr, 1932a)

5   Got the blues; can't be satisfied
    Keep the blues, I'll catch the train and ride
    (Mississippi John Hurt, 1928c)

Whether the verbs *keep* and *be full of* truly fulfill the criteria of the deep-structure predicate of this formula is unclear, but they certainly represent related forms.

Another possible manifestation, which occurs only once in the corpus, seems to include the extraformulaic Neg (see chapter 3 for explanation of abbreviations) within the specific semantic features of the surface-level verb:

6   Oh maybe it's the blues that keeps me worried all the time
    If I could lose these weary blues that's on my mind
    (Thomas A. Dorsey, 1930a)

In the sense that *lose* is the opposite of *contract* in this context, example 6 seems to be a special case of negation (*–contract* or *uncontract*).

These verb variations, however, are quite rare. Almost all examples of this formula generate either *have* or *get*. The more important variation in this formula occurs in the modification of the noun *blues.* It was common for singers to add an Adj element to *blues,* and this element could include virtually any word or phrase:

7   I walked down the street; I couldn't be satisfied
    I had the *no-no* blues; I couldn't keep from, I couldn't keep from
    crying
    (Willie Baker, 1929b)

8   I got the *Maxwell Street* blues, mama, and it just won't pay
    Because the Maxwell Street women going to carry me to my
    grave
    (Papa Charlie Jackson, 1925d)

9   Got the *barrelhousing* blues; feeling awfully dry
    I can't drink moonshine, because I'm afraid I'll die
    (Gertrude Ma Rainey, 1923c)

The adjectival choice is seemingly endless. This extraformulaic modification almost always precedes the word *blues,* but there are a few cases
of it following the word:

10   I've had the blues *about my money;* had the blues because I'm
     feeling bad
     But when my sweet woman quit me, them was the worst blues I
     ever had
     (Clifford Gibson, 1929a)

11   I've got the blues *for my baby;* my babe got the blues for me
     For she went and caught the Big Four; she beat it back to
     Tennessee
     (Charley Jordan, 1930b)

The Emb, common with so many formulas, occurs with this formula
only three times in the corpus:

12   *I can tell* when I've got the blues; I can't help but feel so lowdown
     I can tell when the blues is coming; I can't help but feel so low-
     down
     Then I want to get drunk, and pitch a bugger all over town
     (J.T. Funny Paper Smith, 1931a)

13   Women all singing the blues; I can't raise my right hand
     What make a woman have them blues; when she knows some-
     body's got her man
     (Willie Baker, 1929c)

14 Women all singing the blues; I ain't raise my right hand
What make a woman have them blues; when she knows some-
body's got her man
(Willie Baker, 1929e)

This x-formula occurs approximately 110 times in the corpus. Other
phrases, in which the blues is personified, or at least in which the blues
becomes the A1 argument and the *+human* becomes the A2 argument,
also occur and might be considered as closely related to this formula.
The following are a few examples of these phrases, the first of which is
the most common, occurring eight times in the corpus:

15 I mean I went to the depot, and set my suitcase down
The blues overtake me, and tears come rolling down
(Blind Lemon Jefferson, 1927c)

16 *Blues grabbed mama's child,* and it tore me all upside down
Travel on, poor Bob; just can't turn you around
(Robert Johnson, 1936g)

17 *Now my blues got at me,* Lord, and run me from tree to tree
You should have heard me begging, Mr. Blues don't murder me
(Eurreal Little Brother Montgomery, 1936a)

+human come to some place (x-formula)

This is the most frequently recurring formula in the blues, but at the
same time, the most diffuse. The A1 argument carries a *+human* feature,
while the A2 argument includes the large and general semantic feature of
+some place. The predicate might be described as "movement toward." In
diagram form, the formula looks something like the following:

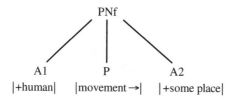

The predicate and A2 argument can generate a vast number of different words and phrases. Under the A2 feature +*some place,* for example, might fall any type of location from human-made structures to natural sites:

18   *Uncle Jim went to jail* with a heavy load
     They gave him thirty days on the country road
     (Bob Robinson, 1928)

19   *I went down to the ocean,* just to get a permanent wave
     My woman got a new way of loving, man, and it won't behave
     (Jake Jones, 1929)

Place names often fill the A2 slot:

20   Still I ain't going to worry; and I ain't going to raise no sand
     I'm going back to Friar's Point, down in sweet old Dixieland
     (Robert Lee McCoy, 1940)

21   *I'm going to Third Alley,* and bring my rider home
     Because these women in Third Alley won't let my rider alone
     (Ivy Smith, 1927)

Or compass directions:

22   *I'm going back south,* where it's warm the whole year round
     I'll be so glad when my train pulls up in town
     (Francis Scrapper Blackwell, 1931c)

23   *Going north, child,* where I can be free
     Where there's no hardships, like in Tennessee
     (Maggie Jones, 1925a)

Or the place might be left unspecified:

24   I got a letter, mama; you ought to heard it read
     Says you coming back, baby, and I'll be almost dead
     (Ashley Thompson, 1928)

25   Say excuse me, mama; I don't mean no harm
     Just come here to sing this little song
     (Charlie Burse, 1932)

26 *Molly man's coming;* I hear his voice
He's got hot tamales, and it's just my choice
(Moses Mason, 1928)

The predicate can vary almost as much as the A2 argument. The most common manifestations of the predicate generate *come* and *go* (see couplets 23 and 24), but such verbs as *hurry to, run to, walk to, reach, get to, start to, roll back to,* and *fly to* also occur. The possible combinations of these many different verbs and places give this formula countless manifestations.

Some of these manifestations occur quite frequently and might be considered more precise formulas in themselves; for example, *+human go to the station/depot* (discussed earlier in this study) occurs 34 times:

27 *I went down to the station,* up to the train
I couldn't buy no ticket for shaking that thing
(Walter Vincson, 1932a)

And *+human come here,* where the *here* can be deleted or be placed before the verb, can occur, as in the following example:

28 *Here come the biggest boy,* coming right from school
Hollering and crying like a doggone fool
(Jesse James, 1936b)

This manifestation occurs 62 times. The phrase *+human go +compass direction* (see examples 22 and 23) occurs 26 times, and *+human go to +place name* (see examples 20 and 21) occurs 118 times in the corpus.

The phrase *+human come back* occurs 30 times, *+human come in here* occurs 26 times, *+human go to/up the mountain* occurs 24 times, *+human go to the river* occurs 25 times, and *+human go downtown* occurs 27 times. The phrase *+human go to +human* might not appear to be a member of this formula, because the A2 argument is not, overtly, "some place," but the semantic feature for the A2 in this manifestation is more accurately *some place where +human is located.* This manifestation occurs 46 times.

The most common manifestations of this formula, as already pointed out, generate the verbs *come* or *go.* One interesting manifestation, however, converts the predication into an equative predication, wherein the predicate becomes the verb *be.* This manifestation might be represented as *+human be some place bound,* and the feature *some place* is usually filled by a place name, as in the following example:

29 *I'm Texas bound;* got no time to lose
    Because my sweet mama quit me; left me with the Texas blues
    (Papa Charlie Jackson, 1925e)

This formula is often prefaced by Embs, but only one such element occurs with any frequency: the Emb *see* prefaces the manifestation *+human come* 15 times, as in the following example:

30 It was early in the evening; sun was going down
    Seen a lassie coming, all dressed in brown
    (Teddy Edwards, 1934)

This formula, in all its many manifestations, occurs approximately 860 times in the corpus and is by far the largest formula uncovered by this study. In terms of the formulaic analysis of individual singers or songs, it might be best to view the different manifestations of this formula as formulas in their own right, but regardless of the manifestation, every phrase in this group entails the deep-level predication *+human movement toward +some place.*

+human go away from some place (x-formula)

This x-formula is obviously related to the previous one. It is, in a sense, a mirror image of the *go someplace* formula. It can also take a number of different A2 arguments and predicates and might be represented by the following diagram:

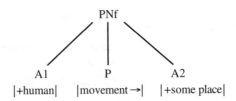

The two most common surface predicates are the verbs *go away* and *leave,* as in the following two examples:

31 *I'm going away;* now don't you want to go
I'm going to stop at a place, I haven't never been before
(Blind Lemon Jefferson, 1927h)

32 *When he was leaving,* I couldn't hear nothing but that whistle blow
And the man at the throttle, Lord, he wasn't coming back to more
(Lucille Bogan, 1934b)

The only other manifestations of the predicate that occur with any frequency are *get away* and *get out,* but these forms are rare in comparison with *leave* and *go away:*

33 You will think you left trouble all behind
Get away from home; then it will roll across your mind
(Lonnie Chatman, 1932a)

Even rarer are the verbs *walk away, run away, scamper away, creep away,* and *move away,* with only one or two examples each in the corpus.

Although this formula allows as much variation in its A2 argument as does the previous formula, in actual usage it seems more limited. In a great many cases, the *place* is unspecified, often identified only as *here.* Thus, the most common A2 argument that accompanies the verb *leave* is either *here* or the deleted *here,* as in example 32. In all, the manifestation +*human leave here* occurs 82 times in the corpus.

Similarly, when the manifestation of the predicate is the verb *go away,* the A2 argument is again most frequently *here.* This manifestation, which might be described as +*human go away from here,* almost always deletes the *from here* in its surface structure, as in example 31, and might even delete the *away,* as in this example:

34 *I'm going, I'm going;* crying won't make me stay
The more you cry, further you drive me away
(Mississippi John Hurt, 1928b)

In all, this manifestation occurs 174 times in the corpus.

Some manifestations with more specific A2 arguments include the following: +*human leave town* occurs 30 times; +*human leave +place name* occurs 20 times; +*human leave home* occurs 9 times; and +*human leave the station* occurs 5 times.

The formula occurs, prefaced by Embs or followed by Advs, although no one extraformulaic element occurs with any frequency. Some of the more interesting manifestations demonstrate multiple verbs, all of which mean *movement away from:*

35 I got the key to the highway; billed out and ready to go
I'm going to leave here running, because walking is most too slow
(Bill Jazz Gillum, 1940)

36 *I'm going to leave here walking;* going down number sixty-one
If I find my baby, we are going to have some fun
(Will Batts, 1933)

37 I've got a girl; her name is Joan
She leaves here walking running fast; chocolate to the bone
(Henry Thomas, 1928b)

These manifestations exhibit extraformulaic modifiers on the verb *leave* in the form of gerunds. In all its manifestations, this formula occurs more than 300 times.

+*human got/have* +*human* (x-formula)

In this formula the A2 argument has the feature of *lover* or *potential lover* of the A1 argument. The predicate has the general meaning of "to possess in a loving relationship."

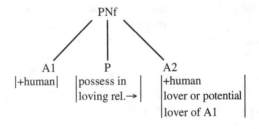

Almost all of examples of this formula fall into one of three surface manifestations: the predicate is *have, got,* or *get.* The predicate manifestations *have* and *got* seem to be synonymous; the predicate *get,* however, implies more activity or a search for someone to possess. The following couplets show these three manifestations:

38   Said I woke up this morning, just about the break of day
     Some man had my woman, and the worried blues had me
     (George Torey, 1937b)

39   *I've got a good girl,* and I've got a lazy friend
     And if I tell about her, he always tell me where she been
     (John D. Fox, 1927)

40   If you don't want me, baby, just leave me alone
     I can get another woman to carry your business on
     (Amos Easton, 1932)

The most numerous manifestation has the *got* predicate (281 occurrences), followed by the *have* predicate (88 occurrences), and the *get* predicate (74 occurrences).

In comparison to other formulas, further manifestations are rare. The only other manifestations that occur more than twice in the corpus preface the formula with Embs: +*human used to have* +*human* (5 times) and +*human wish* +*human have* +*human* (4 times). In all, this formula occurs 460 times in the corpus, with all but 17 examples conforming to one of the three major manifestations.

+*human leave/quit* +*human* (x-formula)

This formula is interesting in that it combines the ideas of the two previous formulas: possessing someone and leaving, thereby dispossessing someone. As with the previous formulas, the second +*human* is usually a lover or potential lover of the first +*human.* The predicate means "to abandon or terminate a love relationship" rather than simply to move away from some person, and it might be represented as follows:

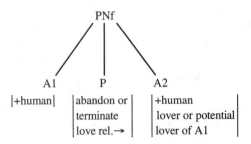

There are only two predicate manifestations of this formula: the verbs *leave* and *quit*. The verb *leave* might imply the actual physical removal of the persona from a place where his or her lover is, as opposed to *quit*, which does not necessarily imply movement, but the two verbs seem to be synonymous as used in the blues. Note the following examples:

41 *Now I'm leaving you, mama,* Lord, and it won't be long
   Now if you don't believe I'm leaving, please count the days I'm
   gone
   (Kokomo Arnold, 1937e)

42 Depot agent, please turn your depot around
   My woman done quit me now; going to leave your town
   (Noah Lewis, 1930a)

The *leave* manifestation occurs 130 times, and the *quit* manifestation occurs 88 times in the corpus.

This formula is prefaced by a number of different Embs: *try to leave +human* (15 times), *hate to leave +human* (4 times), *want to leave +human* (3 times), among others. One of the more numerous minor manifestations includes a temporal Adv as a preface: *the day +human quit +human* (10 times).

Another common manifestation might, in fact, be a combination of two x-formulas: *+human go away* and *+human leave +human*. In its most expanded form it appears as in the following couplet:

43   Early this morning my baby made me sore
I'm going away to leave you; ain't coming back no more
(Blind Blake, 1926a)

But it can also take a more contracted form:

44   What did I ever do that made you leave so all alone
Since you've gone and left me, I do nothing but weep and moan
(Joshua White, 1934)

There are 22 examples of this condensed double x-formula in the corpus. There are approximately 300 examples of this formula in all its manifestations.

+*human love* +*human* (x-formula)

This formula is quite straightforward. Neither the two arguments nor the predicate need any further explanation. The formula can be expressed by the following diagram:

PNf

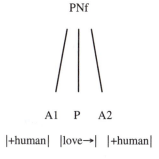

A1   P   A2

|+human| |love→| |+human|

The only manifestation of the predicate is the verb *love,* although there are twenty examples of the phrase +*human like* +*human* in the corpus that might or might not be considered members of this formula.

By far, the most common manifestation is the unembellished one, as in this example:

45   *I love my baby;* my baby don't love me
But I really love that woman; can't stand to leave her be
(Robert Johnson, 1936a)

There are 253 examples of this manifestation in the corpus.

This formula, however, is prone to considerable Emb modification, as the following examples demonstrate:

46   Look here, pretty mama, what you done done
     You done made me love you; now your man done come
     (C.J. Anderson, 1930)

47   I just flutters when I see you, like a little bird up in his nest
     Lord, sometime I think I love you; sometime I think I love my little gal the best
     (Walter Davis, 1940c)

48   Right or wrong, I must be with my little southern Choctaw
     I don't know that she loves me, but she still calls me her southpaw
     (Whistlin' Alex Moore, 1929)

49   *Well I tried to love a sweet mama,* but she couldn't understand
     But I know she realized the trouble, since she met another man
     (Little Hat Jones, 1930a)

50   Had a little girl; she was little and low
     Used to love me, but she don't no more
     (Blind Boy Fuller, 1940a)

51   *Now you wanted me to love you,* and you treated me mean
     You might *give a thought* on my mighty dream
     (Richard Rabbit Brown, 1927)

The occurrences of this formula prefaced by these Embs is as follows: *make,* 25 times; *think,* 13 times; *want,* 12 times; *know,* 8 times; *try,* 8 times; and *used to,* 6 times. This same formula is also prefaced by the Loc *tell* 9 times, as in the following example:

52   *You told me that you loved me;* say you love me all your life
     I caught you around the corner telling the same lie twice
     (Peter Chatman, 1940)

The total number of examples of this formula in the corpus is approximately 350.

+human speak to +human (**x-formula**)

It is difficult to know whether to call this a true formula or to call it merely an upgraded Loc. In example 52, it seems to act as an extraformulaic element, whereas in many other cases it seems to stand on its own. This formula is in fact a more complex predication than any of the formulas previously discussed, because it involves a mandatory downgraded predication within its predicate, as the following diagram shows:

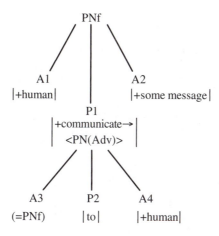

This somewhat complex diagram can be interpreted as follows: there is a predication PNf that might be described as *+human communicate some message.* An adverbial element, PN(Adv), is included within the semantic features of the predicate of the PNf, *+communicate,* wherein the entire PNf is embedded in one argument, A3, of the adverbial predication, PN(Adv). The resulting downgraded predication might be read as *(PNf: +human communicate some message) to +human.*

The most common manifestation of the P1 predicate of this formula is the verb *tell,* and in the most frequent manifestation of the formula, the A2 argument is seemingly deleted, giving the following surface structure:

53 *My mother told me,* don't you weep and moan
   Because, son, there'll be a woman here when you dead and gone
   (Leroy Carr, 1934k)

Of course, the *some message,* or A2 argument, of the formula is filled by the r-formula in the line; in example 53, the A2 *message* is *don't you weep and moan.* This manifestation occurs 430 times in the corpus.

Other verbs can also fill the P1 predicate slot, although none are as common as *tell;* the verbs *ask, talk to,* and *say to* also occur in the corpus. Of these, *ask* is the most frequent, and the following manifestation occurs 80 times:

54 *Anybody ask you* who wrote this worried song
   Tell them you don't know the writer; he'd rather had his happy song
   (Ishman Bracey, 1928d)

Another manifestation of this formula, which occurs 29 times, includes the *message* in its A2 argument, separate from its linked r-formula:

55 *I got something to tell you,* just before you go
   It ain't nothing, baby; turn your lamp down low
   (Otto Virgial, 1935a)

The *some message* slot is filled with the nonspecific word *something.* There can be no doubt that this manifestation is a formula in itself, because it does not rely on the r-formula to complete its internal structure.

A number of Embs preface this formula, of which two occur quite frequently:

56 *Now let me tell you* what that mean old train will do
   It will take your woman, and blow smoke on you
   (Blind Darby, 1931b)

57 Now won't you come here, baby; sit down on my knee
   Now I just want to tell you, black man, how you have treated me
   (Louise Johnson, 1930c)

The manifestation in example 56 occurs 34 times, and the one in example 57 occurs 32 times. In both cases, the A2 argument is sometimes filled with the word *something* and sometimes with the r-formula in the line.

In all its forms, this complex formula occurs approximately 690 times.

+*human treat* +*human in some manner* (**x-formula**)

Structurally, this formula is similar to the preceding one. Thematically, it is close to +*human love* +*human,* because the second +*human* is usually a lover or potential lover of the first +*human.* The predicate might be described as "to behave toward" or "to have a certain effect on." This "treatment" might be physical or mental, and a mandatory adverbial predication *in some manner* describes the nature of this treatment. In diagram form, the formula looks much like +*human speak to* +*human,* because of this mandatory Adv:

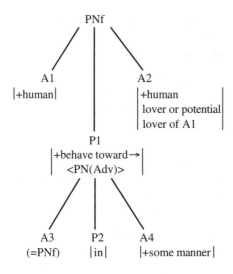

The P1 predicate almost always generates some form of the verb *treat,* although there are five instances in the corpus of the verb *do* and one instance of the verb *misuse.* The most variable element in this predication is the A4 argument, which can take a number of positive or negative images:

58   I'm going to leave this town, baby, and I swear I ain't coming back no more
     I've been treated so bad, I can't be happy no more
     (Sylvester Palmer, 1929)

59   *You treated me wrong;* I treated you right
     I worked for you both day and night
     (Bessie Smith, 1925a)

60   *And you treated me good,* Lord will bless your soul
     If you treated me bad, mama, to hell you surely go
     (Mississippi Moaner, 1935)

61   There's one thing I like about that gal of mine
     She treats me right, and love me all the time
     (William Moore, 1928a)

62   That's all right, mama; that's all right for you
     Treat me lowdown and dirty, any old way you do
     (Arthur Crudup, 1941)

63   *You can treat me mean,* mean as you can be
     But there is coming a day, you will be longing for me
     (Walter Vincson, 1930a)

64   *If you don't treat me no better,* I ain't going to be your man no more
     I love you, it's true, but I will have to let you go
     (Bill Jazz Gillum, 1941c)

65   Judge, I done killed my woman, because she treated me so unkind
     Treated me so unkind, till I swear I lost my mind
     (Leroy Carr, 1934b)

There are several other manifestations of the A4 argument, and although all these manifestations make up a sizeable group, individually they occur rather infrequently in the corpus: example 63 has nine analogues, example 64 occurs six times, and the others occur from one to four times each.

The most common manifestation of this formula places the A4 argument in the position of a morphemic prefix—turning *treat* into *mistreat:*

66   *If I mistreat you, mama,* I sure don't mean no harm
      I'm a honeydripping papa; I don't know right from wrong
      (Kid Prince Moore, 1936)

This manifestation occurs 62 times and is a good example of one of the many possible varieties of surface structure that a deep-level predication can generate.

There are other surface manifestations as well. Note that example 58 is a passive construction: *I've been treated so bad [by someone].* A surface-level reordering of the syntax has occurred here, and most manifestations of this formula allow this type of reordering. Thus, the following example is analogous to example 66, but in a passive position:

67   Ain't no one can change my mind
      I've been mistreated, and I don't mind dying
      (Rosetta Crawford, 1939)

In even more radical surface reorderings, the predicate *treat* is generated as a surface-level noun. Note the following two examples:

68   I worked hard from Monday until late Saturday night
      And you's a dirty mistreater; you ain't treating me right
      (Lucille Bogan, 1929)

69   You can always tell when you woman's got another man
      She will take your bad treatments, and do the best she can
      (Francis Scrapper Blackwell, 1931d)

In example 68, the formulaic predication (PNf) is embedded in an equative predication PN=, where the first argument is equal to the A1 argument of the PNf:

PN=

A1   A2

(=A1 of PNf) (=PNf)

The entire construction might be paraphrased as "you are the one who treats me in a 'mis' manner." The word *me* has been deleted; the *mis* takes its proper place as a prefix to *treat;* the phrase *the one who* becomes the morpheme *er* attached as a suffix to *treat;* and the surface-level sentence becomes *you are a mistreater.* The word *dirty* is an optional Adj.

The italicized phrase in example 69 might be paraphrased as "she will accept the fact that you treat her bad." The phrase *will accept the fact that* might be seen as an Emb (and an Aux *will*); *accept* is transformed into the verb *take;* and the phrase *the fact that* is expressed as the morphemic suffix *-ment* attached to the nominalized verb *treat.* With syntactical reordering, the phrase becomes *she will take your bad treatment of her.* The *of her* is deleted in an optional transformation, leaving the phrase as expressed in example 69.

These more complex manifestations, however, make up only a small portion of all the examples of this formula in the corpus. The second and third most common manifestations do not specify the manner of treatment within the x-formula:

70   Oh Roberta, what in the world you mean
     Honey, the way you treat me beats all I ever seen
     (Huddie Leadbetter, 1935a)

71   I love my mama, and I'll tell the world I do
     Because can't nobody treat me, honey, like my rider do
     (Louie Lasky, 1935)

In example 70, the *some manner* slot is filled by the word *way,* which imparts little information as to the manner of treatment; the description of the "way" is left to the linked r-formula: *beats all I ever seen* (none too specific itself). In example 71, the *some manner* slot is filled directly by the r-formula; that is, the r-formula is embedded in the A4 argument of the x-formula's predication. There are 18 examples of the first phrase and 24 examples of the second phrase in the corpus.

In all, there are more than 160 examples of this formula in the corpus.

some thing worry +human (**x-formula**)

This formula, like the previous one, can take several different syntactical forms. The first argument can be filled by any word or phrase, either *+human* or *–human*, capable of causing worry. The predicate is usually filled by the verb *worry* but can also generate the verbs *trouble* and *bother:*

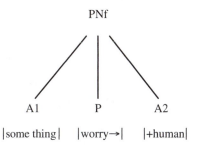

PNf

A1   P   A2

|some thing| |worry→| |+human|

In its simplest form, this formula occurs 15 times, as in this example:

72   Oh baby, what's the matter with you
    You worry me, woman; babe, I don't know what to do
    (Barrel House Buck MacFarland, 1934)

But this formula occurs more frequently in syntactically inverted forms, the most common manifestation exhibiting a passive transformation and the deletion of the A1 argument:

73   Now mmmmm mmmmm
    Said I'm worried now, baby; won't be worried long
    (Billy Bird, 1928)

In this example, a deeper-level paraphrase of the manifestation would be "I am worried by something," but the *by something* has been deleted in the surface structure. This manifestation occurs 41 times in the corpus.

   In another common manifestation, the Emb *keep* is inserted in the passive structure: *something keep you are worried by something*. The equative verb *are* and the phrase *by something* are deleted, forming the surface manifestation:

74 I'm going away, baby, to wear you off my mind
    For you keeps me worried; a-bothered all the time
    (Blue Coat Tom Nelson, 1928)

In this form, the formula occurs 25 times with the verb *worry* and 4 times with the verb *trouble*.

Similar to the passive construction is another transformation that makes the verb *worry* intransitive. The usual A2 of the predication then becomes the subject, and the A1 argument is placed in a prepositional phrase: *+human worry about something.* The phrase *about something* is then deleted, in most cases, leaving the simple phrase *+human worry.* This manifestation is almost always modified by a Neg, as in the following example:

75 *Mother, please don't worry;* this is all my prayer
    Just say your son is gone; I'm out in the world somewhere
    (Jimmy Oden, 1941)

There are 19 examples of this manifestation in the corpus.

In two isolated examples the predicate is realized as a noun:

76 I worried a long time ago, and you was as happy as you could be
    So now it's your worry; I'm glad you have set me free
    (Washboard Sam, 1941c)

77 *She didn't have no worry;* didn't have a lick at a snake
    She didn't even cook her meals; ooo well well, I mean she really had got a break
    (Peetie Wheatstraw, 1936g)

And in one case it is realized as an adjective:

78 *Now the blues so worrisome, mama,* between midnight and day
    Now the blues done caused my woman, hon', to run away
    (Jaybird Coleman, 1927b)

The formula appears with several different Embs, such as *get* (i.e., *become*) and *be no use to,* as well as with several Auxs, such as *have to* and *should.* In all, this formula occurs 170 times in the corpus.

+*human* *have the blues* (r-formula)

The description of this r-formula is the same as that of its x-formula counterpart, previously described. The only major difference is that the A2 argument cannot be followed by an Adj (as in examples 10 and 11), because the word *blues* must be retained at the end of the phrase for rhyming purposes.

The most common manifestation has the verb *get* in its surface predicate:

> 79 Ain't got no stocking; ain't got no shoes
> *Know I've got the Memphis Jug Band blues*
> (Poor Jab, 1928)

The *get* form occurs 43 times, whereas the *have* form occurs only 11 times in the corpus.

One phrase, which might or might not be considered a member of this formula, is the following:

> 80 Hey Mr. Mailman, did you bring me any news
> Because if you didn't, *it will give me those special delivery blues*
> (Sippie Wallace, 1926)

This example might be paraphrased as "it will cause me to have the blues," where the verb *cause* is an Emb attached to the formula. There are 10 examples in the corpus of this interesting manifestation. In all, there are more than 80 examples of this r-formula.

+*human* *cry* (r-formula)

The predication for this r-formula is quite simple, being a one-argument variety:

PNf

A1   P

|+human| |+cry|

The flexibility of blues rhyme allows the conjugation *cried* and *cries,* as well as *cry,* in the surface predicate of this formula. Because this formula is so short, it invariably undergoes modifications by extraformulaic elements, as in the following examples:

81 Well good-bye, Red; *now ain't going to cry*
    Well I ain't going to frown; wouldn't tell you no lie
    (Sonny Boy Williamson, 1938g)

82 One day I sit thinking, when the rain pour down outside
    And the more I thought, *the more I began to cry*
    (Scrapper Blackwell, 1931b)

83 I had a little kitty; I called her mine
    Way in the night, *I could hear her cry*
    (Blind Ben Covington, 1928)

84 Sometimes he makes me happy; *then sometimes he makes me cry*
    He had me to the place, where I wish to God that I could die
    (Memphis Minnie, 1930a)

85 *Once I couldn't stand to see you cry*
    But I feel all the same, mama, if you die
    (Charlie Spand, 1929a)

86 *Sister and brother, you needn't have cried*
    The kids in school are ready to write
    (Unknown artist, 1930c)

The most frequent of these manifestations is example 84, which occurs 13 times in the corpus.

But the formula is also embellished in another way. Often another complete predication is attached to the formula, usually describing the physical movements and gestures that accompany the action of crying. Most of these predications never occur by themselves in blues lyrics and cannot, therefore, be called formulas in their own right. They are, instead, complex Advs, although they cannot be represented semantically in the same way as can other Advs. The following are examples of these strange manifestations:

87 Lord, said the blues jumped a rabbit; run him for a solid mile
    Lord, that fool couldn't catch him, *and he fell right down and cry*
    (James Yank Rachel, 1930)

88 And I locked in the death cell, *and drop my weary head and cry*
    I told the Sing Sing prison board, this ain't like being outside
    (Bob Coleman, 1929)

89 Mama, now she told me, *ooo mmm till I hold her head and cry*
    Well well well, some of these women, now, done made up their
    minds all the time
    (Peetie Wheatstraw, 1930a)

90 I was locked outdoors; *huddled myself all night long and cried*
    I'm going crazy; crazy as I can be
    (Memphis Minnie, 1931a)

91 If my black angel would leave me, I believe that I would die
    And if I see him looking at another woman, *I just scream and
    cry*
    (Lucille Bogan, 1930b)

92 Now that last cruel papa, he blacked my eye
    Then left me alone *to sigh and cry*
    (Ethel Waters, 1923a)

93 Now you see me coming; now mama, heist your window high
    But you know I'm going to leave you; *girl, I know you going to
    grieve and cry*
    (Big Bill Broonzy, 1930a)

94 Many day I sit down; *weep and cry*
    That's why I'm dying to be by your side
    (Big Boy George Owens, 1926)

95 I can't count the times, *I stoled away and cried*
    Sugar, the blues ain't on me, but things ain't going right
    (Blind Lemon Jefferson, 1927e)

96 Boo hoo, *wring my hands and cry*
    I'm thinking about that loving that I let go by
    (Gene Campbell, 1930)

97 I was standing at the terminal; *arms folded up and cried*
    Crying I wonder what train taking that brown of mine
    (Robert Hicks, 1928c)

In each case, the highlighted phrase consists of two predications linked by the conjunction *and*. If the first predication is considered an Adv, then the entire phrase might look like this:

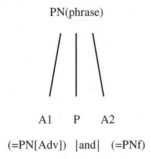

PN(phrase)

A1   P   A2

(=PN[Adv]) |and| (=PNf)

The frequency of these forms in the corpus is the following: example 87, 3 times; example 88, 22 times; examples 89 and 90, 1 time each; example 91, 5 times; example 92, 2 times; examples 93 and 94, 1 time each; example 95, 4 times; example 96, 5 times; and example 97, 2 times.

Whether these different manifestations are to be considered as all members of the same formula is a matter of debate, but in all, there are approximately 85 examples of this formula in the corpus.

+human do unspecified action (r-formula)

This formula manifests itself in a great many ways, using a wide variety of Embs and Auxs. In essence, the formula presents the dilemma of not knowing what action to take. It is usually put in the form of a question and the *unspecified action* usually generates the word *what*.

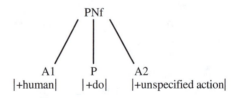

PNf

A1   P   A2
|+human| |+do| |+unspecified action|

Because this is an r-formula, the rhyme word *do* must always fall at the end of the phrase; this means that the deep-level phrase *+human do* *what* is reordered at the surface level to *what +human do*. The following list shows some of this formula's more common surface manifestations:

98 Now look a-here, Sue; *what you trying to do*
Giving away my luggage, and trying to love me too
(Jack Kelly, 1939)

99 When I get drunk, I'm evil; *I don't know what to do*
If I get my good chib, can I get something good from you
(Edith North Johnson, 1929a)

100 The north wind has begin howling, and the skies are pretty blue
And winter is coming; *wonder what the poor people are going to do*
(Walter Davis, 1931)

101 Will you please tell me, judge, don't have a trial till June
Because I got a working baby; *let me see what my woman can do*
(Little Hat Jones, 1929a)

102 *Mmmmm, baby, what are you going to do*
You say you love me, baby, but now you say you are through
(Huddie Leadbetter, 1935d)

103 Lord, I got a pretty mama; lives on Central Avenue
Lord, if that woman left and quite me *now*, *what in the world that I would do*
(Will Day, 1928a)

104 You put the puppies on my mama; you drove me crazy too
You done made me love you; *what can I do*
(Leroy Carr, 1934a)

105 You ought to be grateful, daddy, ???
You are three times seven; *you know just what you want to do*
(Jennie Clayton, 1927)

106 I'm waiting on you; I'm waiting on you
I'm waiting on you, baby; *tell me what you going to do*
(Amos Easton, 1932)

107 Tell all you women, *what you better do*
     You better lay off my pigmeat, or it won't be good for you
     (Mae Glover, 1929a)

Note the many different Embs and Auxs used here to alter the basic
meaning of the formula.

Although most of these examples occur with fairly equal frequency
in the corpus, there are a few manifestations that are especially common.
The formula prefaced by the Emb *want*, where the subject of the Emb is
different from that of the formula (as opposed to example 105), occurs
approximately 35 times in the corpus:

108 *Now pretty mama, what you want me to do*
     I did everything in this world, trying to get along with you
     (Ollie Rupert, 1927b)

The formula prefaced by the Emb *tell*, meaning "to ascertain" (as opposed to example 106), occurs about 10 times:

109 I've got a baby that keeps me feeling blue
     He acts like the weather; *I can't tell what he's going to do*
     (Ruth Willis, 1931b)

The formula prefaced by the Emb and Neg elements *don't care* occurs
about 20 times:

110 Now I love you, baby; *don't care what you do*
     But the way you doing, I swear it's coming back home to you
     (Tommy McClennan, 1940b)

And the formula prefaced by the Adv and Aux elements *more* and *can*
occurs approximately 10 times:

111 I done told you I loved you; *what more can I do*
     And you must a-want me to lay down and die for you
     (Bobby Grant, 1927a)

There are also several manifestations in which the *unspecified action* feature generates a word other than *what*. The majority of these examples
are similar to the following italicized phrase:

112 You can mistreat me, baby; *do anything you want to do*
     Some day you going to want me, but your baby won't want you
     (Charley Jordan, 1930a)

This manifestation occurs about 15 times, but other non-*what* forms also occur:

113 Lord, I don't know what to do, baby; I can't get along with you
Now you may treat me right, babe; *that's all I can do*
(Ed Schaffer, 1930)

114 Been to see the gypsy, hoodoo doctors too
Shook their heads, *and told me nothing they could do*
(Clara Smith, 1924g)

115 I can sit right here, and look on Jackson Avenue
I can see everything *that my good woman do*
(Furry Lewis, 1928c)

In all its many manifestations, this formula occurs approximately 330 times in the corpus.

+*human go some place* (r-formula)

This formula has obvious similarities to the *go some place* x-formula previously discussed, but there are many more limitations on it. Because the argument *some place* is highly variable, it cannot fill the final position in the phrase; the words *go* or *goes* must maintain this position for the purposes of rhyme. The surface syntax of the formula, therefore, becomes *some place +human go*. The verb *go* is highly restricted in the tense it can take, because the conjugations *went, gone,* and *going* would destroy the rhyme of the formula. The deep-level structure of the formula might be represented in the following manner:

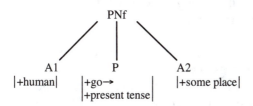

One peculiarity of this formula is that it often includes a part of its linked x-formula within its structure, acting like an Loc, as in the following example:

116   Well it's hard times here, *and it's hard times everywhere I go*
      I've got to make me some money, so I won't have these hard-luck blues no more
      (Bill Jazz Gillum, 1942)

But the formula also occurs as an independent phrase within the line:

117   Skin man's hollering; passing right by my door
      Well he's hollering skin, *everywhere he goes*
      (Hi Henry Brown, 1932)

The *some place* slot is almost always filled by some unspecified location, such as *everywhere, nowhere, any place, anywhere, no matter where, which a-way,* or *no place.* In one of its more common forms, it is prefaced by the Emb and Neg *don't care,* as in this example:

118   Because tricks ain't working, tricks ain't working no more
      And I can't make no money; *don't care where I go*
      (Lucile Bogan, 1930c)

This particular manifestation occurs 9 times in the corpus.

In another manifestation the formula is embedded in the A2 argument of a +*human have something* construction, forming +*human have some place* +*human go*; the two +*humans* must be synonymous, and the entire phrase usually includes a Neg:

119   I woke up this morning; I couldn't even get out my door
      Said this wild water got me covered, *and I ain't got no place to go*
      (Kokomo Arnold, 1937a)

This manifestation forms the single largest group within this formula, with 34 occurrences in the corpus.

There are only 9 examples in the corpus of the *some place* slot being filled by a specific place: *down the road* (twice), *out my door, Riley Springs, to you* (i.e., "to the place where you are"), *hell, Front Street, the valley,* and *the Union Stockyards.*

In all, there are approximately 130 examples of this formula in the corpus.

+*human gone* (r-formula)

The internal structure of this formula is quite simple. The single argument is +*human* and the predicate is the verb *go;* however, this predicate has the further limiting feature that the verb must be in past participle form, such as *be gone, have gone, have been gone, had been gone,* or *done gone.*

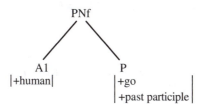

In its simplest form, the predicate is usually some conjugation of *be gone:*

120 I woke up this morning; *my good gal was gone*
     Stood by my bedside, and I hung my head, and I hung my head
     and moaned
     (Willie Baker, 1929b)

121 Lord, it's some of these old mornings; Lordy, know it won't be
     long
     Lord, you know you going to call me, *baby, Lord, and I'll be gone*
     (Big Bill Broonzy, 1932c)

122 I treated her wrong, before she left my home
     I guess I'm not her daddy, *and she would not have been gone*
     (Ed Bell, 1930a)

Because this structure is so simple, the formula often needs embellishment, in a manner similar to that of the x-formula +*human cry.* The most common Emb attachment is the verb *find:*

123 And I got up this morning; a light all in my room
     And I looked behind me, *and I found my faro gone*
     (James Yank Rachel, 1929)

This formula is also similar to the +*human cry* formula in its ability to incorporate other phrases into its structure; that is, the actual formulaic phrase +*human gone* is often prefaced by another action that describes, in greater detail, the method or reason behind the +*human*'s leaving. Thus, the following examples occur:

124 Now if anybody ask you who composed this song
Tell them it's corn-liquor daddy; *he's been here and gone*
(Lewis Black, 1927c)

125 Boy, I may be right, Lord; boy, I may be wrong
But my faro done come here, baby; *caught the train and gone*
(Will Weldon, 1927)

126 I can't stay away; I done cried the whole night long
The good woman I love, *she done packed her trunk and gone*
(Blind Lemon Jefferson, 1926g)

127 I don't mind being in jail, but I got to stay there so long, so long
When every friend I had is done shook hands and gone
(Bessie Smith, 1923b)

128 Love is like water; it turns off and on
When you think you got a good girl, *Lord, she done turn off and gone*
(Bill Day, 1929)

129 Said my love's like water; it turns off and on
When you think I'm loving, *I done took off and gone*
(Edward Thompson, 1929c)

130 Children's in the pulpit, mama, trying to learn the Psalms
Now that lowdown dirty deacon done stole my gal and gone
(Luke Jordan, 1927b)

The frequency of these phrases is as follows: example 124 occurs 14 times; example 125 occurs 7 times; example 126 occurs 3 times; example 127 occurs 2 times; example 128 occurs 5 times; example 129 occurs once (although this seems to have some connection with example 128); and example 130 occurs 11 times.

In all, there are approximately 200 examples of this formula in the corpus.

+human come home (**r-formula**)

In this formula the two arguments are fairly fixed, *+human* and *home*, while the predicate can generate any word or phrase that means "movement toward."

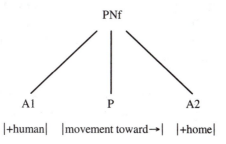

The predicate is often modified by the adverb *back,* and the following examples show some of the different predicate manifestations:

131   *I believe, I believe I'll go back home*
      Lord, acknowledge to my good gal, mama, Lord, that I have done
      you wrong
      (Kokomo Arnold, 1935a)

132   One day ???; we're riding along
      I asked her how about it, *and she walked back home*
      (Pillie Bolling, 1930b)

133   If you see my baby, *tell her to hurry home*
      Ain't had no mmm, since she has been gone
      (Leroy Carr, 1934a)

134   Now I'm going down south, and I'll stay until winter is gone
      Time that wintertime is gone, *I might come back home*
      (John Estes, 1935a)

135   *Crying Lord, I wonder will I ever get back home*
      (Tommy Johnson, 1928a)

136   You may miss my love and kisses, *and you wish you back home*
      But someone else will be picking up your chicken bones
      (Maggie Jones, 1924d)

137 Babe, please forgive me; I know that I done wrong
I'm going to get down on my knees; *I want my little old baby back home*
(Jack Kelly, 1933b)

138 Says I ain't going to give you no more money; ain't going to let you do me wrong
For you would take my money; *then you will slip on home*
(Walter Roland, 1934)

139 When I left town this morning, *I was on my way back home*
I heard the churchbells making a lonesome sound
(Walter Vincson, 1930d)

140 I believe to my soul, my girl got a black cat bone
For when I leave, *sure come creeping home*
(Uncle Bud Walker, 1928a)

Together, these examples occur about 75 times and make up the majority of examples of this formula in the corpus. The verbs *come* and *go* are the most frequent, but these examples show that singers had considerable choice in filling the predicate slot.

The other major group of manifestations embeds the formulaic predication within the A2 of another phrase:

141 You know I love her, Santa Claus; *why don't you bring her home*
If you bring her back to me, I'll never do her wrong
(Buck Turner, 1937b)

142 Way down in Boogie Alley, ain't nothing but skulls and bones
And when I get drunk, *who's going to take me home*
(Lucille Bogan, 1934d)

143 Well wonder where's that black snake gone
Lord, that black snake, mama, done run my darling home
(Blind Lemon Jefferson, 1926h)

144 Well I went out, mama, and I begin to prayer and moan
I want to be good, Lord; Lord, *send my babe back home*
(Sammy Hill, 1929b)

145 If you see my wild cow, *please drive her back home*
   Lord, I ain't had no milk and butter, since he stole my wild cow
   and gone
   (Big Joe Williams, 1935f)

All these italicized phrases might be paraphrased as +*human cause* +*human move toward home*. The deep-structure predicate *cause* generates the surface predicates in these phrases. There are twenty occurrences of this manifestation.

   Every example of this formula falls into one or the other of these two major manifestations, so that in all, there are nearly 100 examples of this formula in the corpus.

time won't be long (**r-formula**)

This is the most invariable of the twenty formulas described here. Its structure is an equative predication, where one argument is equated with another. In addition, there is a mandatory Neg, because the phrase *time will be long* does not seem entirely logical, and it never occurs in the corpus. Equative predications are generally shown as two equative arguments without a predicate:

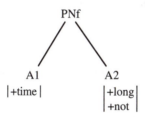

At the semantic level, the verb *be* is only a signal for the equative predication. At the syntactical level, however, the verb must be expressed, complete with tense and modal modification. In the case of this formula, almost all examples place the verb in the future tense. In addition, the word *time* is almost always pronominalized to *it*. The following example is typical of most manifestations of this formula:

146 Tell my dad, I'm going to leave my home
   Now I'm going, I'm going, *and it won't be long*
   (Gertrude Ma Rainey, 1926b)

There are only two examples in the corpus in which the word *time* is not pronominalized:

147   My windows begin rattling, and my doorknob is turning around and around
      My lover's ghost has got me, *and I know my time won't be long*
      (Lonnie Johnson, 1938a)

148   Well I'm going away; *swear the time ain't long*
      If you don't believe I'm leaving, daddy, count them days I'm gone
      (Louise Johnson, 1930a)

In example 147, the pronoun *it* cannot replace the word *time*, because of the qualifying word *my*. In fact, the sense of example 147 is quite different from that of the other manifestations of this formula, and it is debatable whether this phrase should be included in the formula group at all. In example 148, however, the singer definitely chose the nominal form over the pronominal form for the A1 argument.

There are only four other atypical manifestations:

149   So bye bye, baby, if you call it gone
      I know it's going to worry me, *but it won't last long*
      (Peter Chatman, 1941)

150   I'll sing you these verses, *and it didn't take long*
      If you want to hear any more, you'll have to buy this song
      (Jim Jackson, 1930)

151   Folks, I'm going to tell you about a brand new song
      I'm going to beat some dirt, *and it won't take long*
      (Frankie Half Pint Jaxon, 1929)

152   All last night, *baby, it seemed so long*
      All I've done, I ain't done nothing wrong
      (Francis Scrapper Blackwell, 1928b)

In examples 149 to 151, the predicate generates verbs other than *be;* whether this should eliminate these phrases from the formula group is problematic. In example 152, there is no negation, which is probably made possible by the insertion of the verb *seem* in the predicate. Again, it is debatable whether this example should be considered a member of the formula.

In all, there are more than 50 examples of this formula in the corpus.

+*human have some thing on* +*human's mind* (**r-formula**)

The structure of this formula is somewhat complex, in that it involves embedded predications within embedded predications. The A1 argument is +*human,* and its predicate is similar to that of the +*human have the blues* formulas; that is, it may be described as "to contract or come down with, as with a cold." The A2 argument is an embedded equative predication with two arguments: *some thing* and a further embedded predication. This final predication also has *some thing* as its first argument, the preposition *on* as its predicate, and the rhyme word *mind* as its second argument. In diagram form, this complex formulaic predication looks like this:

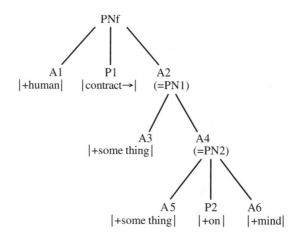

The *some thing* under A3 must be synonymous with the *some thing* under A5. In addition, the A6 argument must be modified by a possessive synonymous with the A1 argument. Otherwise, incongruous statements such as *I got something on your mind* would occur.

A paraphrase of this deep structure is something like *+human has something that is the something on +human's mind*. Obviously, certain deletion transformations must take place; namely, the A3 argument is deleted, because two *some things* are redundant in the surface structure. The final form of the formula appears as in this example:

153   I'm kind of worried; *got something on my mind*
      That's why I drink my whisky; make my faro wait behind
      (Robert Hicks, 1928a)

There are, however, other deletions that can be made from the deep structure, forming different surface manifestations. The A1 argument and the P1 predicate can be deleted, as well as the A5 argument of the PN2 embedded predication. What is left becomes an equative manifestation of the formula, as in this example:

154   Early one morning, *baby, something was on my mind*
      I thinking about my welfare, and I just couldn't keep from crying
      (Robert Wilkins, 1935a)

Note that when the equative predication (PN1) becomes the surface structure, the verb *be* must fill the empty predicate slot.

It is also possible, however, to delete everything but the most deeply embedded predication (PN2) *some thing on my mind:*

155   I woke up this morning; *thousand things on my mind*
      Lord, I thought about my troubles; could not keep from crying
      (Roosevelt Sykes, 1929d)

In a similar manifestation, the A1 and P1 elements are not so much deleted as transformed into the preposition *with* in the surface structure:

156   Got up this morning, *with the same thing on my mind*
      And the girl I'm loving, but she don't pay me no mind
      (Big Bill Broonzy, 1930a)

One of the most common forms of this formula transforms the statement into a question. Invariably, the *some thing* slot is filled by the word *what*, as these two examples demonstrate:

157 Now tell me, daddy, *what you got on your worried mind*
     Tell your little mama your troubles; swear I'll tell you mine
     (Rosie Mae Moore, 1928b)

158 *Sweet mama, sweet mama, what's on your mind*
     Say you can't quit me; no need of trying
     (Peg Leg Howell, 1926a)

In all of these examples, the *some thing* slot has been filled by a non-specific word: *something, thing,* and *what.* The slot can also be filled by concrete words and phrases, both *+human* and *−human.* In fact, the *+human on my mind* manifestations make up a whole subgroup:

159 I can hear my back door slamming; seem like I can hear my little baby crying
     Lord, I wonder, baby, *have you got me on your mind*
     (Walter Davis, 1940a)

160 I'm so blue, baby, I'm so blue, baby; I can't keep from drinking; hardly talk for crying
     You know, baby, you know, baby, you are always forever on my mind
     (Lonnie Chatman, 1932c)

161 I can't sleep for dreaming; I can't eat for crying
     I lay down last night *with that gal all on my mind*
     (Sam Collins, 1927c)

The third major group consists of phrases that have concrete human words and phrases in their *some thing* slots:

162 *Mmmmm corn liquor on my mind*
     If you catch me out drinking, I'm not drinking just to keep from crying
     (Lewis Black, 1927c)

163 The clothes look lonesome hanging out on the line
You can tell by that *I've got rambling on my mind*
(Tommie Bradley, 1931a)

164 I woke up this morning moaning *with the worried blues on my mind*
I was thinking about someone, who were left behind
(Bill Day, 1929)

When the *–human some thing* is a gerund, as in example 163, a further syntactical transformation is possible, which converts the A2 argument into a noun modified by an adjective:

165 I got a rambling woman; *she got a rambling mind*
I buy her a ticket; let her ease on down the line
(George Noble, 1935)

The three major categories within this formula, then, are dependent on the nature of the *some thing* features: nonspecific, specific and *+human,* specific and *–human.* These three categories occur approximately 40 times each, for a total of about 120 examples in the corpus.

+human treat +human right (r-formula)

Structurally, this formula is the same as its x-formula counterpart previously described. Because it is an r-formula, however, there are more restrictions on it. Instead of the A4 argument being *some manner,* it is more specifically the word *right,* because this word carries the rhyme. Because of the rhyme factor, the word *right* must always remain at the end of the line. Thus, although the phrases *you mistreat me* and *you don't treat me right* are virtually synonymous, only the latter is a member of this formula.

This formula can take a number of Embs and Advs:

166 Now when I was a schoolboy, I would not take no one's advice
Now I'm just a broke man; *nobody seems to want to treat me right*
(Kokomo Arnold, 1937f)

167 Walk with my good girl in the daytime; walk with her at night
Said I taught my kitchen *teller* how to treat a good man right
(Joe Calicott, 1930)

168 I often tell my honey, don't have to fight
     The gal that gets you *has got to try to treat you right*
     (Bo Weavil Jackson, 1926a)

Although the predicate usually generates the verb *treat* (approximately 35 times in the corpus), it can also generate at least two other verbs:

169 *Now you know, 'Berta, you ain't doing me right*
     And when you come home, we'll go to fuss and fight
     (Tommy McClennan, 1940d)

170 Baby, you been gone all day, that you may make whoopee all night
     If I going to take my razor and cut your late hours, *you wouldn't think I be serving you right*
     (King Solomon Hill, 1932a)

These other manifestations occur 7 and 2 times, respectively. Overall, this formula occurs about 45 times in the corpus.

* * *

To demonstrate the scope of particular formulas, I list every manifestation of the following last two formulas. In doing so, not only will the varied surface-level manifestations of these formulas reveal themselves but the varied juxtapositions of these formulas within the line and stanza will become clear. As always, whether all examples of these formulas are truly members of their respective groups or—especially in the case of some of the more anomalous manifestations—whether my list has been too inclusive is problematic.

+*human wake up* (x-formula)

As I discuss later in this study, this formula is symbolic of an "awakening" to a change in state or situation. Its denotation, however, is +*human emerge from sleep,* and it can be represented by the following diagram:

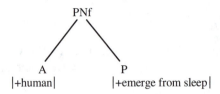

Some examples tend more toward the denotation, such as couplet 171.46 below, in which sleep is induced by the dentist's gas, while others are clearly symbolic, such as example 171.260, in which the "waking up" refers to the persona's realization of how his lover has been exploiting him. In a few cases, such as example 171.263, it is not clear whether the feature "emergence from sleep" is being employed at all, and therefore the inclusion of this phrase in the list might not be justified.

The vast majority of cases, however, unquestionably fulfill the criteria of the predication described earlier. The predicate allows four possible manifestations: *wake up,* as in example 171.205; *get up,* as in example 171.193; *rise,* as in example 171.181; and the equative verb *be,* as in example 171.125. The first two predicate manifestations are, by far, the most frequent. The verb *rise* occurs only three times (171.1, 171.157, and 171.181) and the equative *be* form occurs only twice (171.125 and 171.214). In fact, the equative predicates might fall outside the semantic criteria of this formula, because they do not imply "emergence from sleep" as much as "the state of being fully awake."

The temporal Adv *in the morning* or *this morning* almost always accompanies this formula, although it must not be thought of as an essential part of the structure. Not only does this same extraformulaic element occur with other formulas but also this formula often occurs without such modification; for example, see couplets 171.89, 171.110, 171.128, and 171.164. In addition, the predicate of this formula might be modified by a number of other Advs: *in my stockings,* example 171.60; *moaning,* example 171.66; *with the blues,* examples 171.87 and 171.157; *lonesome,* example 171.271; and *weak and dizzy,* example 171.46.

There are four examples (171.29, 171.48, 171.159, and 171.218) in which the verb *wake* is transitive rather than intransitive, and consequently the semantic deep structure of these phrases has two arguments: *+human wake up +human.* This indicates that perhaps the true deep structure of this formula might indeed have two arguments and that in most cases the second argument is synonymous with the first: *+human1 wake up +human1.* In the surface structure this can be represented by the use of the reflexive pronoun, as in *I woke up myself*, but there are no examples in the corpus of the reflexive being used with this formula. In every case, this hypothetical reflexive has been deleted in a syntactical transformation.

There are two examples of *lay awake* included in this list (171.106 and 171.119), which show another x-position usage of the "wake" image, but they are clearly not members of this formula.

171.1 And I rolled and I tumbled, and I cried the whole night long
And I rose this morning, and I didn't know right from wrong
(Garfield Akers, 1930a)

171.2 *Have you ever woke up*, and found your dough-roller gone
Then you wring your hands, and you cry the whole day long
(Garfield Akers, 1930a)

171.3 *She will get up early in the morning*, just a while before day
Then cook your breakfast; man, rush you away
(Texas Alexander, 1928b)

171.4 *I'm going to get up in the morning;* do like Buddy Brown
I'm going to eat my breakfast, man, and lay back down
(Texas Alexander, 1929)

171.5 *Did you ever wake up* between midnight and day
And you felt for your rider; she done eased away
(Blind Joe Amos, 1927)

171.6 *I woke up this morning*, about half past four
Told my girl I couldn't use her no more
(C.J. Anderson, 1930)

171.7 Baby, baby, baby, I got all my clothes out on pawn
I'm going to wake up one morning, and have all my glad-rags gone
(Jelly Roll Anderson, 1927)

171.8 *Says I woke up this morning*, and I looked outdoors
Says I know my mamlish milkcow, pretty mama, Lord, by the way she lows
(Kokomo Arnold, 1934)

171.9   *Lord, I woke up this morning* with my Port China tickets in my hand
Lord, if you can't send me no woman, please send me some sissy man
(Kokomo Arnold, 1935a)

171.10 *Now if you wake up in the morning;* ain't got nothing on your mind
Play that old country number that you call three sixty-nine
(Kokomo Arnold, 1935g)

171.11 *I woke up this morning;* I couldn't even get out of my door
Said this wild water got me covered, and I ain't got no place to go
(Kokomo Arnold, 1937a)

171.12 *Now I'm going to get up in the morning;* do just like old Buddy Brown
Says I'm going to eat my breakfast, please and lay back down
(Kokomo Arnold, 1937c)

171.13 Well I dreamed last night now that my old shack was falling down
And when I woke up this morning, my poor head was going round and round
(Kokomo Arnold, 1937f)

171.14 I'm getting so tired of running from town to town
For when I wake up in the morning, my head is going around and around
(Kokomo Arnold, 1938a)

171.15 I'm scared to stay here; scared to leave this old bad-luck town
So when I wake up every morning, my head is going round and round
(Kokomo Arnold, 1938c)

171.16 *I woke up this morning;* my good gal was gone
Stood by my bedside, and I hung my head and, hung my head and moaned
(Willie Baker, 1929b)

171.17   *She got up last night;* she crawled around my bed
Going to love you long time, daddy; I guess I will see you
dead
(Willie Baker, 1929c)

171.18   *She got up last night;* she crawled around my bed
Going to love you long time, daddy; guess I will see you
dead
(Willie Baker, 1929e)

171.19   *Well I woke up this morning,* half past four
A long tall gal rapping at my door
(Willie Baker, 1929f)

171.20   *Have you ever waked up, babe,* between midnight and day
Turn over and grab the pillow where your great gal used to
lay
(Wiley Barner, 1927)

171.21   *I wake up this morning;* blues all around my bed
Well I had a high fever going up to my head
(Wiley Barner, 1927)

171.22   *And I got up this morning,* just about the dawn of day
Mean I ain't got no job; I ain't got no place to stay
(Big Bill Broonzy, 1928)

171.23   *Got up this morning* with the same thing on my mind
And the girl I'm loving, but she don't pay me no mind
(Big Bill Broonzy, 1930a)

171.24   *Got up this morning,* about half past four
Somebody's knocking on my back door
(Big Bill Broonzy, 1930b)

171.25   *I got up this morning,* mama, about half past four
Somebody was knocking on my back door
(Big Bill Broonzy, 1930c)

171.26   *I got up this morning;* hear the train whistle blow
Lord, I thought about my baby; I sure did want to go
(Big Bill Broonzy, 1932a)

171.27   *Lord, I got up this morning,* just about the break of day
          Lord, I'm thinking about my baby; Lord, the one that went
          away
          (Big Bill Broonzy, 1932c)

171.28   Now you can put me in the alley; my gal is name is Sally
          You wake me up in the morning; mama, I still got that old
          habit
          (Big Bill Broonzy, 1932c)

171.29   *Now I wake up in the morning,* holding a bottle tight
          When I lay down at night, mama, just a gallon out of sight
          (Big Bill Broonzy, 1935c)

171.30   *I woke up this morning* with rambling on my mind
          And I lit out to walking just to pass away the time
          (Francis Scrapper Blackwell, 1931a)

171.31   *I woke up this morning;* worried in my mind
          Thinking about that girl I left behind
          (Blind Blake, 1926c)

171.32   *I got up this morning;* put on my walking shoes
          I'm going back to Tampa, just to kill my lowdown blues
          (Blind Blake, 1926d)

171.33   Take me; mama, I'll tell you what I'll do
          I'll get up every morning; work hard all day for you
          (Blind Blake, 1927a)

171.34   It must be a black cat bone; jomo can't work that hard
          Every time I wake up, Jim Tampa's in my yard
          (Lucille Bogan, 1927b)

171.35   I boogie all night; all the night before
          When I woke up this morning, I want to boogie some more
          (Lucille Bogan, 1930a)

171.36   *I got up this morning* with the rising sun
          Been working all day, and I ain't caught a one
          (Lucille Bogan, 1930c)

171.37　*I got up this morning,* feeling tough
　　　　I've got to call in my tricks in the rough, rough, rough
　　　　(Lucille Bogan, 1930c)

171.38　*Got up this morning* by the rising sun
　　　　Didn't have no whisky; I tried to buy me some
　　　　(Lucille Bogan, 1933)

171.39　*He gets up every morning,* and before he goes
　　　　Say he don't want me to put my head out of my front door
　　　　(Lucille Bogan, 1934a)

171.40　*Woke up this morning;* mama was treating me night and day
　　　　I reached for my sugar, and the fool had stoled away
　　　　(Ishman Bracey, 1928e)

171.41　*Woke up this morning* with my face up to the ground
　　　　I didn't have no sugar, not to pick up in my arms
　　　　(Ishman Bracey, 1928e)

171.42　*I woke up this morning;* had the blues all around my bed
　　　　I couldn't help but to think about what my good gal said
　　　　(Ishman Bracey, 1930b)

171.43　*Woke up this morning;* couldn't even walk in my shoes
　　　　My baby just quit me; she left me with the bust up blues
　　　　(Ishman Bracey, 1930c)

171.44　*Have you ever woke up in the morning;* *you weep and
　　　　moan*
　　　　Your best girl quit you; left you all alone
　　　　(Ishman Bracey, 1930d)

171.45　*Lord, when I got up this morning,* snow was on my window
　　　　pane
　　　　I couldn't even see my baby; couldn't even hear her name
　　　　(Tommie Bradley, 1932)

171.46　*I woke up weak and dizzy;* he told me that I would
　　　　But all my pain had left me; he really done me good
　　　　(Laura Bryant, 1929)

171.47   I don't want no woman that wears a number nine
        I wake up in the morning; I can't tell her shoes from mine
        (Charlie Campbell, 1937)

171.48   *Woke up my baby;* come my love
        Unlock the door; the sky's above
        (Leroy Carr, 1929)

171.49   *Now I woke up this morning;* my woman was standing over me
        She had a big forty-five, and she was mad as she could be
        (Leroy Carr, 1934c)

171.50   *When she gets up in the morning,* she starts to drink her corn
        Every time I think of that woman, I wished I had never been born
        (Leroy Carr, 1934e)

171.51   *I woke up this morning;* didn't find you there
        Wondering what man had his hand running down through your hair down there
        (Leroy Carr, 1934i)

171.52   *Says I woke up this morning,* half past four
        I want to roll your lemon, baby, just before I go
        (Bo Chatman, 1935)

171.53   She shook me this morning at half past one
        Oh wake up, daddy; rolling must go on
        (Bo Chatman, 1936)

171.54   She shook me again at half past two
        Oh wake up, daddy; rolling ain't near through
        (Bo Chatman, 1936)

171.55   *And I woke up this morning;* my pillow slip wringing wet
        I looked around for my baby; daddy, I can't use you yet
        (Kid Cole, 1928b)

171.56   I'm so worried; don't know what to do
        I waked up this morning, mama, feeling sad and blue
        (Jaybird Coleman, 1927a)

171.57   *I woke up this morning;* *things are worrying on a-* poor me
(Jaybird Coleman, 1930)

171.58   *When you get up in the morning,* when the ding-dong rings
You make it to the station; see the same old thing
(Sam Collins, 1927f)

171.59   *I got up this morning;* looked at the rising sun
Can't nobody run me like them bloodhounds done
(Sam Collins, 1931d)

171.60   *I got up in my stockings;* tipped across the floor
Scared the bloodhounds are rapping upon my door
(Sam Collins, 1931d)

171.61   *I got up this morning,* just about the break of day
I could hear *a bunch of* bloodhounds a-coming down my
way
(Sam Collins, 1931d)

171.62   *I got up this morning;* fell down across my bed
I could hear something pushing all around my head
(Sam Collins, 1931d)

171.63   *My woman woke up this morning;* dollar in her hand
Two bits for the monkey; six bits for her man
(Robert Cooksey, 1927)

171.64   *Mama, I woke up this morning;* mama, had the sundown
blues
And my fair brown told me I refuse to go
(Daddy Stovepipe, 1924)

171.65   *Woke up this morning,* and I was half most dead
I was bone-down weary, a low and ache aching head
(Blind Darby, 1929)

171.66   *I woke up this morning moaning* with the worried blues on
my mind
I was thinking about someone who were left behind
(Bill Day, 1929)

171.67   *You got to get up early in the morning;* fix your lunch
And get out early with that scuffling bunch
(Thomas A. Dorsey, 1932)

171.68   *If I wake up at night* and wants to eat
It's up to you to get me some of that western meat
(Thomas A. Dorsey, 1932)

171.69   *Get up every morning* at half past three
Ease out to your job without disturbing me
(Joe Edwards, 1924)

171.70   *How you get up every morning* at half past three
Bring the coal and kindling; make a fire for me
(Susie Edwards, 1924)

171.71   *Now I got up this morning;* couldn't make no time
I didn't have no blues; messed all up in mind
(John Estes, 1930a)

171.72   *Get up in the morning;* grey towel around your head
Ask her to cook your breakfast, but she never did
(John Estes, 1930a)

171.73   *Now I got up this morning;* blues all around my bed
I turned back to my *chivver*; blues all in my bed
(John Estes, 1930c)

171.74   *Now I get up every morning,* and I walk to Third and Field
And I'm just standing and I'm wondering, Lord, just how to
make a meal
(John Estes, 1935a)

171.75   *Now I'm going to get up in the morning,* and I'm going to do
like Buddy Brown
Know I'm going to eat my breakfast; I believe I'll lay back
down
(John Estes, 1935b)

171.76   *Now woke up this morning;* couldn't hardly see
Snow on the ground about eight foot deep
(John Estes, 1938b)

171.77   I washed my clothes; I hanged them by the fire
Get up in the morning; they be finally dry
(John Estes, 1938d)

171.78   *I woke up this morning* about half past four
Somebody knocking on my back door
(Blind Boy Fuller, 1935)

171.79   When I called this morning about half past one
Wake up, baby; loving has just begun
(Blind Boy Fuller, 1940c)

171.80   Says I told my baby about half past two
Wake up, mama; loving ain't half through
(Blind Boy Fuller, 1940c)

171.81   Then I called her this morning about half past ten
Wake up, mama; loving is just began
(Blind Boy Fuller, 1940c)

171.82   *Did you ever wake up in the morning,* and find your rider
gone
I know just how it feels; that's why I composed this song
(Clifford Gibson, 1929d)

171.83   *Wake up, baby;* please don't be so still
Unless you fixing a good way to get your daddy killed
(Clifford Gibson, 1929e)

171.84   *Says I woke up this morning* feeling so bad
Thinking about the good times that I once have had
(Bill Jazz Gillum, 1938)

171.85   *I woke up this morning,* Lord, and my baby was gone
I didn't have no sweet woman just to hold me in her arms
(Bill Jazz Gillum, 1939)

171.86   Had a strange feeling this morning; I swear I've had it all
day
I'll wake up one of these mornings; that feeling will be here to
stay
(George Hannah, 1930)

171.87   *Did you ever wake up with the blues,* and didn't have no place to go
And you couldn't do nothing but just walk from door to door
(Otis Harris, 1928)

171.88   *Got up this morning,* and I could not keep from crying
Thinking about my rider; she done put me down
(William Harris, 1927)

171.89   *Have you ever woke up* with them bull frogs on your mind
(William Harris, 1928)

171.90   *When I woke up this morning,* folks, I just started to scream
Why when I came to find out that it was just a lonesome midnight dream
(Willie Harris, 1930)

171.91   *I woke up this morning* feeling sad and blue
Couldn't find my yo yo; didn't know what to do
(Hattie Hart, 1929)

171.92   *You going to wake up one of these mornings,* mama, baby, and I'll be gone
And you may not never, mama, see me in your town no more
(Walter Buddy Boy Hawkins, 1927b)

171.93   *When I wake up in the morning,* my heart it feels like lead
When I go to bed at midnight, sometimes I wish I was dead
(Bertha Henderson, 1928a)

171.94   *Now woke up this morning;* my gal had the worried blues
I looked over in the corner; my poor grandma *what* had them too
(Hound Head Henry, 1928)

171.95   *Woke up this morning* twixt midnight and day
With my hand around my pillow where my brownie used to lay
(Robert Hicks, 1927a)

171.96   *Woke up this morning;* my clock was striking four
           Someone started knocking, knocking on my door
           (Robert Hicks, 1928b)

171.97   *Did you ever wake up in the morning, baby;* same thing all on
           your mind
           Something keep you bothered, mama; honey, worried all the
           time
           (Sammy Hill, 1929a)

171.98   I wrung my hands and I wanted to scream
           But when I woke up, I found it was only a dream
           (Mattie Hite, 1923)

171.99   *Well I woke up this morning,* half past four
           Met a big crowd at the ??? store
           (Tony Hollins, 1941)

171.100   *Well I woke up this morning,* half past two
           Streets was crowded and I couldn't get through
           (Tony Hollins, 1941)

171.101   *Woke up this morning* about five o'clock
           Get me some eggs and a nice pork chop
           (Peg Leg Howell, 1926a)

171.102   *I woke up this morning* between midnight and day
           I felt for my rider; she done walked away
           (Peg Leg Howell, 1926b)

171.103   *I woke up this morning* 'tween midnight and day
           I woke up this morning just before day
           I looked at the pillow where my good gal used to lay
           (Peg Leg Howell, 1927)

171.104   *Now I woke up this morning, mama;* blues all around my bed
           Thinking about the kind words that my mama had said
           (Bo Weavil Jackson, 1926a)

171.105   *I woke up this morning;* blues all around my bed
           Thinking about the wire that my brown had sent
           (Bo Weavil Jackson, 1926b)

171.106   I walked the streets all day; hung my head and cried
I laid awake all night trying to make myself satisfied
(Papa Charlie Jackson, 1925c)

171.107   *I get up early in the morning,* sweet mama, and I comb and curry my horse
Because I don't want nobody not to *see my pause*
(Papa Charlie Jackson, 1927c)

171.108   *Ah wake up, mama; wake up* and don't sleep so sound
Give me what you promised me, before you lay down
(Jesse James, 1936a)

171.109   *I woke up this morning;* looked at the special rising sun
I prayed to the Lord, my special rider would come
(Skip James, 1931e)

171.110   I wring my hands, baby, and I want to scream
And I woke up; I found it was all a dream
(Skip James, 1931f)

171.111   *I got up this morning;* the blues all around my bed
Went in to eat my breakfast, and the blues all in my bread
(Blind Lemon Jefferson, 1926a)

171.112   *I got up this morning;* my sure-enough on my mind
I had to raise a conversation with the landlady to keep from crying
(Blind Lemon Jefferson, 1926b)

171.113   *I got up this morning,* rambling for my shoes
The little woman sung me a song of her worried blues
(Blind Lemon Jefferson, 1926c)

171.114   *Well I got up this morning* with my same thing on my mind
The woman I love, she keeps a good man worried all the time
(Blind Lemon Jefferson, 1927d)

171.115   *I woke up this morning;* took a walk till the break of day
I asked a woman to marry me, and I just made my get-away
(Blind Lemon Jefferson, 1928b)

171.116   *I woke up this morning; woke up* about half past ten
Ease my head in the window; she's singing Lemon's worried
blues again
(Blind Lemon Jefferson, 1928b)

171.117   *I got up this morning;* sure was feeling fine
I heard a rap at my door; must be that bad-cat woman of
mine
(Blind Lemon Jefferson, 1928c)

171.118   *I got up this morning;* I was easing across the floor
Now my bad cat's leaving me; ain't going to catch my mice no
more
(Blind Lemon Jefferson, 1928c)

171.119   *Lay awake at night,* and just can't eat a bite
Used to be my rider, but she just won't treat me right
(Blind Lemon Jefferson, 1928d)

171.120   On better find my mama soon
I woke up this morning; black snake was making *easy rukus*
in my room
(Blind Lemon Jefferson, 1929b)

171.121   Black snake is evil; black snake is all I see
I woke up this morning; black snake was moving in on me
(Blind Lemon Jefferson, 1929b)

171.122   *I wake up every morning* with the rising sun
Oh thinking about my honey dripper, and all the wrongs he
done
(Edith North Johnson, 1929b)

171.123   *I woke up this morning* with the blues all around my bed
I felt just like somebody in my family was dead
(Lil Johnson, 1929)

171.124   *I woke up this morning;* couldn't even get out my door
I was snowbound in my cabin; had water seeping up through
my floor
(Lonnie Johnson, 1938b)

171.125   *We're up before sunrise,* slaving sixteen hours a day
We pay our house rent and grocery bills, and the pimps get the rest of our pay
(Lonnie Johnson, 1941)

171.126   *I woke up this morning;* blues all around my bed
I never had no good man, I mean to ease my aching head
(Louise Johnson, 1930a)

171.127   *Lord, I woke up this morning;* blues all around my bed
I never had no good man, I mean to ease my worried head
(Louise Johnson, 1930b)

171.128   *I'm going to wake up* between midnight and day
You going to ??? *my need* baby, and I swear I'll be gone away
(Louise Johnson, 1930c)

171.129   *I'm going to get up in the morning;* I believe I'll dust my broom
Because then the black man you been loving, girl friend, can get my room
(Robert Johnson, 1936b)

171.130   *I woke up this morning,* and all my shrimps was dead and gone
I was thinking about you, baby; will you hear my weep and moan
(Robert Johnson, 1936e)

171.131   *I woke up this morning* feeling around for my shoes
Know by that, I got these old walking blues
(Robert Johnson, 1936f)

171.132   Lord, I feel like blowing my poor lonesome horn
Got up this morning; my little Bernice was gone
(Robert Johnson, 1936f)

171.133   Lord, I feel like blowing my lonesome horn
Well I got up this morning; all I had was gone
(Robert Johnson, 1936f)

171.134 *I got up this morning;* the blues walking like a man
Worried blues, give me your right hand
(Robert Johnson, 1936g)

171.135 *I got up this morning;* the blues walking like a man
Worried blues, give me your right hand
(Robert Johnson, 1936h)

171.136 And I rolled and I tumbled, and I cried the whole night long
When I woke up this morning, my biscuit-roller's gone
(Robert Johnson, 1936i)

171.137 *I woke up this morning* with canned heat on my mind
(Tommy Johnson, 1928d)

171.138 *I woke up, up this morning;* crying canned heat around my
bed
Run here, somebody; take these canned heat blues
(Tommy Johnson, 1928d)

171.139 *I woke up this morning;* said my morning prayers
(Tommy Johnson, 1928e)

171.140 *I woke up this morning;* said my morning prayers
I ain't got no woman to speak in my behalf
(Tommy Johnson, 1928f)

171.141 *Lord, I woke up this morning;* blues all around my bed
Had the blues so bad, mama, till I couldn't raise my head
(Tommy Johnson, 1928g)

171.142 *Woke up this morning;* blues all around my bed
I didn't have my daddy to hold my aching head
(Anna Jones, 1923)

171.143 Won't you tell me, baby, who can your good man be
I woke up this morning, baby, with a hex all over me
(Charley Jordan, 1936a)

171.144 Lord, my girl got something, sure, Lord, worries me
I woke up soon this morning; had that thing all over me
(Charley Jordan, 1936b)

171.145   *Woke up this morning;* *to stab* me with the worried blues
Now *must've* peep over in the corner; poor grandmammy
had them too
(Luke Jordan, 1927a)

171.146   *Woke up this morning;* the family had the weary blues
Poked my head over in the corner; poor grandmammy had
them too
(Luke Jordan, 1927b)

171.147   *I woke up this morning* with traveling on my mind
Kept a-feeling my pocket, and I didn't have a lousy dime
(Luke Jordan, 1929)

171.148   *Well I woke up this morning,* and I feeling bad
I thinking about the good times that I used to have
(Eddie Kelly, 1937)

171.149   *Woke up this morning;* look at the rising sun
I thought about my good gal, who done gone along
(King David, 1930)

171.150   *I woke up this morning;* those blues were on my mind
I was so downhearted, I couldn't do nothing but cry
(Charlie Kyle, 1928)

171.151   *I woke up this morning, I woke up this morning* with the blues
right there around my bed
Went to eat my breakfast, and the blues all in my bread
(Huddie Leadbetter, 1935c)

171.152   *I got up this morning;* hung all around my brown
Because she told me which a-way the Red River was a-run-
ning down
(Huddie Leadbetter, 1935f)

171.153   *I woke up this morning,* and I looked up against the wall
Roaches and bedbugs playing a game of ball
(Furry Lewis, 1929b)

171.154   *When I woke up this morning,* I looked down on the floor
Bedbug had been in my pocket, and pulled out all my
dough
(Furry Lewis, 1929b)

171.155   *Did you ever wake up* twixt night and day
Had your arm around the pillow where your good gal used to
lay
(Charley Lincoln, 1927c)

171.156   I believe to my soul my brown's got a stingaree
When I woke up this morning, say she was singing poor me
(Charley Lincoln, 1927c)

171.157   *I rise with the blues,* and I work with the blues
Nothing I can get but bad news
(Charley Lincoln, 1927d)

171.158   Sprinkle goofer dust around your bed
Wake up some morning; find your own self dead
(Cripple Clarence Lofton, 1936–38)

171.159   *Trouble wake me in the morning;* put me to bed late at night
Now if I get out of trouble, going to start living right
(Jane Lucas, 1930)

171.160   Now my baby got ways soon in the morning just like a squir-
rel
Get up every morning, grabbing them *covers* on the world
(Tommy McClennan, 1940e)

171.161   *Woke up this morning;* found something wrong
My loving babe had caught that train and gone
(Charlie McCoy, 1930)

171.162   *I got up this morning;* said my morning prayers
Didn't have nobody to speak in my behalf
(Joe McCoy, 1931b)

171.163   *Wake up, mama;* don't you sleep so hard
For these old blues walking all over your yard
(Blind Willie McTell, 1927b)

171.164   *Wake up, mama;* turn your lamp down low
Have you got the nerve to drive Papa McTell from your door
(Blind Willie McTell, 1928)

171.165   *We woke up this morning;* we had them Statesboro blues
I looked over in the corner; grandma and grandpa had them too
(Blind Willie McTell, 1928)

171.166   *Get up, fellow;* ride all around the world
Poor boy, you ain't got no girl
(Blind Willie McTell, 1929b)

171.167   *Wake up in the morning* about half past three
Think my baby done quit poor me
(Blind Willie McTell, 1929c)

171.168   *Wake up in the morning* at half past three
Think pretty mama done fell on me
(Blind Willie McTell, 1929d)

171.169   This Bell Street whisky make you sleep all in your clothes
And when you wake up next morning, feel like you done laid outdoors
(Blind Willie McTell, 1935a)

171.170   I give you my money, baby; my last dime
Soon as you got up, mama, you changed your mind
(Blind Willie McTell, 1935c)

171.171   *I woke up this morning;* got on a stroll
Met my baby; got her told
(Carl Martin, 1935a)

171.172   *Now I woke up this morning,* doggone my soul
My flour barrel was empty; swear I didn't have no coal
(Carl Martin, 1935b)

171.173   *I woke up this morning* about half past five
My baby turned over; cried just like a child
(Memphis Minnie, 1929b)

171.174 I got a Hudson Super Six; I got me *a little old* Cadillac
Eight
I woke up this morning; my Cadillac standing at my back
gate
(Memphis Minnie, 1930g)

171.175 *I got up this morning;* I made a fire in my stove
And made up my bread, and stuck my pan outdoors
(Memphis Minnie, 1931a)

171.176 *I got up this morning;* I went outdoors
I'd know my cow by the way she lows
(Memphis Minnie, 1931b)

171.177 *I got up this morning;* one stung me on the leg
I can't sleep at night, because he keeps me awake
(Memphis Minnie, 1934a)

171.178 Have you ever been drunk, and slept in all your clothes
And when you wake up, feel like you want a dose
(Lillian Miller, 1928)

171.179 *I get up early every morning* to toil the whole day through
Baby, it wouldn't be so hard, if I was getting up from beside of
you
(Whistlin' Alex Moore, 1929)

171.180 *I woke up here this morning,* feeling bad
I was dreaming about, sweet mama, the time once I've had
(Blue Coat Tom Nelson, 1928)

171.181 And I rolled and I tumbled, and I cried the whole night long
And I rosed this morning, mama, and I didn't know right from
wrong
(Hambone Willie Newbern, 1929b)

171.182 *Did you ever wake up,* and find your dough-roller gone
And you wring your hands, and you cry the whole day long
(Hambone Willie Newbern, 1929b)

171.183 *I woke up this morning,* baby, and feeling bad
(Big Boy George Owens, 1926)

171.184 *Oh I woke up this morning,* honey, about the break of day
I hugging the pillow where my fair brown did lay
(Marshall Owens, 1932a)

171.185 *Woke up this morning;* get my shoes
I love a woman that I can't give it to
(Marshall Owens, 1932b)

171.186 *Woke up this morning* to get my coat
My brown knocking on a-my back door
(Marshall Owens, 1932b)

171.187 *Woke up this morning* to get my tie
I can't get you, woman, because you let me die
(Marshall Owens, 1932b)

171.188 *Woke up this morning* about the break of day
Hugging the pillow where that fair brown lay
(Marshall Owens, 1932b)

171.189 *I woke up this morning;* jinx all around my bed
Turned my face to the wall, and I didn't have a word to say
(Charley Patton, 1929a)

171.190 She's a long tall woman; tall like a cherry tree
She gets up before day, and she puts that thing on me
(Charley Patton, 1929d)

171.191 I lay down last night, hoping I would have my peace
But when I woke up, Tom Rushen was shaking me
(Charley Patton, 1929e)

171.192 *I got up this morning;* Tom Day was standing around
If he lose his office now, he's running from town to town
(Charley Patton, 1929e)

171.193 *I got up this morning;* my hat in my hand
Didn't have no other brown, didn't have no man
(Charley Patton, 1929f)

171.194 *I got up this morning,* something after five
And the morning sun, Lord, was beginning to rise
(Charley Patton, 1929i)

171.195 *I got up this morning,* feeling mighty bad
And it must not have been them Belzoni jail I had
(Charley Patton, 1934b)

171.196 *Aw I wake up every morning,* now with the jinx all around my bed
I have been a good provider, but I believe I've been misled
(Charley Patton, 1934d)

171.197 *Wake up every morning,* when everything look blue
Go see the one you love; the blues will soon leave you
(Arthur Petties, 1930)

171.198 *Have you ever woke up* with whisky-drinking on your mind
You send away to that bootlegger, and you did not have a dime
(Jenny Pope, 1929)

171.199 *I woke up this morning* to make a fire in the stove
Bull frogs in the bread pan; *bacon and eggs ??? they go*
(Jenny Pope, 1930)

171.200 *I woke up this morning;* couldn't even get out of my bed
I was just thinking about that black woman, and it almost killed me dead
(Joe Pullum, 1934)

171.201 *And I got up this morning;* a light all in my room
And I looked behind me, and I found my faro gone
(James Yank Rachel, 1929)

171.202 *Did you ever wake up,* just at the break of day
With your arms around the pillow where your daddy used to lay
(Gertrude Ma Rainey, 1923a)

171.203   *Woke up this morning* with my head bowed down
I had that mean old feeling; I was in the wrong man's town
(Gertrude Ma Rainey, 1923f)

171.204   *Woke up this morning,* looking for my darn old shoes
Because mama's going home singing the Bessemer blues
(Gertrude Ma Rainey, 1926a)

171.205   *I woke up this morning;* the crying blues on my mind
I done got to the place, baby, that I hardly know my right
mind
(Ben Ramey, 1929)

171.206   *Well I got up this morning,* feeling bad
Thinking about the times that I once have had
(Allen Shaw, 1934a)

171.207   *Well I woke up this morning,* feeling blue
Thinking about no other one but you
(Allen Shaw, 1934a)

171.208   *When I woke up this morning,* mama's feeling bad
Got to thinking about the time I once have had
(Allen Shaw, 1934b)

171.209   *Woke up this morning,* when the chickens was crowing for
day
Turned on the right side of my pillow; my man had gone
away
(Bessie Smith, 1926)

171.210   *I woke up this morning;* can't even get out my door
There's enough trouble to make a poor girl wonder where she
want to go
(Bessie Smith, 1927a)

171.211   *I woke up this morning* with an awful aching head
My new man had left me just a room and an empty bed
(Bessie Smith, 1928)

171.212 I had a nightmare last night, when I lay down
When I woke up this morning, my sweet man couldn't be found
(Bessie Smith, 1933)

171.213 *When I woke up,* my pillow was wet with tears
Just one day from that man of mine seem like a thousand years
(Bessie Smith, 1933)

171.214 He eats his supper; throws his clothes on the floor
And he's up every morning at half past four
(Clara Smith, 1924h)

171.215 Last night you called me a lowdown dirty name
Woke up Monday morning and done the same old thing
(J.T. Funny Paper Smith, 1931b)

171.216 *I woke up this morning;* clock was striking four
And my baby told me, pack your things and go
(Charlie Spand, 1929b)

171.217 Say my bed seem lonely; my pillow now it sure do
Say my bed is lonesome; my pillow now it sure do
I wake up out of the midnight; I really have those milkcow blues
(Freddie Spruell, 1926a)

171.218 *My baby woke me up this morning;* she told me she's Joliet bound
She want to find Four-A Highway; that's the main highway out of town
(Freddie Spruell, 1935a)

171.219 *Woke up early this morning;* blues around my bed
And the ??? running everywhere
(Vol Stevens, 1927a)

171.220 *Woke up early this morning,* feeling awful low
And the blues they had me *running up the wall*
(Vol Stevens, 1927a)

171.221 *Woke up early this morning;* got out of my bed
And the blues had started climbing up the bed
(Vol Stevens, 1928a)

171.222 *Woke up early this morning* with the blues all around my bed
And the blues, they tell me, crying man oh man
(Vol Stevens, 1928a)

171.223 *Woke up early this morning;* blues all around my bed
And the blues ain't there; they easing everywhere
(Vol Stevens, 1928b)

171.224 *Lord, I woke up this morning* with the blues all around my baby's bed
I turned my face to the wall; baby, these are the words I said
(Frank Stokes, 1927a)

171.225 Lord, I got a little cabin; Lord, it's number forty-four
Lord, I wake up every morning; the world be scratching on my door
(Roosevelt Sykes, 1929a)

171.226 *I woke up this morning,* just as sick as I could be
Now nothing but these blues almost killing poor me
(Roosevelt Sykes, 1929b)

171.227 *I woke up this morning;* thousand things on my mind
Lord, I thought about my troubles; could not keep from crying
(Roosevelt Sykes, 1929d)

171.228 Drink some rooster soup before going to bed
Wake up in the morning; find your own self dead
(Tampa Red, 1929a)

171.229 *Have you ever woke up in the morning;* your bed going around and around
You know by that, baby; you have done throwed me down
(Johnnie Temple, 1937a)

171.230   She sleeps late every morning; I can't hardly get her woke
She will wake up in one second, when she hears a car horn blow
(Ramblin' Thomas, 1928b)

171.231   *Now you will wake up in the morning* and find me gone
Because I'm a rambling man; I can't stay at one place long
(Ramblin' Thomas, 1928g)

171.232   *Lord, I got up this morning* with a rambling mind, feeling fine
Thinking about the good times I had five years ago
And I'm leaving town this morning; and I sure don't want to go
(Ramblin' Thomas, 1928h)

171.233   *I woke up this morning;* I had the blues three different ways
I had one mind to stay here, and two to leave this place
(Ramblin' Thomas, 1928h)

171.234   *Got up one of these mornings;* looked down in the sea
What see the way them fishes do the shivaree
(Edward Thompson, 1929a)

171.235   *Wake up soon every morning;* babe wear a rag all around her head
Every time you speak to her, she'll swear she nearly dead
(George Torey, 1937a)

171.236   *Said I woke up this morning,* just about the dawn of day
Some man had my woman, and the worried blues had me
(George Torey, 1937b)

171.237   *I woke up this morning,* feeling mighty bad
I done lost my daddy; best man I ever had
(Bessie Tucker, 1928a)

171.238   *Woke up this morning;* woke up before day
Woke up this morning with the same thing on my mind
(Unknown artist, 1928a)

171.239 *Say wake up, mama;* the children done come home
(Unknown artist, 1930a)

171.240 *Say wake up, mama;* hear your rooster crow
One at your window; one at your door
(Unknown artist, 1930b)

171.241 *Wake up, mama;* hear your rooster crow
One at your window; one at your door
(Unknown artist, 1930c)

171.242 *Say I woke up this morning* about the break of day
I hugged the pillow where you used to lay
(Unknown artist, 1930d)

171.243 *Wake up, mama;* hear the rooster crow
One at your window; one at your door
(Unknown artist, 1930d)

171.244 *When you get up in the morning,* begin to sing this lonesome song
I had a good man; he caught the train and gone
(Walter Vincson, 1930a)

171.245 I went to a country girl's house, and only one night I spent
I got up next morning and came back home; been running ever since
(Walter Vincson, 1930b)

171.246 I rammed my gun every morning before day
When I woke up this morning, my ramrod was gone away
(Walter Vincson, 1930c)

171.247 I lay down last night; I was awful sick
I woke up this morning; she had my pocket picked
(Walter Vincson, 1932a)

171.248 *She got up this morning;* she looking mighty sweet
The mens all thought she was something good to eat
(Walter Vincson, 1932b)

171.249   *Oh I woke up this morning;* sure was feeling bad
Don't know about the good times that I, oh that I once have had
(Otto Virgial, 1935b)

171.250   Said I walked from noon, honey, way up north
I got up this morning, crying, mama, I got to go
(Uncle Bud Walker, 1928b)

171.251   *I woke up this morning,* feeling mighty sad
Was the worst old feeling that I ever had
(Minnie Wallace, 1935)

171.252   Have you ever been drunk; slept in all of your clothes
And when you woke up, you found that you were out of dough
(Sippie Wallace, 1927a)

171.253   *Wake up, man;* see how bright the sun does shine
Get up in that section gang, and bring me up some time
(Sippie Wallace, 1927c)

171.254   *Woke up this morning;* the day was dawning, and I was feeling all sad and blue
I had nobody to tell my troubles to
I felt so worried, I didn't know what to do
(Ethel Waters, 1921)

171.255   Did you ever feel like you lost the best friend you had
You wake up in the morning, and you feel so bad
Thinking about your brownie, and your heart's so sad
(Ethel Waters, 1923b)

171.256   *I got up this morning* about half past four
Big Bill *Johnny* had his *spenders* on the floor
(Curley Weaver, 1928a)

171.257   *Got up this morning;* my good gal was gone
Stood by my bedside long many, long many morn
(Curley Weaver, 1928b)

171.258   *Said I woke up this morning;* I was feeling so bad
          Thinking about the good times that I once have had
          (Will Weldon, 1937)

171.259   *Lord, I woke up this morning,* when everything was still
          Well, well, well I seen my little mama as she come creeping
          up the hill
          (Peetie Wheatstraw, 1930b)

171.260   *Well, well, well did you ever wake up, mama,* baby, now be-
          tween midnight and day
          Oh with your head on your pillow, babe, where your good
          man he once have lay
          (Peetie Wheatstraw, 1930b)

171.261   *You got up this morning* with a big rag around your head
          Asked you to cook my breakfast; babe, you went back to bed
          (Peetie Wheatstraw, 1934b)

171.262   *And I got up this morning;* went down in old *alleycan*
          Now the women there was hollering, ooo, well, well here
          come that old cocktail man
          (Peetie Wheatstraw, 1935)

171.263   Now men, when you're down, one thing you must do
          When you get up, try to remember everybody that mistreated
          you
          (Peetie Wheatstraw, 1936i)

171.264   *I wake up this morning* just crazy with the blues
          I can't even tell you, oh well, well the difference in my shoes
          (Peetie Wheatstraw, 1937a)

171.265   Working on the project; my gal's spending all my dough
          Now I have waked up on her, oh well, well and I won't be that
          weak no more
          (Peetie Wheatstraw, 1937c)

171.266   *Going to get up in the morning,* baby, with the rising sun
          If the train don't run, going to be some walking down
          (Washington White, 1937a)

171.267   *I wake up every morning* with leaving on my mind
Because my mama's so evil, and she treats me so unkind
(James Boodle It Wiggins, 1928)

171.268   Now I got a little old Chevy; Lord, number is forty-four
I wake up every morning; wolves sitting in my door
(James Boodle It Wiggins, 1929a)

171.269   *I woke up this morning* about half past five
My baby turned over and tried to cop a jive
(James Boodle It Wiggins, 1929b)

171.270   *When you wake up Monday morning* with the stock yard
blues
Come and talk to Mr. Owens about his good-looking mules
(Robert Wilkins, 1935b)

171.271   *Did you ever wake up lonesome,* all by yourself
And the one you love off loving someone else
(Henry Williams, 1928)

171.272   Little leg woman do just like a squirrel
Get up in the morning; *caught that* on the world
(Big Joe Williams, 1935a)

171.273   *I got up this morning,* feeling bad
Thinking about that stuff I had
(Big Joe Williams, 1935b)

171.274   *Well, well get up in the morning;* catch the Highway Forty-
Nine
Well, well I'm going to look for little Malvina; ooo man, don't
say she can't be found
(Big Joe Williams, 1935c)

171.275   I got a long tall woman; live on Highway Forty-Nine
Well, well I get up in the morning; ooo Lord, boys, she's down
on my mind
(Big Joe Williams, 1935c)

171.276 *I'm going to get up in the morning, Malvina;* I believe I'll dust my bed
If I get up in the morning, Malvina, I believe I'll dust my bed
I'm going down Highway Forty-Nine; boys, I'm going to be rocking to my head
(Big Joe Williams, 1935c)

171.277 *Yeah I got up this morning;* I was feeling awful bad
I was thinking about the good time, mama, mmm Lord, me and my baby once have had
(Big Joe Williams, 1935f)

171.278 *Babe, I woke up this morning;* I looked down the road
I think I heard my wild cow, mama, when she being to low
(Big Joe Williams, 1935f)

171.279 *I woke up this morning;* I looked down the line
Couldn't hear nothing but my babe's train crying
(Big Joe Williams, 1937)

171.280 You have got me to the place, I hate to see that evening sun go down
Well when I get up in the morning, ooo well peach orchard man, she's on my mind
(Big Joe Williams, 1941b)

171.281 *Well I'm going to get up in the morning;* get to Highway Forty-Nine
Well *about* my sweet woman, ooo well, well she don't pay poor Joey no mind
(Big Joe Williams, 1941c)

171.282 *I'm going to wake up in the morning;* I believe I'll dust my bed
Well I'm going to get up in the morning; I believe I'll dust my bed
Going down the Highway Forty-Nine; ooo well, boys, I be rocking to my head
(Big Joe Williams, 1941c)

171.283 Now you done got me so, I hate to see that evening sun go down
I wake up in the morning; peach orchard woman on my mind
(Joe Williams, 1938)

171.284 *I woke up one morning,* walking across the floor
I'm going away to leave you, baby; I don't mean you no good no more
(Ruth Willis, 1931a)

171.285 *Woke up this morning* at the break of day
Looked on my pillow where my man used to lay
(Ruth Willis, 1933)

171.286 *Woke up this morning* about half past nine, and I just could not keep from crying
I was worried about that stevedore man of mine
(Leola B. Wilson, 1926a)

171.287 *You ever wake up,* just about the break of day
With your arms around the pillow, where Mr. so-and-so used to lay
(Leola B. Wilson, 1926b)

+*human leave town* (**r-formula**)

This formula alludes to an underlying theme in the blues—travel—although it also has overtones of abandonment and unfaithfulness. Its semantic structure is quite simple: an A1 argument that can generate any +*human* word or phrase; an A2 argument that must be the rhyme word *town;* and a predicate that has the sense of "move away from."

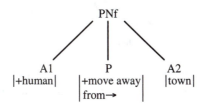

The most variable part of this formula is its predicate. In about 75 percent of the examples, it generates the verb *leave* (examples 172.1, 172.7, 172.8, and so on), but it can also generate a number of other interesting and imaginative words and phrases. The most frequent of these other predicate manifestations is *blow* (172.6, 172.26, 172.46, and 172.81), while others occur only one or two times in the corpus: *go away from* (172.41), *get out of* (172.10 and 172.12), *hobo out of* (172.50), *blind it from* (172.4), and *cadillaced out of* (172.49).

In addition, this formula also expresses itself as an equative: +*human be out of town* (172.21, 172.29, 172.44, 172.45, 172.56, and 172.61). This equative form conveys the sense of a completed action; that is, the +*human* has completed the movement away from town.

A small group of examples exhibit the following manifestations: +*human drive* +*human from town* (172.30), +*human run* +*human out of town* (172.84), and +*human take* +*human away from or out of town* (172.33, 172.63, and 172.78). These all include a hidden Emb: +*human cause PNf.* The surface-level verbs are actually more complex than they appear because of their causative qualities.

There are two examples in the corpus that play on the theme of abandonment more than on movement, and they might, in fact, not belong to this formula at all: +*human leave* +*human in town* (172.17 and 172.59). This phrase indirectly implies that the first +*human* has left or is out of town and is related thematically, if not structurally, to this formula. Another questionable member of this formula is example 172.83: +*human move to another town*. This phrase implies that +*human* has left one town to go to another, but its sense of "movement toward" rather than "movement away from" probably places it beyond the boundaries of this formula.

Among the great majority of examples that generate the verb *leave* in their predicates, there are a number of different Embs, although none occur more than twice in the corpus: *worry about* (172.65), *try to* (172.60), *make* (172.55), *ready to* (172.79), *feel like* (172.77), *fixing to* (172.19 and 172.80), *watch* (172.32), *see* (172.14 and 172.64), *scared to* (172.3), and *mind* (172.5).

172.1   And I told my woman *just before I left town*
          Don't let nobody tear the barrelhouse down
          (Garfield Akers, 1930a)

172.2   Said now I got a notion *to leave this lonesome town*
          Says my gal, she caught the Southern, and I know she done
          put me down
          (Kokomo Arnold, 1935a)

172.3   I'm scared to stay here; *scared to leave this old bad-luck town*
         So when I wake up every morning, my head is going round
         and round
         (Kokomo Arnold, 1938a)

172.4   *I just want to blind it from this half-good town*
         When she blows for the crossing, I'm going ease it on
         (Ed Bell, 1927b)

172.5   I got a mind to ramble; *mind to leave this town*
         (Lewis Black, 1927a)

172.6   Ah the rising sun going down
         I ain't got nobody, *since my baby's blowed this town*
         (Blind Blake, 1927a)

172.7   I got the bad-feeling blues; keeps me so lowdown
         I'm going to pack my grip; *leave this lonesome town*
         (Blind Blake, 1927b)

172.8   Packing my duffle; *going to leave this town*
         And I'm going to hustle to catch that train southbound
         (Blind Blake, 1929c)

172.9   The gals from the alley slipping all around
         Telling everybody *they're leaving town*
         (Blind Blake, 1930)

172.10   Ain't no need of sitting with my head hung down
         Your black man ought to get out of town
         (Blind Blake, 1932)

172.11   Now I tell you, mama, *now I'm sure going to leave this town*
         Because I been in trouble, ever since I set my suitcase down
         (Ishman Bracey, 1928a)

172.12   It's hard, it's hard, it's hard *to get out of this* town
         Get another ???
         (Ishman Bracey, 1930b)

172.13 He's got to rob and steal; *don't he got to leave out of this man's town*
Know he'll say going back to the country; going to sow some more cotton seed down
(Bo Chatman, 1938b)

172.14 Make your lamp up higher, and turn your lamp around
Look out your back door; *see me leave this town*
(Sam Collins, 1931b)

172.15 I helped you, baby, when your kinfolks turned you down
Now you loving someone else, baby, *and you done left this town*
(Blind Darby, 1929)

172.16 Please don't mistreat me, if you don't want me around
Lord, don't be mad with me, baby, *because your good man have left this town*
(Walter Davis, 1940b)

172.17 *Boy, I'd *better see my good gal* leave me in this town*
I'd beat the train to the *crossroads*, and I'd burn the depot down
(Will Day, 1928a)

172.18 I got my mind all made up, *and I'm going to leave this town*
I'm a-going so far, till the women can't run me down
(Thomas A. Dorsey, 1930c)

172.19 Lord, my eyes are sorrow; tears come a-rolling down
Now you know by that, babe, *fixed to leave your town*
(John Estes, 1929b)

172.20 I hate to see that evening sun go down
Lord, I got a notion, *my woman done and left this town*
(Blind Boy Fuller, 1940b)

172.21 Now my woman, please don't worry, *baby, while I'm out of your town*
Now the love I have for you, mama, God knows it can't be turned around
(Blind Boy Fuller, 1940e)

172.22 Let's get our gauge up, papa; let our love come down
Get leaping drunk, *and leave this lowdown town*
(Bertha Henderson, 1928b)

172.23 If you quit me, daddy, *I'm going to leave this town*
Can't get my gauge up, and let my love come down
(Bertha Henderson, 1928b)

172.24 I hate to see that evening sun go down
Because my daddy, he's done left this town
(Katherine Henderson, 1928a)

172.25 I went to see what the noise was all about
Someone told me *your brown done left this town*
(Robert Hicks, 1928b)

172.26 Take me, mama; please don't throw me down
I'm going to pack my suitcase; *I'm going to blow this town*
(Peg Leg Howell, 1927)

172.27 I'm Alabama bound; I'm Alabama bound
Then if you want me to love you, babe, *you got to leave this town*
(Papa Charlie Jackson, 1925b)

172.28 I'm leaving today; *going to leave this southern town*
Because my baby caught a plane that was up the way bound
(Papa Charlie Jackson, 1926a)

172.29 The woman I love, *she must be out of town*
She left me this morning with a face that's full of frowns
(Blind Lemon Jefferson, 1927c)

172.30 Brownskin girl is deceitful, till she gets you all worn down
She get all your pocket change; *she going to drive you from her town*
(Blind Lemon Jefferson, 1927k)

172.31 It makes a man feel bad, when competition ???
Now there's so much competition, *I believe I'll leave your town*
(Blind Lemon Jefferson, 1928e)

172.32   Standing at the station; *watch my baby leave town*
I feel disgusted; no peace can be found
(Blind Lemon Jefferson, 1928f)

172.33   Mmmmm going to run that black snake down
I ain't seen my mama, *since black snake taken her away from town*
(Blind Lemon Jefferson, 1929b)

172.34   I have to see that evening sun go down
That's the time my baby left this town
I get the blues, when the evening sun goes down
(Alec Johnson, 1928a)

172.35   Straight for the madhouse I'm surely bound
Thinking about the gal *who left this town*
How I despair, when the evening sun goes down
(Alec Johnson, 1928a)

172.36   Oh your time now; be mine after a while
Give me my fare; *I sure will leave this town*
(Elizabeth Johnson, 1928)

172.37   I hate to see that evening sun go down
Because that's the time my baby left this town
And I get so blue, when the evening sun go down
(Lonnie Johnson, 1929a)

172.38   My friends gave up, and they cannot be found
Because my gal done quit, *and she left this town*
Oh how it grieves me, when that evening sun goes down
(Lonnie Johnson, 1929a)

172.39   Strait for the madhouse I am surely bound
Thinking about that gal *who left this town*
How I feel desperate, when that evening sun goes down
(Lonnie Johnson, 1929a)

172.40   The chief of police done tore my playhouse down
No use grieving; *I'm going to leave this town*
(Maggie Jones, 1924c)

172.41   When your money's gone; friends have turned you down
          And you wander around just like a hound
          Then you got to say, *let me go away from this old town*
          (Maggie Jones, 1925b)

172.42   I remember the day when I was living at Lula town
          My man did so many wrong things, *that I had to leave the town*
          (Bertha Lee, 1934)

172.43   Depot agent, please turn your depot around
          My woman done quit me now; *going to leave your town*
          (Noah Lewis, 1930a)

172.44   Now I've rambled and I've rambled, until I broke my poor self down
          I believe to my soul *that the little girl is out of town*
          (Robert Lockwood, 1941a)

172.45   Now baby, don't you worry, *just because I'm out of town*
          All my love I have for you, darling; swear it can't be turned around
          (Tommy McClennan, 1940b)

172.46   Mr. depot agent, close your depot down
          The woman I'm loving, *she's fixing to blow this town*
          (Charlie McCoy, 1930)

172.47   If you don't want me, please don't dog me around
          Oh just hand me my suitcase; *I'll leave your Dallas town*
          (William McCoy, 1928)

172.48   Now if you don't want me, baby, please don't dog me around
          My home ain't here, *and I can leave your town*
          (Blind Willie McTell, 1931c)

172.49   Oh Lord, Lord, wonder where is my chauffeur now
          Got my Cadillac Eight; *done cadillaced out of town*
          (Memphis Minnie, 1930g)

172.50   Hey believe I'll get drunk; tear this old barrelhouse down
Because I ain't got no money, *but I can hobo out of town*
(Memphis Minnie, 1934b)

172.51   Reason why I start; why I lowdown
My gal done quit me; *I got to leave this town*
(Buddy Moss, 1933b)

172.52   And I told my woman, Lord, *just before I left her town*
Don't she let nobody tear her barrelhouse down
(Hambone Willie Newbern, 1929b)

172.53   What will you do, when your good friend throws you down
Going to catch me a plane; *babe, going to leave your town*
(Big Boy George Owens, 1926)

172.54   Lord, the Lula woman, Lord, ??? up and down
Lord, you ought to been there; *Lord, see these womens all leaving town*
(Charley Patton, 1930a)

172.55   And I keeps on telling my rider, well she was *shivering* down
Lord, that jelly-baking strut will make a monkey-man leave his town
(Charley Patton, 1934c)

172.56   The man I love, *I know he's out of town*
And when I find him, he better not be messing around
(Gertrude Perkins, 1927)

172.57   Boys, I can't stand up; I can't sit down
The man I love has done left this town
(Gertrude Ma Rainey, 1923e)

172.58   My head's going around and around, *since my daddy left town*
I don't know if the river is running up or down
But there's one thing certain; *babe, mama's going to leave town*
(Gertrude Ma Rainey, 1923e)

172.59   Lord, pretty mama, what's the matter now
You know if you don't want me, *why didn't you leave me back
in town*
(Willie Reed, 1928b)

172.60   Ticket agent, ease your window down
Because my man's done quit me, *and tried to leave this town*
(Bessie Smith, 1924a)

172.61   When you broken-hearted, *and your man is out of town*
Go to the river; take a chair and sit down
(Bessie Smith, 1924b)

172.62   I hate to see that evening sun go down
For my baby, he's done left this town
(Bessie Smith, 1929)

172.63   Uncle Sam has told me that things are ??? bound
He took all the booze away, *and my good brown from town*
(Clara Smith, 1923d)

172.64   I stood at the station, I said station; *saw my man leaving
town*
When that man quit me, that's what brought me down
(Clara Smith, 1924d)

172.65   If I had my machine, *I wouldn't worry about leaving town*
I'd get on the Four-A Highway, and God knows I'd roll that
highway down
(Freddie Spruell, 1935a)

172.66   Colored man take the blues; he walk to the river and set
down
Get stuck by a nehi mama, and he turn right short around
Well mama wonder what's going on, mama, *since I left town*
(Frank Stokes, 1928b)

172.67   Now I'm a lonely guy, following the browns
I think about the times, *since I left town*
(Frank Stokes, 1928c)

172.68   The woman I love treat me too unkind
         Going to pack my grip, *and leave this lonesome town*
         (Tampa Red, 1928)

172.69   You got ways, dragging my heart around
         Some of these days, baby, *I'm going to leave this town*
         (Johnnie Temple, 1937a)

172.70   *And before I would stand to see my baby leave this town*
         I would beat the train to the crossing, and burn that doggone
         bridge down
         (Ramblin' Thomas, 1928f)

172.71   I believe to my soul, mama, *got to leave your town*
         I got no pretty mama, talk baby-talk to me
         (Unknown artist, 1928a)

172.72   I felt like falling from the treetop to the ground
         Should have been my old babe, *and she was leaving town*
         (Unknown artist, 1928b)

172.73   Says the rooster crow and the hen walk around
         I ain't seen my woman, *since she left this town*
         (Unknown artist, 1930d)

172.74   They sent out a law *for everybody to leave town*
         But when I got the news, I was high-water bound
         (Sippie Wallace, 1927d)

172.75   Well the blues in my house from the rooftop to the ground
         And the blues everywhere, *because my good gal have left this
         town*
         (Will Weldon, 1936)

172.76   Now the prosecutor questioned me, partner; the clerk he
         wrote it down
         The judge say I'll give you one chance, Nolan, *but you would
         not leave this town*
         (Nolan Welsh, 1926a)

172.77   Oh the blues ain't nothing but a feeling that will get you down
Falling out with your man; *you feel like leaving town*
(Georgia White, 1938)

172.78   Aberdeen is my home, but the mens don't want me around
They know I will take these women, *and take them out of town*
(Washington White, 1940c)

172.79   My train is made up; *ready to leave this town*
You can think about your baby when the sun goes down
(James Boodle It Wiggins, 1928)

172.80   Now the judge going to sentence me, and the clerk going to write it down
So they accuse me of stealing; *I fixing to leave your town*
(Robert Wilkins, 1928a)

172.81   Ohhhh look where the sun going down
I ain't had no righteous woman, *since my baby blowed this town*
(Henry Williams, 1928)

172.82   I got a brownskin woman; she don't pay me no mind
And I know you going to miss me, *baby, when I leave this town*
(Big Joe Williams, 1935d)

172.83   Now my baby have changed her way of living; I mean she's changed all around
Because she even changed her house number; *oh you know she done moved to another town*
(Sonny Boy Williamson, 1941a)

172.84   Now you going to keep on, baby, you know fooling around
Oh you know the police is going to run you clean out of town
(Sonny Boy Williamson, 1941b)

172.85   And it's hey, mama, *I'm going to leave your town*
I ain't got no man to put my arms around
(Hosea Woods, 1929a)

* * *

The overall popularity of these formulas with blues singers indicates something of the "message" of the blues. Any conclusions about the meaning of the blues, based on a thematic analysis of this song form is difficult, because as Sterling Brown wrote, "There are so many blues that any preconception might be proved about Negro life, as well as its opposite" (1930, p. 325). Virtually every aspect of black life was grist for the singer's mill; thematically, the blues is a mixture of many social images, some of which, as Brown correctly observed, are in conflict with each other.

If, for instance, one wished to assess the role of alcohol in African American culture by analyzing blues lyrics, one would find as many statements critical of drink as statements in favor of it:

173   If the river was whisky, baby, and I was a duck
      I'd dive to the bottom, Lord, and I'd never come up
      (Furry Lewis, 1928b)

174   Lord, Lord, whisky is killing me
      And why can't I stop drinking whisky, Lord, Lord, I just can't see
      (Black Bottom McPhail, 1932b)

Through a formulaic analysis, rather than a thematic one, however, certain aspects of African American society take on special significance in blues lyrics. By studying the highly recurrent formulas in the blues, one might learn which sentiments the singers most often expressed in their songs. Whatever themes they touched on, what messages emerge again and again through the recurrent formulas? Such a quantitative analysis not only reveals something about early twentieth-century African American society but also hints at why the blues became so popular among African Americans of that era.

Why were the blues so popular in the first four decades of the twentieth century? What was happening in African American society that would account for the growth and popularity of this song form? I stated previously that the blues is fundamentally a love lyric, but the theme of love alone would not necessarily make the blues popular in African American society. There were many other song forms, in both black and white culture, that were concerned with love. The answer to these questions lies in the recurrent themes that the singers expressed through their use of formulas.

If there are recurrent themes in the blues, they should manifest themselves in the twenty most frequent formulas outlined in this chapter.

The very frequency of these formulas linked blues songs in a thematic matrix that both the singers and their audience understood at either a conscious or an unconscious level. These formulas are evocative of the blues as a whole and are the clues to the meaning of the song form.

To review these most frequent formulas, I list a representative manifestation of each one:

1. I have the blues
2. I come to some place
3. I go away from some place
4. I have a woman
5. I quit my woman
6. I love you
7. I tell you
8. I treat you good/bad
9. I woke up this morning
10. I am worried
11. I have the blues
12. I cry
13. What am I going to do
14. Everywhere I go
15. I will be gone
16. I'm going back home
17. It won't be long
18. Some thing is on my mind
19. I treat you right
20. I'm leaving town

Clearly, some of these formulas speak directly to the love theme in the blues: 4. *I have a woman;* 5. *I quit my woman;* 6. *I love you;* 8. *I treat you good/bad;* and 19. *I treat you right.* The formula *I tell you,* though not overtly about love, also speaks to the main theme of the blues, in that it establishes a one-to-one, personal mode of communication between the blues persona and someone else, thereby reflecting the love theme. The x- and r-formulas *I have the blues* define the song genre.

The high frequency of the other formulas, however, are not so easily explained, because they do not directly refer to love or the song genre as a whole. It is these formulas that reflect the nonlove recurrent themes in the blues. The largest proportion of them deals with some aspect of travel: 2. *I come to some place;* 3. *I go away from some place;* 14. *Everywhere I go;* 15. *I will be gone;* 16. *I'm going back home;* and 20. *I'm leaving town.*

This travel motif reflects the state of African American society in the first part of the twentieth century, for the out-migration of blacks from the rural south started in the late 1870s and reached its peak during World War I (see Groh, 1972; and Kennedy, 1930). Although this migration is often thought of as being a northward movement, this was not entirely the case:

> The migration of Negroes ... was a movement from country to city. In proportion to their size, the southern cities have received as substantial increases in their Negro population as have northern cities; but the increases of northern cities have been more spectacular by reason of the fact that before the movement began the Negro population of these cities was negligible, and because the trend has been toward industrial cities, a majority of which are found in the North. (Woofter, 1928, p. 26)

During the years when the blues was growing in popularity, then, African American society in general was undergoing massive urbanization. The reasons for this phenomenon were many: oppressive Jim Crow laws in the South, lack of proper educational opportunities, exploitative sharecropping and plantation systems, low wages, racism, and other hardships of southern rural life. Certainly one large factor was the boll weevil infestation that began in 1892 and ultimately caused an economic depression in the cotton-growing areas of the South (Woodson, 1918, pp. 171–72).

From the turn of the century to World War I, traveling was on the minds of African Americans, and this is reflected in the high frequency of "traveling" formulas in the blues. If a theme of a particular song was love or love troubles, there was a good chance that its underlying theme was movement: leaving town, going to some place, not having a place to go, going back home. As Brown observed, "Blues often express a wish to be somewhere else, a dislike for this hard-hearted town, this no-good place, this sun-down job" (1943, p. 21). The importance of movement in the blues is such that the formula *go to some place* is the most frequently recurring formula in the corpus.

How did this movement affect African American society? Certainly, it was not just a move from a rural to an urban environment; it was also a move from a familiar lifestyle to a strange and uncertain existence. If the harsh social and economic conditions at the turn of the century upset the security of rural African American society, then the move to an urban atmosphere must have been that much more unsettling. Such a change in lifestyle undoubtedly produced anxiety; the feeling of rootlessness that accompanied the move to the city—the move from farm to factory—must have left a deep impression on the African American psyche.

The anxiety brought about by this state of flux was also reflected in these most common blues formulas. Just as some of the twenty formulas are concerned with love, and others with travel, a third group is concerned with anxiety and a sense of instability. Three of the formulas speak directly of an unsettled mind: 10. *I am worried;* 13. *What am I going to do;* and 18. *Some thing is on my mind.* Another formula describes a common reaction to anxiety: 12. *I cry.*

The formula *it won't be long* shows yet another perspective on this anxiety. It emphasizes an impending change and disruption to the status quo: time is short, and the threat of something new and perhaps unpleasant is just around the corner. Note the way the formula is used in the following example:

175 Some day you'll want me, *and it won't be long*
    Then you'll be sorry, you ever done me wrong
    (Clara Smith, 1924a)

Even though the singer is ostensibly talking about a love situation, the general feeling of anxiety over a change of state is a strong undertone in the couplet.

The most interesting of the "anxiety" formulas is *I woke up this morning.* By itself, it does not imply any anxiety at all, but as used in the context of the blues couplet, it almost always points to some change of state. Although the formula denotes an "emergence from sleep," it connotes a "waking up to a realization that there has been a change in the situation."

176 *I woke up this morning* feeling mighty sad
    Was the worst old feeling that I ever had
    (Minnie Wallace, 1935)

This sudden realization of a new situation is almost always for the worse. Generally, the figurative "waking up" is from a situation in which the persona feels good or in which the persona is in a good, stable love relationship to a situation in which the persona feels bad or in which the love relationship has gone awry.

The strong identification of the Adv *in the morning* with the formula *I woke up* adds to this feeling of anxiety and instability. Rosenberg pointed out that the formula *in the morning* has special connotations in African American folk preaching: "'In the Morning' is a phrase which [preacher Rubin] Lacy and others associate with *Revelation,* since the apocalypse is supposed to fall then" (1975, p. 99). The same audience that listened to these sermons listened to the blues, and while the blues does not allude to the final "change" of the apocalypse, its use of the symbol "morning" would not be entirely lost on the blues audience.

Although the main theme of the blues is love, then, its supplementary themes are movement and the anxiety caused by this movement. It might be said that the theme of love is a vehicle for expressing the worries and fears that accompany a fundamental change in the lifestyle of a culture. Conversely, the anxieties brought about by change affected love relationships, the cohesion of the family, and normal courting patterns; the kind of uncertainty and the volatile nature of the love described in so many blues songs was perhaps a reflection of the disruptions going on in contemporary African American social relationships. African Americans could identify with these themes, even if they themselves had not moved to the city. Even if they remained on the farm, they undoubtedly knew of someone who had moved away. The great migration of African Americans to the cities, in this sense, touched everyone in the culture.

It is no coincidence that the blues gained its greatest popularity in the first decades of the twentieth century. Rowe recognized the connections outlined here (1975, pp. 26–39), but the evidence supplied by the most frequently recurrent images in the blues—the twenty formulas described in this chapter—adds weight to the conjectures of blues scholars on this matter. If these highly recurrent formulas are any indication, the meaning of the blues includes more than "problems in love relationships." It also includes "movement, change, flux, and anxiety." By contrast, themes of alcohol, poverty, racism, or other such social phenomena were of secondary importance to blues singers and their audience.

CHAPTER 6

One Singer's Formulaic Tradition: The Repertoire of Garfield Akers

Although the preceding chapter examined actual blues performances, its main concern was still competence: the frequency of generalized—perhaps even idealized—formulaic predications. To understand blues compositional performance requires an examination of the songs themselves. To show how the blues singer manipulated the rules of compositional competence outlined in previous chapters, I analyze in this chapter the repertoire of one particular artist—Garfield Akers.

As I stated earlier, the boundaries of any given blues formula become clearer as one moves from generalities to specific cases. Where formulas are nothing more than abstract entities—outside the context of the songs in which they appear—they tend to lose their shape and melt away. In examining song texts, however, individual formulas that the singer chose assume a concrete form and become clearly distinguishable as the basic units of blues composition.

Especially in structural studies, the application of the theory is at least as enlightening as its description. Propp applied his theory of the morphology of the Russian folktale to one short *Märchen* and in the process made clear many of the theoretical points of his study (1928, pp. 96–99). In the same way, a formulaic study of the repertoire of one singer will do much to clarify the theories presented in this study.

I hesitate to call Akers a "typical" blues singer, though he was certainly not atypical. I chose him for this case study for several reasons. His recorded repertoire of four songs is manageable for the practical purposes of this study—a singer who recorded many songs would have required a book-length analysis. His singing is clear enough that there are no questionable passages in my transcriptions of his songs (see Taft, 2005, pp. 1–2), and because he was highly formulaic in his compositions, he demonstrates well the thesis of this study.

Little is known about Akers. He was born around 1902 in Brights, Mississippi, and, like many other singers, he spent most of his performing career playing at country suppers and local juke joints (Ankeny, 2004; Oliver, 1969; Santelli, 1993). On September 23, 1929, and again on February 21, 1930, he made recordings for a field unit of the Vocalion Record Company in the Peabody Hotel, Memphis, Tennessee. On both occasions, his performing partner, Joe Calicott, traveled with him to Memphis; Calicott played second guitar behind Akers at the 1929 session and recorded his own songs at the 1930 session (see Dixon, Godrich, and Rye, 1997, pp. 2, 133). In all, Akers recorded four songs—two at each session—all issued on the Vocalion label. He died sometime between 1959 and 1962, never having recorded again, so these four songs are all that is known about his repertoire.

Akers's style of singing is almost chantlike and seems somewhat like field-holler singing. Three of his songs show the typical AAB stanzaic pattern, whereas "Cottonfield Blues—Part 2" exhibits a varied textural pattern from stanza to stanza: AB, AABB, AB, AAB, and AB, respectively. His guitar playing establishes a simple, repetitive rhythm with little embellishment; the most notable feature of his playing is his tendency to dampen the strings immediately after striking them, causing a muffled, staccato sound.

In the following four song transcriptions (given in the order in which Akers recorded them), I have reduced each stanza to its basic couplet form. There are no substantial differences in the repeated lines of his AAB or AABB stanzas; at most, he varies a Voc (see chapter 3 for explanation of abbreviations) between his first and second singing of a repeated line. Those phrases that are formulaic—in the sense that they have analogues in the corpus—are italicized.

Cottonfield Blues—Part 1

1   *I said look a-here, mama; what in the world are you trying to do*
    You want to make me love you; you going to break my heart in
    two

    I said you don't want me; what made you want to lie
    Now the day you quit me, fair brown, baby, that's the day you die

5   *I'd rather see you dead; buried in some cypress grove*
    Than to hear some gossip, mama, *that she had done you so*

    It was early one morning, just about the break of day
    And along brownskin coming, man, and drove me away

    Lord, my baby quit me; she set my trunk outdoors
10 That put the poor boy wandering, Lord, along the road
    I said trouble here, mama, and trouble everywhere you go

    And it's trouble here, mama; baby, good gal, I don't know

Cottonfield Blues—Part 2

1   *I got something I'm going to tell you; mama, keep it all to yourself*
    Don't tell your mama; don't you tell nobody else

    I'm going to write you a letter; I'm going to mail it in the air
    Then I know you going to catch it, *babe, in this world somewhere*

5   *I'm going to write you a letter;* I'm going to mail it in the sky
    Mama, I know you going to catch it, when the wind blows on the
    line

    Ohhhh, mama, I don't know what to do
    I knows you'll go; leave me all lowdown and blue

    Ohhhh that's the last word you said
10 *And I just can't remember, babe, the last old words you said*

Dough Roller Blues

1   *And I rolled and I tumbled, and I cried the whole night long*
    And I rose this morning, and I didn't know right from wrong

Have you ever woke up, and found your dough-roller gone
Then you wring your hands, and you cry the whole day long

5 *And I told my woman, just before I left your town*
Don't you let nobody tear the barrelhouse down

And I fold my arms, and I begin to walk away
I said that's all right, sweet mama; your trouble's going to come
some day

Jumpin' and Shoutin' Blues

1 *Lord, I know my baby sure going to jump and shout*
When the train get here; I come a-rolling out

Lord, I tell you it wasn't no need of, mama, trying to be so kind
Ah you know you don't love me; you ain't got me on your mind

5 *Mmmmm you ain't got me on your mind*
And what is the need of, baby, trying to be so kind

Mmmmm tried to treat her right
But you started with another man, and stayed out every day and
night

Says I ain't going down this big road by myself
10 *If I can't get you, mama, I'm going to get somebody else*

Mmmmm what you want your babe to do
Says I know it's something; gal, it ain't no use

In the following analysis, I list each phrase in these songs separately and comment on features of these phrases that are especially interesting. Where phrases are formulaic, I list analogues (within their stanzaic contexts) from the rest of the corpus. Although I list all analogues for many of the phrases, for those where there might be thirty or more analogues, I select from the corpus only those phrases that are most similar to the ones Akers used.

Note especially the following aspects of this analysis:

1. The variety of ways in which Akers's formulas manifest themselves in other singer's songs
2. The different extraformulaic elements and formula conjunctions that singers employed when working with the same formula

3. The different degrees of popularity of these formulas among singers

Cottonfield Blues—Part 1

I said look a-here, mama (line 1, x-formula)

This formula is common in the blues and acts in some ways as a Loc. Less common, but still widespread, is the similar phrase *listen here.* Akers added the Loc *I said* and the Voc *mama* to this formula in a manner similar to that of other singers. The following analogues are among the eighty or more examples of this formula in the corpus; I chose these particular examples because the formula is juxtaposed with the same r-formula used by Akers. This x-formula, however, is linked with a wide variety of other r-formulas as well.

1 *Look a-here, mama;* what you want me to do
 I work all the time; bring my money home to you
 (Blind Blake, 1927b)

2 *Now look here, man;* what more you want me to do
 Give you my stew meat, and credit you too
 (Lucille Bogan, 1935b)

3 *Look a-here, baby;* what more you want me to do
 I sacrificed my mother just to get along with you
 (Blind Darby, 1929)

4 *Now look a-here, Sue;* what you trying to do
 Giving away my luggage, and trying to love me too
 (Jack Kelly, 1939)

5 *Now look here, mama;* what am I to do
 I ain't got nobody; tell my troubles to
 (Joe McCoy, 1929b)

6 *Look a-here, look a-here;* what you want me to do
 Give you my jelly; then die for you
 (Memphis Minnie, 1929b)

7 *Now look a-here, mama;* what you trying to do
 I believe to my soul, you break my heart in two
 (Uncle Bud Walker, 1928a)

8 *Look a-here, look a-here;* what you want me to do
   You knew my jelly didn't die for you
   (James Boodle It Wiggins, 1929b)

9 *Now look a-here, baby;* now tell me what you going to do
   You can't marry me, and somebody else too
   (Sonny Boy Williamson, 1938f)

what in the world are you trying to do (line 1, r-formula)

This is one of the ten most frequent r-formulas in the corpus (see the preceding chapter). The surface manifestation that Akers chose is not unusual. An important feature of this manifestation is the inclusion of the Emb *try to* within the structure of the formula *what you do.* The phrase *in the world* is an optional Adj that singers often attached to the word *what.* The following examples are analogues with similar surface manifestations to the ones used by Akers.

10 *Woman, woman, woman, woman, Lord, what in the world you trying to do*
    Baby, the way you treat me, break my heart in two
    (Ishman Bracey, 1930a)

11 *Lord, pretty mama, I wonder what you trying to do*
    She make it trying to run with me, and my buddy too
    (Will Day, 1928a)

12 Just tell me, pretty mama; *what you trying to do*
    You didn't do no more, than I looked for you to do
    (Will Day, 1928b)

13 Now you trying to take my life, and all my loving too
    You laid a passway for me; *now what you trying to do*
    (Robert Johnson, 1937a)

14 Now look a-here, Sue; *what you trying to do*
    Giving away my luggage, and trying to love me too
    (Jack Kelly, 1939)

15 *Black Minnie, black Minnie, what in the world are you trying to do*
    I believe trying to love me, black Minnie, and my partner too
    (Tommy McClennan, 1940f)

16 Baby, you treat me *so unkind*; you always keep me feeling blue
    Lord, I sometimes wonder, honey, what you trying to do
    (Charley Taylor, 1930b)

17 Now look a-here, Louise; *what you trying to do*
    You trying to give some man my loving, and me too
    (Johnnie Temple, 1936)

18 Now look a-here, mama; *what you trying to do*
    I believe to my soul, you break my heart in two
    (Bud Walker, 1928a)

19 Now tell me, baby, *what you trying to do*
    You trying to love me, and some other man too
    (Sonny Boy Williamson, 1941c)

You want to make me love you (line 2, x-formula)

This is a manifestation of one of the ten most frequent x-formulas: +*human love* +*human*. The particular manifestation that Akers chose features the Emb *make*, but Akers is unique in the corpus in prefacing this manifestation with yet another Emb, *want*. The following list shows how other singers used this formula, prefaced by the Emb *make*.

20 Look here, pretty mama, what you done done
    You done made me love you; now your man done come
    (C.J. Anderson, 1930)

21 Can't you see, mama, what you done done
    You done made me love you; now your man done come
    (Lewis Black, 1927a)

22 You put the puppies on my mama; you drove me crazy too
    You done made me love you; what can I do
    (Leroy Carr, 1934a)

23 Now look here, baby; see what you done done
    Made me love you; now your man done come
    (John Estes, 1935e)

24 Now look a-here, baby; see what you done done
    Done made me love you; now your man done come
    (John Estes, 1935g)

25 Now look a-here, baby; see what you done done
    You done made me love you; now your man done come
    (John Estes, 1938e)

26 Look here, baby; see what you done done
    You made me love you; now your man done come
    (John Estes, 1940)

27 I don't mind you going; please don't stay the whole night long
    Because you made me love you, baby, and I miss you when you
    go
    (Clifford Gibson, 1929b)

28 Don't you let your gal fix you like my gal fixed me
    She made me love her; now she's way down in Tennessee
    (Robert Hicks, 1929b)

29 *Oh you done made me love you;* now you got me for your slave
    From now on you'll be making whoopee, baby, in your lonesome
    grave
    (King Solomon Hill, 1932a)

30 Furnish you wood; furnish you coal
    Make me love you; doggone your soul
    (Peg Leg Howell, 1926a)

31 See, see, rider; you see what you done done
    Made me love you, and now your friend is come
    (Blind Lemon Jefferson, 1926e)

32 I'm going to shoot my pistol; going to shoot my Gatling gun
    You made me love you; now your man done come
    (Robert Johnson, 1936d)

33 Mmm see, see, rider; see what you done done
    You done made me love you; now you're trying to put me down
    (Tommy Johnson, 1928c)

34 Mmmmm, baby, honey, don't you think I know
    Said I wouldn't make a man love her, if he wouldn't shake hands
    and go
    (Little Hat Jones, 1929a)

35   Baby, is all I want, mama, just one more crack at you
     If I can't make you love me, then I don't care what you do
     (Charley Jordan, 1930b)

36   See, see, rider; see what you done done
     You made me love you; now your man done come
     (Huddie Leadbetter, 1935b)

37   Feel like a broke-down engine; ain't got no drivers at all
     What makes me love my woman; she can really do the Georgia
     crawl
     (Blind Willie McTell, 1931b)

38   Hey, baby, see what you done done
     You went made me love you; now your man did come
     (Blue Coat Tom Nelson, 1928)

39   I love my baby, and I tell the world I do
     What made me love her; you'll come and love her too
     (Charley Patton, 1929h)

40   My heart is aching all over that man
     What makes me love him, I can't understand
     (Gertrude Ma Rainey, 1924a)

41   *What makes me love you, baby;* she loved me when I was down
     Well now she was nice and kind; ooo well, well she did not dog
     me around
     (Peetie Wheatstraw, 1936c)

42   See, see, mama; what you done done
     Made me love you; now your man done come
     (Washington White, 1937b)

you going to break my heart in two (line 2, r-formula)

This formula occurs only two other times in the corpus. Note that in
every case it is attached to a different x-formula but rhymed with the
same first-line r-formula in the couplet.

43   Woman, woman, woman, woman, Lord, what in the world you
     trying to do
     Baby, the way you treat me, *break my heart in two*
     (Ishman Bracey, 1930a)

44   Now look a-here, mama; what you trying to do
     I believe to my soul, *you break my heart in two*
     (Uncle Bud Walker, 1928a)

I said you don't want me (line 3, x-formula)

This is a common formula in the corpus. As Akers used it, the formula
is placed in an *if … then* equation, although he deleted the words *if* and
then in an optional transformation. The following are only a few of the
more than seventy-five occurrences of this formula in the corpus. Note
that the word *if* is usually present.

45   *I said if you don't want me,* why don't you tell me so
     Because it ain't like a man that ain't got nowhere to go
     (Richard Rabbit Brown, 1927)

46   *If he didn't want me,* he didn't have to lie
     The day I see him; that's the day he'll die
     (Rosetta Crawford, 1939)

47   *If you don't want me,* why don't you tell me why
     Because you flirting with the undertaker; I mean it ain't no lie
     (Papa Charlie Jackson, 1925c)

48   *Girl, if you don't want me,* why don't you let me know
     So I can leave at once, and hunt me somewhere else to go
     (Blind Lemon Jefferson, 1926i)

49   *Now if you don't want me, baby,* why don't you tell me so
     Then I can sleep at night, and won't have to dream no more
     (Black Bottom McPhail, 1932a)

50   *Now if you don't want me,* baby, give me your right hand
     I'll go back to my woman; you go back to your man
     (Blind Willie McTell, 1931c)

51 *If you don't want me, mama,* now let your daddy be
    For me I may find someone that cares for me
    (Eurreal Little Brother Montgomery, 1935b)

52 *And if you don't want me, baby,* you don't have to pay me no
    mind
    Because I done got tired of you driving me; ???ing me all the
    time
    (Ben Ramey, 1929)

53 Every time you leave me, I hang my head and cry
    If you don't want me, baby, please tell me the reason why
    (Bessie Mae Smith, 1930b)

54 *Don't want me, mama,* don't you tell no lies
    Because the day you quit me; that's the day you die
    (Unknown artist, 1930c)

what made you want to lie (line 3, r-formula)

This is another common formula. It usually manifests itself in one of
two ways: +*human tell* +*human a lie*, where the word *lie* is a noun, and
+*human lie to* +*human*, where the word *lie* is a verb. In the latter case,
the second +*human* is always deleted in the surface structure, so that
lie becomes the rhyme word. This second +*human* argument can also
be deleted in the former case, but this deletion is optional (compare
examples 55 and 56). Akers's use of two Embs, *make* and *want*, with this
formula is unique in the corpus, as was his use of *make* in the second
line of the song. The following list includes a portion of the more than
forty instances of this formula in the corpus.

55 I ain't going to tell you no story; *tell you no doggone lie*
    Say when you get to loving, man, I near about die
    (Texas Alexander, 1934)

56 You said you loved me; *you know you told a lie*
    Oh never mind, never mind
    (Georgia Boyd, 1933)

57 Now down on Smith Street, where you can get your rockin' rye
    Boy, that's what I'm talking about, *and I ain't talking no lie*
    (Leroy Carr, 1934f)

58 I'll tell you what I'll do, *and I sure, God, ain't going to tell no lie*
I believe I'll lay down; take morphine and die
(Sam Collins, 1927a)

59 I want to tell you something; *I wouldn't tell you a lie*
Wild women are the only kind that do ???
(Ida Cox, 1924)

60 I can't keep from worrying; *Lord, I can't keep from telling you lies*
Lord, I would do all right with you, baby, but you know you try to
be too wise
(Walter Davis, 1940c)

61 *Now, depot agent, don't tell me no lie*
Did my baby stop here; did she keep on going
(John Estes, 1930a)

62 Stinging is my trade; *I don't have to lie*
If you feel my stinger, you want to until you die
(Hattie Hart, 1934)

63 Now tell me, pretty mama, tell me; *please don't lie*
Can your sweet papa stop by here, or must I pass on by
(Charlie Jackson, 1925a)

64 Don't tell no stories; *please don't tell no lies*
Did my gal stop here; Lord, did mama keep on by
(Blind Lemon Jefferson, 1927f)

65 It's eighteen hundred and it's ninety-five
This people in town don't do nothing, *but tell, tell dirty lies*
(Will Shade, 1928a)

66 I'm going to Newport News, just to see Aunt Caroline Dyer
She's the fortune-telling woman; *oh Lord, she don't tell no lies*
(Vol Stevens, 1930a)

67 I'm going to shoot you, woman, as long as my pistol will fire
Because this is Jesse James, *and you should not tell him a lie*
(Washboard Sam, 1935)

68   You told everybody *I didn't do nothing but lie*
       I wouldn't give you women even time to die
       (Peetie Wheatstraw, 1936e)

Now the day you quit me, fair brown (line 4, x-formula)

This x-formula is one of the ten most frequent in the corpus. The formulaic predication generates either the verb *leave* or the verb *quit*. The time-adverbial *the day* that prefaces Akers's manifestation of the formula is not unusual, and the following list shows the use of this formula with both the time-adverbial and the choice of the verb *quit* in the surface predicate.

69   I love you, pretty mama; believe me, it ain't no lie
       The day you dare to quit me, baby, that's the day you die
       (Blind Blake, 1926a)

70   *The day you quit me,* that's the day you die
       (Blind Blake, 1927e)

71   Now you three times seven; you know what you want to do
       Now the day that you quit me, I won't be mad with you
       (John Estes, 1929b)

72   You three times seven, you three times seven; you ought to know
       what you want, you ought to know what you want to do
       Now the day that you quit me, and I won't be mad with, I won't be
       mad with you
       (John Estes, 1935h)

73   Honey, honey, I'm going to tell you the truth
       The day you quit me, that's the day you die
       (Robert Hicks, 1927c)

74   Black Minnie, black Minnie, you know you ain't doing me right
       But the day you quit me, black Minnie, I swear that's the day you
       die
       (Tommy McClennan, 1940f)

75   Well I love you, Mr. Charlie; honey, God knows I do
       But the day you try to quit me; brother, that's the day you die
       (Rosie Mae Moore, 1928a)

76   It may be a week; it may be a month or two
     But the day you quit me, honey, it's coming home to you
     (Bessie Smith, 1923a)

77   Don't want me, mama; don't you tell no lies
     Because the day you quit me, that's the day you die
     (Unknown artist, 1930c)

baby, that's the day you die (line 4, r-formula)

This formula is often linked with the preceding one, but as some of the following examples show, it can also be linked with other x-formulas.

78   Ah watch her, boy, as she pass by
     Because the day I catch you with her, *boy, that's the day you're going to die*
     (Big Bill Broonzy, 1935b)

79   I love you, pretty mama; believe me, it ain't no lie
     The day you dare to quit me; *baby, that's the day you die*
     (Blind Blake, 1926a)

80   Love you, pretty mama; believe me, it ain't no lie
     The day you try to quit me; *baby, that's the day you die*
     (Blind Blake, 1926b)

81   Hey, hey love you *till the day you die*
     Nobody but me, you know the reason why
     (Blind Blake, 1927c)

82   The day you quit me, *that's the day you die*
     (Blind Blake, 1927e)

83   Love you, mama, till the sea run dry
     Lord, I love you, rider, Lord, *till the day you die*
     (Ishman Bracey, 1928d)

84   If he didn't want me, he didn't have to lie
     The day I see him; *that's the day he'll die*
     (Rosetta Crawford, 1939)

85   Well it's so long, so long, baby; I must say good-bye
     I'm going to roam this highway, *until the day I die*
     (Bill Jazz Gillum, 1940)

86   Honey, honey, I'm going to tell you the truth
     The day you quit me, *that's the day you die*
     (Robert Hicks, 1927c)

87   Black Minnie, black Minnie, you know you ain't doing me right
     But the day you quit me, black Minnie, *I swear that's the day you die*
     (Tommy McClennan, 1940f)

88   Going to tell you this; ain't going to tell no lie
     Day you leave me; *that's the day you die*
     (Joe McCoy, 1930a)

89   Well I love you, Mr. Charlie; honey, God knows I do
     But the day you try to quit me; *brother, that's the day you die*
     (Rosie Mae Moore, 1928a)

90   I've got the freight train blues, but I'm too darn mean to cry
     I'm going to love that man *till the day he dies*
     (Trixie Smith, 1938)

91   Lord, I'm going to leave here walking; chance is that I may ride
     Because I'm going to ramble *until the day I die*
     (Ramblin' Thomas, 1928g)

92   Don't want me, mama; don't you tell no lies
     Because the day you quit me, *that's the day you die*
     (Unknown artist, 1930c)

93   You couldn't see my baby passing by
     Mama, be your crawling king snake *till the day I die*
     (Big Joe Williams, 1941a)

I'd rather see you dead (line 5, x-formula)

This formula is part of a logical equation *rather X than Y,* which is fairly rare in the blues. Akers's addition of the Emb *see* is not common, but there are analogues in examples 100 and 102.

94 *I'd rather be dead;* buried in the sea
    Than to have that man I love say he don't want me
    (Ida Cox, 1923)

95 *Now I'd rather be dead;* sleep in an old hollow log
    And to be here, baby, and you doing me like a dog
    (John Estes, 1930b)

96 *I'd rather be dead* in some lonesome place
    Than for my man treating me this a-way
    (Nellie Florence, 1928)

97 *Lord, I'd rather be dead, mama,* mouldering in the clay
    Seeing my sweet baby treated this a-way
    (Harvey Hull, 1927b)

98 *I would rather be dead,* and six feet in my grave
    To be way up here, honey, treated this a-way
    (Skip James, 1931b)

99 *I'd rather be dead, baby;* buried in the deep blue sea
    Than to be so far from home, baby; people making a fool of me
    (Charley Jordan, 1936b)

100 *See you dead, now,* in some cedar grove
     Than to see some man, now, bothering with your clothes
     (Joe McCoy, 1930d)

101 I'm going to kill my man; than I'm going to kill myself
     I'd rather we both be dead, than to see him with someone else
     (Rosie Mae Moore, 1928c)

102 *I'd rather see you dead;* straight down in your grave
     To see you give another man, Lord, my *roof* and *plate*
     (Mooch Richardson, 1928a)

103 Lord, my good man don't want me no more
     Well I wished I was dead, and in the land I'm doomed to go
     (Victoria Spivey, 1936)

104 *I'd rather be dead,* and in my horrible tomb
To hear my woman; some man done taken my room
(Johnnie Temple, 1935)

105 *Because I'd rather be dead;* buried on my face
Than to love you woman; you treat me this a-way
(Robert Wilkins, 1928b)

buried in some cypress grove (line 5, r-formula)

This is an interesting and unusual poetic image. Although it is often associated with Skip James's "Cypress Grove Blues" (1931b), both Akers and Joe McCoy used this formula before James made his recording.

106 *I would rather be buried in some cypress grove*
To have some woman, Lord, I can't control
(Skip James, 1931b)

107 See you dead, now, *in some cedar grove*
Than to see some man, now, bothering with your clothes
(Joe McCoy, 1930d)

Than to hear some gossip (line 6, x-position)

This phrase is unique in the corpus.

That she had done you so (line 6, r-formula)

This is one manifestation of a formula that also allows the verb *treat* in its surface predicate. It might also allow the verb *hurt*, as in example 109, but this might be stretching the boundaries of the formula a bit far.

108 *Baby, baby, what makes you treat me so*
I've done all that a poor boy could do
(Blind Darby, 1929)

109 I never earned nothing, *oh so much to hurt me so*
Oh when I was talking to my babe that morning, and she told me that I didn't ???
(Little Hat Jones, 1929b)

110 When you used to be my gypsy, *done just so and so*
Now I got another baby; I can't use you no more
(Furry Lewis, 1929a)

111 *I never would have thought that my baby would treat me so*
Oh she broke my heart when she grabbed that B & O
(Willie McTell, 1933c)

112 *You wonder why I treat you so*
You should have sense enough to know
(Charlie Spand, 1929a)

113 Because I'm going up the country; coming here no more
Oh I love you, woman, *but you always treat me so*
(Robert Wilkins, 1928b)

It was early one morning (line 7, x-formula)

This formula is an "upgraded" Adv. The time-adverbial does not refer directly to any particular action and, therefore, becomes a surface-level sentence with an empty *it* as its subject. The *it was* is sometimes deleted (see examples 116, 122, and 124); whether this manifestation is an Adv of the r-formula or an x-formula in its own right is problematic. There are more than fifty-five examples of this formula in the corpus, from which the following list is taken.

114 *Say it's in the morning;* so late in the night
When she's loving you, man, she loves you just right
(Texas Alexander, 1934)

115 *Now it was early one morning, mama;* I was on my way to school
Lord, that's when I got the notion to break my mama's rule
(Kokomo Arnold, 1930)

116 *Soon one morning,* I heard a panther squawl
Tell your mama caught the local; you catch the cannonball
(Lewis Black, 1927b)

117 *Lord, it's soon in the morning;* going to believe I'll leave here
(Ishman Bracey, 1928b)

118 *Lord, it's early this morning,* Lord, about four o'clock
There was something in my bedroom began to reel and rock
(Tommie Bradley, 1931b)

119 *Lord, it was early in the morning,* about the break of day
With my head on the pillow, where my goat, Lord, used to lay
(John Byrd, 1930a)

120 *It was soon this morning;* I heard my doorbell ring
I thought Slim was working, and he wasn't doing a doggone thing
(Hattie Hart, 1934)

121 *It was early one morning,* just about the break of day
Says I thought I heard my sweet baby say
(Papa Charlie Jackson, 1927b)

122 *Lord, early one morning,* just about the break of day
A passenger train carried my man away
(Ollie Rupert, 1927a)

123 *It was early this morning;* I was lying out on my floor
I was keeping daily watch on my wall, so that granddaddy won't crawl in my house no more
(Jaydee Short, 1932c)

124 *Early one morning,* baby, something was on my mind
I thinking about my welfare, and I just couldn't keep from crying
(Robert Wilkins, 1935a)

125 *It was early one morning,* about the break of day
Don't you hear me crying; won't you lead me where to stay
(Oscar Woods, 1937)

just about the break of day (line 7, r-formula)

This formula is quite common and usually follows some allusion to "morning" in the x-formula. The following are a few of the more than thirty-five occurrences of this formula in the corpus.

126 Captain rung the bell this morning, *just about the break of day*
Said now it's time for you to go rolling; buddy, why don't you be on your way
(Kokomo Arnold, 1937c)

127 I got up this morning, *just about the break of day*
   I could hear a *bunch of* bloodhounds a-coming my way
   (Sam Collins, 1931d)

128 My man quit me this morning, *just about the break of day*
   And he told me he was going away to stay
   (Lena Henry, 1924)

129 He met me one sunny morning, *just about the break of day*
   I was drinking my moonshine; he made me throw my knife
   away
   (Memphis Minnie, 1935)

130 Went home this morning, *about the break of day*
   Ha baby, he's just staying away
   (Unknown artist, 1930b)

131 And hey what makes a rooster crow *at the break of day*
   That's to let the rounder know the workingman is on his way
   (Hosea Woods, 1929b)

And along brownskin coming (line 8, x-formula)

This phrase is a member of one of the most frequent (and most diffuse) formulas in the corpus: +*human moves toward some place*. The surface manifestation Akers used might be represented as +*human come along (here)*, where the place *here* is deleted in a surface-level transformation. The following are other examples of this particular manifestation.

132 If you got a good bull-cow, better feed him every day
   Because may come along some young cow, and tow your bull
   away
   (Big Bill Broonzy, 1932b)

133 Standing on the corner, *all ??? man*
   Police come along; take me by the hand
   (Teddy Edwards, 1934)

134 *Said come along, mama;* give me a hug
   You got the world; I got the stopper and the jug
   (Robert Hicks, 1929a)

135 Oh up in my room, I bowed down to pray
Say the blues come along, and they drove my spirit away
(Son House, 1930b)

136 I bought all her clothes; I bought her a diamond ring
Then along come a fatmouth; keep me shaking that thing
(Papa Charlie Jackson, 1927a)

137 Now January, February, and March too
The women come along, and showed her just what to do
(Papa Charlie Jackson, 1927d)

138 If you got a no-good bull-cow, you ought to keep your bull, bull at home
Say may come along a young heifer, and just tow your bull from home
(Charley Patton, 1934a)

139 I picking up the newspaper, and I looking in the ads
And the policeman came along, and he arrested me for vag
(Ramblin' Thomas, 1928e)

140 *Along came John,* who's my best friend
Cut his head, till it was a sin
(Kid Wesley Wilson, 1929)

Lord, and drove me away (line 8, r-formula)

This formula often includes the Adv *further* and, with this element, is always adjoined to the x -formula *the more you cry* in the corpus. Akers, however, did not use this manifestation of the formula, preferring an unembellished predication.

141 I wonder what can the matter with poor Betsy Mae
Lord, she got mad, *and drove poor me away*
(Texas Alexander, 1930)

142 That's all right, baby; *sorry* *you drove me away*
Well now you don't think, ooo well, well, that you may need my help some day
(Andrew Hogg, 1937)

143   I'm going to Tishamingo, because I'm sad today
Say the woman I love, *she done drove me away*
(Peg Leg Howell, 1926b)

144   I'm going, I'm going; crying won't make me stay
The more you cry, *further you drive me away*
(Mississippi John Hurt, 1928b)

145   I'm leaving town; crying won't make me stay
Baby, the more you cry, *the further you drive me away*
(Blind Lemon Jefferson, 1927b)

146   Oh because I'm brown, *Lord, he want to drive me away*
He knows he's a good honey dripper; Lord, I want him every
day
(Edith North Johnson, 1929b)

147   I'm going, I'm going; your crying won't make me stay
For the more you cry, gal, *the further you drive me away*
(Furry Lewis, 1927a)

148   I'm going, babe, I'm going; and crying won't make me stay
Because the more you cry, now, now, babe, *the further you drive
me away*
(Tommy McClennan, 1941b)

149   How my poor heart weeped and worried, *baby, when you drove
me away*
It was crying for poor boy McTell, some old rainy day
(Blind Willie McTell, 1929e)

150   I'm going, I'm going; crying won't make me stay
The more you cry, *the further it drive me away*
(Memphis Minnie, 1929a)

151   And I'm going, I'm going, mama; and your crying won't make me
stay
And the more you cry, mama, *the farther that you drive me away*
(Eurreal Little Brother Montgomery, 1936b)

152 I'm going to leave you, but I'll be back some old day
     I'm going to make you remember *how you drove me away*
     (Willie Reed, 1928a)

153 Now you done drove me, baby, *until you drove me away*
     Now someone has done something, mama; about to take your place
     (Will Shade, 1929c)

154 I hate to leave St. Louis, and I tried so hard to stay
     But the meanest treatment is driving me away
     (Bessie Mae Smith, 1929)

155 And I'm going and I'm going, and your crying won't make me stay
     Baby, the more you cry, *the further you drive me away*
     (Frank Stokes, 1927e)

156 And I'm going, I'm going, and your crying won't make me stay
     Because the more you cry, gal, *the further you drive me away*
     (Frank Stokes, 1929e)

157 She give me her love; even let me draw her pay
     She was a real good woman, *but unkindness drove her away*
     (Tampa Red, 1937)

158 *I said please, mama, please don't drive me away*
     Because I'd be a good fellow, mama, if you would please let me stay
     (Buck Turner, 1937a)

159 I'm standing on my mother's grave, and I wished I could see her face
     I be glad when that day comes, *ooo well, when these blues drive me away*
     (Washington White, 1940a)

160 Well my mother, she gone, and I hope she gone to stay
     I have a mean stepfather; *he done drove me away*
     (Big Joe Williams, 1935e)

Lord, my baby quit me (line 9, x-formula)
This is another manifestation of the x-formula in line 4.

161 Says I can't live for loving, but I just can't help myself
Now the little woman I'm loving quit me; well I sure don't want
nobody else
(Kokomo Arnold, 1936)

162 Woke up this morning; couldn't even walk in my shoes
My baby just quit me; she left me with the bust up blues
(Ishman Bracey, 1930c)

163 Have you woke up in the morning; *you weep and moan*
Your best girl quit you; left you all alone
(Ishman Bracey, 1930d)

164 *Because my woman had done quit me,* didn't have nowhere to go
(Jaybird Coleman, 1927a)

165 *Say my gal just quit me, now man;* pulled in another lane
Didn't want to come back, till I bought an airplane
(Frank Edwards, 1941)

166 *Says my woman, she quit me;* keep me worried and blue
Take me in your arms, and love me like you used to do
(Blind Boy Fuller, 1940c)

167 When you see me coming; my head hanging all down
It's that my woman done quit me; the news all over town
(Clifford Gibson, 1929f)

168 I used to didn't blow gauge; drink nothing of the kind
But my man quit me, and that changed my mind
(Lil Green, 1941a)

169 *My man quit me this morning,* about the break of day
And he told me he was going away to stay
(Lena Henry, 1924)

170 *Cherry Ball quit me;* she quit me in a calm good way
Lordy, what to take to get her; I carried it every day
(Skip James, 1931c)

171 I'm going to run to town; talk with that chief of police
Tell him my good gal has quit me, and I can't live in no peace
(Blind Lemon Jefferson, 1926f)

172 *My wife has quit me,* and my best pigmeat gal has too
All of ??? *Lord* here with the chinch bug blues
(Blind Lemon Jefferson, 1927j)

173 Lord, I'm going to the station; going to tell the chief of police
Roberta done quit me, and I can't see no peace
(Huddie Leadbetter, 1935a)

174 *You up and quit me;* do anything you want to do
Some day you'll want me, and I won't want you
(Memphis Minnie, 1930d)

175 *Lord, I quit my kid-man,* because I caught him in a lie
And all I can hear now is his moaning and his mournful cry
(Alice Moore, 1930b)

176 *You quit me, pretty mama,* because you couldn't be my boss
But a rolling stone don't gather no moss
(Charlie Bozo Nickerson, 1930b)

177 Mmmmm now my poor heart is aching for me
My black woman has quit me; I'm going back to Culver City
(Joe Pullum, 1934)

178 I did something last winter; Lord, I ain't going to do it no more
I quit a thousand-dollar woman, *but it wasn't worth ???*
(Will Shade, 1929a)

179 *Ever since you quit me, mama,* I ain't wanted nobody else
For I'd rather be with nobody, than I'd rather be howling by myself
(J.T. Funny Paper Smith, 1930a)

180 Say some strange something is easing down on me
Because my best baby has quit me, and the world she cared for me
(Henry Spaulding, 1929b)

181 *And she quit me;* she left me to sing this song
You never miss your friend, till you caught your train and gone
(Frank Stokes, 1928a)

182 *Last time my baby quit me,* I say I didn't no more want her around
But every time I see her smiling face, my kind-hearted feeling come down
(Roosevelt Sykes, 1931b)

183 There's so many women; there's so many different kinds
When one quit me, it's sure to worry my mind
(Ramblin' Thomas, 1928c)

184 Go bring me my shotgun, my *biskins* and my shells
You know my woman, she done quit me, and I'm going to start to raising hell
(Sonny Boy Williamson, 1941b)

she done set my trunk outdoors (line 9, r-formula)

The four other manifestations of this formula show interesting variations in both their arguments and their predicates.

185 I ain't got no shoes, and I ain't got no clothes
The house-rent man has done put my things outdoors
(Leroy Carr, 1934j)

186 I'm going to ask my rider, *would she set my trunk outdoors*
I don't mean quitting you, but I got another place to go
(Tom Dickson, 1928a)

187 Listen here, mama; black snake is wearing my clothes
And I told you about it, *and you put my trunk outdoors*
(Blind Lemon Jefferson, 1927g)

188 Mmm little girl got buggy; *she throwed all my clothes outdoors*
Well, well right now I wonder will a shopping bag hold my clothes
(Peetie Wheatstraw, 1930c)

That put the poor boy wandering, Lord, along the road (line 10, r-position)

This phrase is unique in the corpus, although there are some phrases that are quite similar to it. It might be considered part of the formula +*human move upon the road*. The predicate *move upon* might generate a number of different surface-level verbs. The following list includes some of the possible manifestations of this formula (if, indeed, it is a formula).

189 *I been rolling and drifting along the road*
    Just looking for my room and board
    (Lottie Beaman, 1929)

190 When the bell started ringing, conductor holler all aboard
    Lord, I picked up my suitcase; *started walking down the road*
    (Big Bill Broonzy, 1932a)

191 I grabbed my suitcase; *I took on up the road*
    I got there; she was laying on the cooling board
    (Son House, 1930a)

192 Now my first love is in Texas; my next one lives in Kokomo
    Now my first love is in Texas; my second lives in Kokomo
    I'm going to catch me a freight train, *and I'm going on down the road*
    (Jack Kelly, 1933c)

193 I got a babe up in a *slumber*; I put on my shoes and clothes
    I'm going to try to find my woman; *I know she's strolling, babe, on the road*
    (James Yank Rachel, 1934)

194 Mmmmm oh Lord, Lord, Lordy, Lord
    My suitcase is too heavy *to walk down that dusty road*
    (Charley Taylor, 1930a)

195 *So many days I would be walking down the road*
    I could hardly walk with looking down on my clothes
    (Washington White, 1940b)

I said trouble here, mama (line 11, x-formula)

The three other manifestations of this formula show a deeper-level construction: *it is trouble here.* Akers chose to delete the *it is* in his use of the formula.

196   *Now it's trouble, trouble;* I been had it all my days
      Well it seems like trouble going to follow me to my grave
      (Kokomo Arnold, 1935d)

197   *And it's trouble here;* and it's trouble everywhere
      So much trouble floating in the air
      (Furry Lewis, 1928d)

198   *And it's trouble here;* it's trouble in the air
      Says I want to go home, but I know it's trouble there
      (Noah Lewis, 1930b)

and trouble everywhere you go (line 11, r-formula)

This is one of the most frequent r-formulas in the corpus. It has the peculiar feature of incorporating a part of the x-formula within its structure. The essence of the formula is *everywhere +human go,* and the following list shows some of the different ways in which this r-formula is attached to x-formulas.

199   I got a bed in my bedroom, a pallet on my floor
      Got to do the alley boogie, *everywhere I go*
      (Lucille Bogan, 1930a)

200   Well it's hard times here, and *it's hard times everywhere I go*
      I've got to make me some money, so I won't have these hard-luck
      blues no more
      (Bill Jazz Gillum, 1942)

201   Out in the rain, hail, sleet, and snow
      I'm so downhearted, *everywhere I go*
      (Lil Green, 1942)

202   Hard times here, *everywhere you go*
      Times is harder than I ever seen before
      (Skip James, 1931d)

203   I used to be a drunkard, *rowdy everywhere I go*
      If I ever get out of this trouble I'm in, man, I won't be rowdy no
      more
      (Blind Lemon Jefferson, 1928a)

204   Lord, I'm worried here; *worried everywhere I go*
      I worried my rider so late last night, she had a mule-wagon
      backed up to my door
      (Blind Lemon Jefferson, 1928b)

205   Mosquitoes all around me; *mosquitoes everywhere I go*
      No matter where I go, well they sticks their bills in me
      (Blind Lemon Jefferson, 1929d)

206   You sprinkled hot-foot powder mmm around my door
      It keeps me with a rambling mind, rider, *every old place I go*
      (Robert Johnson, 1937c)

207   I'm going to sing this old song; ain't going to sing it no more
      I'm going to sing this old song, *everywhere I go*
      (Jack Kelly, 1933a)

208   Said my good girl said she didn't want me no more
      But she don't mind *dancing**, *Lord, everywhere I go*
      (Furry Lewis, 1927c)

209   I'm a guitar king; singing the blues *everywhere I go*
      I'm going to sing these blues, till I get back in Territor'
      (Tommy McClennan, 1941c)

210   Here comes grandpa, staring up and down the road
      With that pipe in his hand, he'll find you *everywhere you go*
      (Memphis Minnie, 1930f)

211   You have seen a lots of cats, and you going to see a lots more
      I got one-eyed cats, *everywhere I go*
      (Memphis Minnie, 1936a)

212   Hey, boll weevil, don't sing the blues no more
      Boll weevil's here; *boll weevil's everywhere you go*
      (Gertrude Ma Rainey, 1923b)

213 I am a snake doctor; *gang of womens everywhere I go*
And when I get to flying sometime, I can see a gang of women
standing out in the door
(Jaydee Short, 1932a)

214 Said now Mary had a little lamb; I mean his fleece was white as
snow
Mary take that little lamb with her *to most every place that she
go*
(Freddie Spruell, 1935d)

215 I said a-weeping Mary, now Mary don't you weep no more
And now stop and take your time, and do your work *everywhere
you go*
(Frank Stokes, 1927a)

216 Take me in your arms, mama, and rock me good and slow
So I can take my time, and do my work *everywhere I go*
(Frank Stokes, 1927e)

217 Now little batch of posies laid on my door
The Nehi women keep me, *everywhere I go*
(Frank Stokes, 1928b)

218 There's only four places in Memphis that I'd like to go
Where I could have a good time, and do my work *everywhere I
go*
(Frank Stokes, 1929f)

219 But I can't tell you, because you don't know
People talking, *everywhere I go*
(Roosevelt Sykes, 1930)

220 Well it's blues, it's blues, *everywhere I go*
Well, well I'm going to find my good girl, ooo and I won't be blue
no more
(Will Weldon, 1936)

221 I try to be good, *every place I go*
But now you know there will come a day, ooo well, well I will
have some place I know
(Peetie Wheatstraw, 1936b)

222 People talk; I can hear them whisper, *everywhere I go*
     All my friends come to see me, and say well I told you so
     (Joshua White, 1934)

223 I'm a rooting groundhog, and *I root everywhere I go*
     Well my baby had the nerve to tell me that she didn't want me no
     more
     (Big Joe Williams, 1935e)

224 I say bad luck and trouble, *every place I go*
     I believe somebody put bad luck on me; ooo well I believe now it's
     time to go
     (Big Joe Williams, 1935f)

225 Then I turn right around; went to the next door
     And the gypsy told me I have a woman, *every place I go*
     (Blind Richard Yates, 1927)

And it's trouble here, mama (line 12, x-formula)

See line 11, x-formula. Note that in this instance, Akers chose to retain
the *it is* in the surface manifestation of this formula.

baby, good gal, I don't know (line 12, r-formula)

In most manifestations of this formula, the +*human* argument is filled
with *you*. Akers was one of only two singers to opt for the first-person *I*
(see example 237).

226 Don't never drive a stranger from your door
     He may be your best friend; *mama, says you don't know*
     (Texas Alexander, 1928c)

227 *Mmmmm, baby, you don't know, you don't know*
     Papa's already going back to Kokomo
     (Francis Scrapper Blackwell, 1928a)

228 Loaded in the *dog* wagon, and down the road we go
     Oh baby, oh baby, you don't know
     (Francis Scrapper Blackwell, 1928b)

229 Now she doing things *that you don't never know*
     (Joe Calicott, 1930)

230   Easy, mama; somebody knocking at my door
      It may be my yellow woman; *mama, you sure don't know*
      (Lonnie Clark, 1929)

231   You're walking for miles; no place to go
      You're talking to yourself; *Lord, but you don't know*
      (Katherine Henderson, 1928b)

232   My gal, she's easy; some say she's slow
      There's things about her, *you don't know*
      (Robert Hicks, 1929a)

233   Don't never drive a stranger from your door
      It could be your best friend; *mama, you don't know*
      (Blind Lemon Jefferson, 1927f)

234   I said don't ever drive a stranger from your door
      May be your sister or brother; *say you don't never know*
      (Jack Kelly, 1933c)

235   Baby, you know it may be my last time; *rider, you sure don't know*
      It may be my last time, baby, knocking on your door
      (Charlie McCoy, 1929)

236   Lord, I'm going down south, where the weather sure do suit my clothes
      Well my baby said look, daddy, *I swear to God you sure don't know*
      (Robert Petway, 1942a)

237   The reason why, *I don't know*
      Sometimes I'm certain it's polio
      (Gertrude Ma Rainey, 1924b)

238   *Crying mmmmm don't nobody know*
      (Allen Shaw, 1934b)

239 I'm going to fly by easy; man, you know I ain't going to fly very
low
What I got in these sacks on my back, man, *you don't know, honey, know*
(Jaydee Short, 1932a)

240 Baby, please don't, baby, please don't, I mean please don't go
Here's one thing *that you don't know*
(J.T. Funny Paper Smith, 1930c)

241 Lord, I'm a poor boy; I'm going to and fro
What's on my mind, *don't nobody know*
(Roosevelt Sykes, 1929e)

242 But I can't tell you, *because you don't know*
People talking, everywhere I go
(Roosevelt Sykes, 1930)

243 What is it tastes like gravy; *boys, I bet you don't know*
Can you guess what tastes like gravy; it's tight if you really want
to know
(Tampa Red, 1929b)

244 Mama, never drive a stranger from your door
He may be your best friend; *baby, you don't know*
(Edward Thompson, 1929a)

245 How do you feel when you drive a good man from your door
Well, well now you must stop, look, and listen; may be your best
friend; *you don't know*
(Peetie Wheatstraw, 1934a)

246 Honey, that's why I tell you; don't drive a good man from your
door
Well, well now you may need his help some day, baby; *oh well,
well you don't know*
(Peetie Wheatstraw, 1934a)

247 *Well my little red hen just don't know*
Well now she say she love me; she wild about Mr. so-and-so
(Sonny Boy Williamson, 1938g)

Cottonfield Blues—Part 2

I got something I'm going to tell you (line 1, x-formula)

This x-formula is one of the ten most frequent in the corpus. At times it is difficult to decide whether some manifestations of this formula are indeed formulas or whether they are merely Loc. The manifestation Akers used, however, is clearly an x-formula in its own right. Akers was unique in the corpus in retaining the *I'm going* part of the phrase; other singers shortened the formula to *I got something to tell you*. A syntactical reordering of this formula, *I will tell you something*, is just as frequent in the corpus, but the following list includes only those manifestations with the same syntax as used by Akers.

248 *I've got something to tell you;* make the hair rise on your head
Got a new way of loving a woman; make the springs screech on her bed
(Texas Alexander, 1929)

249 *Now I got something to tell you, mama,* and I really want you to understand
Every man you see wearing britches; he sure God ain't no monkey-man
(Kokomo Arnold, 1937b)

250 *I've got something to tell you, baby;* don't let it break your heart
So long together; now we got to part
(Peter Chatman, 1940)

251 I am traveling this lonesome road, if I ever get back no more
I have something to tell you, people, just before I go
(Walter Davis, 1935a)

252 *Now something to tell you;* keep it to yourself
Don't tell your sister; don't tell nobody else
(John Estes, 1935g)

253 *I'm got something to tell you,* and I know it ain't good news
Because a hesitating woman give me the hesitating blues
(Jim Jackson, 1930)

254 *Got something to tell you;* make the hair rise on your head
Got a new way of getting down; make the springs tremble on
your bed
(Blind Lemon Jefferson, 1929c)

255 *Now I got something to tell you;* make the hair rise on your head
I got a-this old Elgin movement; make the springs tremble on
your bed
(Charley Jordan, 1936b)

256 *Got something to tell you;* don't let it make you mad
I ain't going long down here, honey, you heard I had
(Huddie Leadbetter, 1935h)

257 *I've got something to tell you;* know it's going to break your heart
We been together a good while, but now we got to part
(Memphis Minnie, 1929a)

258 *I got something to tell you;* hope it don't make you mad
I got something for you; make you feel glad
(Memphis Minnie, 1929b)

259 *I got something to tell you;* hope I don't make you mad
I got something for you that you never had
(Memphis Minnie, 1930e)

260 *I got something to tell you,* when I gets a chance
I don't want to marry; just want to be your man
(Charley Patton, 1929c)

261 Now will you please be kind, babe; let me speak just one more
time
Because I have something to tell you, baby; will ease your trouble
in mind
(Henry Spaulding, 1929b)

262 Now daddy, daddy, daddy, listen; turn your lights down low
I got something good to tell you, she *holler* just before you go
(Freddie Spruell, 1926b)

263 *I got something to tell you;* going to make you mad
I got something for you; going to make you feel glad
(James Boodle It Wiggins, 1929b)

264 *I got something to tell you;* is going to break your heart
Been together so long; now got to get apart
(James Boodle It Wiggins, 1929b)

265 *I got something to tell you,* just before I go
Getting out of trouble this time; woman, I won't do wrong no more
(Robert Wilkins, 1928a)

266 *I got something to tell you;* tell you before I go
Because I'm going up the country; coming here no more
(Robert Wilkins, 1928b)

267 *Well I got something to tell you,* mama, when I get a chance
Well I don't want to marry; baby, just want to be your man
(Big Joe Williams, 1935d)

268 *I got something to ask you;* I done got scared
I got to wait now, before I go to bed
(Joe Williams, 1929a)

269 *I got something to ask you;* don't you get mad
I want you to give me something, I ain't never had
(Joe Williams, 1929a)

270 *Well I got something to tell you;* I ain't going to tell you no more
About fooling around with Mr. so-and-so
(Sonny Boy Williamson, 1938c)

271 *Now I got something to tell you, baby;* you can't do
You can't love me, and some other man too
(Sonny Boy Williamson, 1941d)

mama, keep it all to yourself (line 1, r-formula)

Once again, Akers demonstrated his individuality by being the only singer in the corpus to insert the Adv *all* into this formula.

272   Now something to tell you; *keep it to yourself*
      Don't tell your sister; don't tell nobody else
      (John Estes, 1935g)

273   But that ain't none of your business; *keep it to yourself*
      Don't you tell your kid-man; please don't tell nobody else
      (Tommy McClennan, 1941c)

274   I'll tell you something; *keep it to yourself*
      Please don't tell your husband, Lord, and no one else
      (Charley Patton, 1929d)

275   I'm going to tell you something, baby; *want you to keep it to your-
      self*
      If you don't give me all your sugar, you won't give it to no one
      else
      (Bessie Mae Smith, 1930b)

276   I'm going to tell you something; *keep it to yourself*
      Don't tell your kid-man, and nobody else
      (Sonny Boy Williamson, 1938c)

Don't tell your mama (line 2, x-formula)

This is another manifestation of the x-formula in line 1 of this song:
+*human tell* +*human*. The following are those manifestations that, like
Akers's, include a Neg.

277   Now something to tell you; keep it to yourself
      Don't tell your sister; don't tell nobody else
      (John Estes, 1935g)

278   *If you don't want to tell your mother* that you soon will be coming
      home
      You better cut your late hours, and let other mens alone
      (Bill Jazz Gillum, 1941c)

279   But that ain't none of your business; keep it to yourself
      Don't tell your kid-man; please don't tell nobody else
      (Tommy McClennan, 1941c)

280   I'll tell you something; keep it to yourself
Please don't tell your husband, Lord, and no one else
(Charley Patton, 1929d)

281   *Don't never tell nobody* what your perfect man can do
You just get them anxious to try some of his good points too
(Clara Smith, 1923c)

282   *Baby, please don't tell you mother;* please don't let my sister know
Sure as you appreciate my death, baby; will you please hang crepe
on your door
(Freddie Spruell, 1935b)

283   If you see my mama before I do
Don't tell her, faro, what road I'm on
(Henry Thomas, 1927a)

284   *Don't tell all the girls* what that Peetie Wheatstraw can do
That will cause suspicion, now; you know they will try him too
(Peetie Wheatstraw, 1937b)

285   I'm going to tell you something; keep it to yourself
Don't tell your kid-man, and nobody else
(Sonny Boy Williamson, 1938c)

don't you tell nobody else (line 2, r-formula)

The use of this formula in the corpus is restricted in terms of the stanzaic contexts in which it appears. The four examples below, as well as Akers's stanza, seem to indicate that the formula has become "ossified" within a particular stanzaic framework. There was, however, always the potential for new and innovative combinations of this formula with others in the poetic tradition.

286   Now something to tell you; keep it to yourself
Don't tell your sister; *don't tell nobody else*
(John Estes, 1935g)

287   But that ain't none of your business; keep it to yourself
Don't tell your kid-man; *please don't tell nobody else*
(Tommy McClennan, 1941c)

288 I'll tell you something; keep it to yourself
     Please don't tell your husband, *Lord, and no one else*
     (Charley Patton, 1929d)

289 I'm going to tell you something; keep it to yourself
     Don't tell your kid-man, *and nobody else*
     (Sonny Boy Williamson, 1938c)

I'm going to write you a letter (line 3, x-formula)

Interestingly, in the corpus under analysis, the predicate of this formula always manifests itself as the verb *write* and never *send*, although there is a formula *send a telegram*. There is also a related formula, *+human receive/get a letter*, that appears about thirty times in the corpus.

290 *Says she won't write me no letter;* she won't send me no telegram
     She just a hard-headed woman, and she don't even give a damn
     (Kokomo Arnold, 1937d)

291 *I'm going to write a letter;* mail it in the air
     I'm going to find this gal; she's in the world somewhere
     (Lewis Black, 1927a)

292 The day you left me, won't wear black
     I write you a letter; come sneaking back
     (Sam Collins, 1931c)

293 *I'm going to write you a letter;* my wife and I ain't going to do right
     no more
     I know the way you treat me, baby; Lord, you did not want me no
     more
     (Walter Davis, 1936)

294 Now I met Alberta way out across the sea
     Now she didn't write no letter, and she didn't care for me
     (John Estes, 1935d)

295 *Now I wrote little Martha a letter;* five day it return back to me
     You know little Martha Hardin's house done burnt down; she
     done moved on Bathurst Street
     (John Estes, 1938c)

296 *Write me a letter,* and send it by mail
I want you to tell my dear old mother, I'm in the New Huntsville
Jail
(Joe Evans, 1931)

297 *Now I'm going to write a letter;* mail it in the air
Because the March wind blows; it blows news everywhere
(Bo Weavil Jackson, 1926a)

298 *Going to write a letter;* mailed it in the air
Mail it by the window; love yous everywhere
(Bo Weavil Jackson, 1926b)

299 *I'm going to write a letter;* telephone every town I know
If I can't find her in West Selma, she must be in East Monroe I
know
(Robert Johnson, 1936b)

300 *Yes she wrote me a letter;* what you reckon it read
Come home, big papa; your loving baby's dead
(Huddie Leadbetter, 1935e)

301 Get me a pencil and paper; I'm going to sit right down
I'm going to write me a letter, back to Youngstown
(Furry Lewis, 1928a)

302 *I wrote her a letter;* I mailed it in the air
You may know by that, I got a friend somewhere
(Noah Lewis, 1929)

303 *I'm going to write you a letter soon in the morning;* mail it in the
air
You can tell by that, babe I got a-somewhere
(Tommy McClennan, 1940e)

304 I met my Mary way across the sea
She wouldn't write me no letter; she didn't care for me
(Joe McCoy, 1930c)

305 *I wrote you a letter, mama;* put it in your front yard
I would love to come to see you, but your good mens got me barred
(Blind Willie McTell, 1927a)

306 *Oh you wrote me a letter* to come back to Newport News
To leave the town, and don't spread the news
(Blind Willie McTell, 1927a)

307 *I wrote you a letter, mama;* sent you a telegram
Not to meet me in Memphis, but meet me in Birmingham
(Blind Willie McTell, 1927a)

308 *I wrote my gal a letter,* way down in Tennessee
Because I was up here hungry; hurry up and ??? to me
(Charlie Bozo Nickerson, 1930a)

309 *Somebody write, write me a letter, baby;* I'm going to write it, just you see
See if my baby, my baby, do she thinking a little old thing of me
(Robert Petway, 1941)

310 *Going to write a letter;* going to mail it in the air
When the north wind blows, blows news everywhere
(Ollie Rupert, 1927b)

311 *My gal wrote a letter;* how do you reckon it read
Come home, little daddy; your father's might near dead
(Vol Stevens, 1930b)

312 *I wrote my baby a letter;* she send me a telegram
She said, daddy, the reason I love you, you got ways just like a lamb
(Roosevelt Sykes, 1929c)

313 *Mmm going to write me a letter;* mama, going to mail it in the air
Well, well, well going to send it up the country; mama, now to see if my little girl is there
(Peetie Wheatstraw, 1931)

314 Corrina, Corrina, what's the matter now
   You didn't write no letter; you didn't love me nohow
   (James Boodle It Wiggins, 1930)

315 *I'm going to write a letter now;* going to mail it in the air
   I'm going to ask Dr. Jesus, if the devil ever been there
   (Joe Williams, 1929b)

I'm going to mail it in the air (line 3, r-formula)

This formula always appears with some manifestation of the previous formula, at least in the corpus under analysis.

316 I'm going to write a letter; *mail it in the air*
   I'm going to find this gal; she's in the world somewhere
   (Lewis Black, 1927a)

317 Now I'm going to write a letter; *mail it in the air*
   Because the March wind blows; it blows news everywhere
   (Bo Weavil Jackson, 1926a)

318 Going to write a letter; *mailed it in the air*
   Mail it by the window; love yous everywhere
   (Bo Weavil Jackson, 1926b)

319 I wrote her a letter; *I mailed it in the air*
   You may know by that, I got a friend somewhere
   (Noah Lewis, 1929)

320 I'm going to write you a letter soon in the morning; *mail it in the air*
   You can tell by that, babe I got a-somewhere
   (Tommy McClennan, 1940e)

321 Going to write a letter; *going to mail it in the air*
   When the north wind blows, blows news everywhere
   (Ollie Rupert, 1927b)

322 Mmm going to write me a letter; *mama, going to mail it in the air*
   Well, well, well going to send it up the country; mama, now see if my little girl is there
   (Peetie Wheatstraw, 1931)

323 I'm going to write a letter now; *going to mail it in the air*
I'm going to ask Dr. Jesus, if the devil ever been there
(Joe Williams, 1929b)

Then I know you going to catch it (line 4, x-position)

This phrase is unique in the corpus.

babe, in this world somewhere (line 4, r-formula)

This formula usually acts as a modifier on the predicate of its linked x-formula. Just as the formula *at the break of day* places its preceding formula within a temporal context, this formula places its x-formula within a locative context. It can manifest itself as a prepositional phrase, or it can take the form of a complete sentence (see examples 325, 326, 328, 329, 330, and 333).

324 Now I'm going to ring up China, year man; see can I find my good gal over there
Says the Good Book tells me that I got a gal *in this world somewhere*
(Kokomo Arnold, 1935a)

325 I'm going to write a letter; mail it in the air
I'm going to find this gal; *she's in the world somewhere*
(Lewis Black, 1927a)

326 I'm going to go to the station, and try to find her there
And if the Lord has not got her, *she's in the world somewhere*
(Leroy Carr, 1934k)

327 Hitch up my buggy; saddle up my black mare
You'll find me riding, *mama, Lord, Lord, in this world somewhere*
(Skip James, 1931h)

328 Go and get my black horse, and saddle up my grey mare
I'm going home to my good gal; *she's in the world somewhere*
(Blind Lemon Jefferson, 1926d)

329 Won't you wash my jumper; starch my overalls
I'm going to find my woman; *says she's in the world somewhere*
(Tommy Johnson, 1928e)

330   Won't you wash my jumper; starch my overalls
      I'm going to find my woman; *says she's in this world somewhere*
      (Tommy Johnson, 1928f)

331   Hitch up my buggy; saddle up my black mare
      Find my woman, *because she's out in the world somewhere*
      (Tommy Johnson, 1929b)

332   Just as sure as a sparrow, mama, babe, flying in the air
      I got a loving sweet mama *in this world somewhere*
      (Charley Lincoln, 1927a)

333   Mother, please don't worry; this is all my prayer
      Just say your son is gone; *I'm out in this world somewhere*
      (Jimmy Oden, 1941)

334   You can catch my pony; saddle up my black mare
      I'm going to find a rider, *baby, in the world somewhere*
      (Charley Patton, 1929c)

335   Good-bye, pretty mama; oh, babe, fare-thee-well
      Lord, I'm afraid to meet you *in that other world somewhere*
      (Robert Wilkins, 1935a)

336   I got me a grey pony down in my pasture somewhere
      I'm going to find my woman, *baby, in this world somewhere*
      (Big Joe Williams, 1935d)

I'm going to write you a letter (line 5, x-formula)

See the x-formula of line 3 of this song.

I'm going to mail it in the sky (line 5, r-position)

This phrase is unique in the corpus, although it has obvious similarities to the formula *I'm going to mail it in the air*. The substitution of the word *sky* for the word *air* does not seem to change the imagery, but it does change the rhyme of the line.

Mama, I know you going to catch it (line 6, x-position)

See the x-position of line 4 of this song.

when the wind blows on the line (line 6, r-position)

This phrase is unique in the corpus. It seems to combine two images: wind spreading the news (see examples 297 and 310), and a telegraph or telephone carrying the message. This second image was also used by Ma Rainey:

337 I'm going to the Western Union; *type the news all down the line*
Because my man's on the Wabash, darling, and I don't mind dy-
ing
(Gertrude Ma Rainey, 1925a)

Ohhhh, mama, I don't know what to do (line 7, r-formula)

This is another manifestation of one of the ten most frequent r-formulas in the corpus (see "Cottonfield Blues—Part 1," line 1). The prefacing of the formula *what +human do* with the Emb *know* and the addition of a Neg is quite common in surface manifestations of this formula. By adding a Para and Voc *ohhhh, mama* to the front of this phrase, Akers stretched the r-formula to fill the entire first line of the couplet. The fol-lowing are other examples of this formula that are prefaced by the Emb *know* and include the Neg.

338 Now my poor heart is aching, *and I really don't know what to do*
Say I got a strong notion; coming right on back home to you
(Kokomo Arnold, 1937f)

339 Mmmmm, mama, come to my rescue
I'm feeling so bad, *till I don't know what to do*
(Willie Baker, 1929d)

340 If the blues don't kill me, they will drive me through and
through
Woman I love don't know what to do
(Blind Blake, 1926c)

341 I keep the blues all night, and the whole day through
I'm so full of blues, *I don't know what to do*
(Leroy Carr, 1932a)

342 I've been worried; *I didn't know what to do*
So I guess that's why I've had these midnight hour blues
(Leroy Carr, 1932b)

343 I'm so worried; *don't know what to do*
I waked up this morning, mama, feeling sad and blue
(Jaybird Coleman, 1927a)

344 I've got the rickets and the rackets, and my baby's got the Mobile blues
I've got the Rock Island blues, *and I don't know what to do*
(Lonnie Coleman, 1929)

345 I ain't got me nobody, carry my troubles to
I tell you peoples; *I don't know what to do*
(Sam Collins, 1927d)

346 I'm so sorry you heard; *I don't know what to do*
I'm sorry for the time I made you blue
(Lil Green, 1941b)

347 I woke up this morning feeling sad and blue
Couldn't find my yo yo; *didn't know what to do*
(Hattie Hart, 1929)

348 You so downhearted; *you don't know what to do*
You ain't got nobody to tell your troubles to
(Katherine Henderson, 1928b)

349 Got a gang of brownskin sweet women; got a gang of high yellows too
I got so many womens; *I don't know what to do*
(Papa Harvey Hull, 1927a)

350 I'm worried and bothered; *don't know what to do*
Reason I'm worried and bothered; it's all on account of you
(Blind Lemon Jefferson, 1927i)

351 Sometime I feel disgusted, and I feel so blue
I hardly know what in the world, baby, a good man can do
(Blind Lemon Jefferson, 1928f)

352 When I get drunk, I'm evil; *I don't know what to do*
If I get my good chib, can get something good from you
(Edith North Johnson, 1929a)

353 Now back in eighteen hundred and sixty-two
Folks mess around, *but they didn't know what to do*
(Bobby Leecan, 1927)

354 Got a gang of brownskin womens; bunch of high yellows too
I got so many brownskins, *I don't know what to do*
(Cripple Clarence Lofton, 1935)

355 Oh, babe, what's the matter with you
You worry me, woman; *babe, I don't know what to do*
(Barrel House Buck MacFarland, 1934)

356 My head and neck was paining me; seem like my back going to
break in two
I hurried to the neighbors that morning; *I didn't know what in the
world to do*
(Memphis Minnie, 1930b)

357 My head and neck was paining me; seem like my back going to
break in two
Lord, I had such a mood that morning, *I didn't know what in the
world to do*
(Memphis Minnie, 1930c)

358 When the blues is trailing you, *you don't know what to do*
Go back to the one you love, now; the blues will soon leave you
(Arthur Petties, 1928)

359 I have a man I can't control; *I don't know what to do*
My man left me two this morning; now he's trying to come back
at noon
(Gertrude Ma Rainey, 1925b)

360 I asked my captain for to give me his best pair of shoes
For I'm barefoot; I ain't got nothing to wear, Lord; *I don't know
what to do*
(Mooch Richardson, 1928b)

361 Mmmmm, baby, when can I speak to you
If you don't talk to me soon, *baby, I don't know what I'm going to
do*
(Jaydee Short, 1930a)

362   I'm so wild about you, sugar; *don't know what to do*
      It's that granulated sugar; ain't nobody got it but you
      (Bessie Mae Smith, 1930a)

363   I felt so low; *don't know what to do*
      Ain't got nobody to tell my troubles to
      (Clara Smith, 1923b)

364   I'm feeling blue; *don't know what to do*
      Ain't got nobody to tell my troubles to
      (Clara Smith, 1923b)

365   All day long I'm worried; all night long I'm blue
      I'm so awfully lonesome; *I don't know what to do*
      (Clara Smith, 1924g)

366   So they can eagle rock me; they can talk me about the things that
      I used to do
      I got the Nehi blues, mama; *don't know what in the world to do*
      (Frank Stokes, 1928b)

367   I'm so lonesome, lonesome; *I don't know what to do*
      If you don't have no good woman, you'd be lonesome too
      (Ramblin' Thomas, 1928a)

368   It's war in Ethiopia, and mama's feeling blue
      I tell the cockeyed world *I don't know what to do*
      (Minnie Wallace, 1935)

369   Now that was down in Tallahassee, where I had these Tallahassee
      blues
      I got these blues so bad, *don't know what in the world to do*
      (Louis Washington, 1934a)

370   Everybody's bragging about your sugar, sugar, mama, and I'm al-
      most going bragging too
      And if I can't get that sugar, mama, *ooo well, well I don't know
      what I will do*
      (Peetie Wheatstraw, 1938)

371   Well I don't know, baby; *I don't know what to do*
      Baby, you is so sweet, but you just won't be true
      (Sonny Boy Williamson, 1940b)

372   Well I don't know, baby; *I don't know what to do*
      You know I don't want to hurt your feelings; baby, even getting
      mad at you
      (Sonny Boy Williamson, 1940b)

I knows you'll go (line 8, x-formula)

This is a manifestation of one of the ten most frequent x-formulas in
the corpus: +*human go away from some place.* Akers left the "place" unspecified and deleted the word *away* from the surface structure of the
phrase. Akers is unique in the corpus in prefacing this formula with the
Emb *know.* The following list includes those manifestations closest to
Akers's use of the formula.

373   *You can go;* do anything you want to do
      Some day you want me, mama, and I won't want you
      (Blind Blake, 1927d)

374   *Why did you go,* and leave me cold in hand
      I know what it's all about; it was on account of your other man
      (Leroy Carr, 1934g)

375   *Now you may go, honey, you may go;* you may stray all alone
      But one of these days, now little sweet old honey, you'll be out of
      house and home
      (Bo Chatman, 1940)

376   High water rising; get me troubled in mind
      I got to go, and leave my daddy behind
      (Mattie Delaney, 1930b)

377   *Well you won't have to go;* well you won't have to go
      You can get what you want to right here in my liquor store
      (John Estes, 1938a)

378   *You can go;* you can stay
      But you'll come home some old lonesome day
      (Ruby Glaze, 1932)

379 *Now if you go,* have to bring my good clothes back
I says go on home, mama; you got *ruses* all in your back
(Smoky Harrison, 1929)

380 Now don't you leave me here; don't you leave me here
Just before you and your partner get ready to go, leave a dime for beer
(Papa Charlie Jackson, 1925b)

381 *Now you may go,* but you'll come back some day
And you'll be sorry that you went away
(Maggie Jones, 1924d)

382 Now listen folks; don't mean no harm
I got to go, and beat my way back home
(Joe McCoy, 1931a)

383 *I got to go;* got to leave my baby be
And I love my woman, but my woman do not care for me
(Barrel House Buck MacFarland, 1934)

384 *You may go, babe;* you may have your way
But when you think of your loving, I know that you cannot behave
(Alice Moore, 1930a)

385 *You may go;* you may stay
But she'll come back some sweet day
(Charley Patton, 1934e)

386 *Now I believe I'll go, mama;* don't feel welcome here
You're a no-good woman; you don't feel in your hard-working man's care
(Jaydee Short, 1932b)

387 *When I go;* please don't talk after me
Because I'm going where; to my supposed-to-be
(Henry Sims, 1929)

388 All I want is your picture; it must be in a frame
When you go, I can see you just the same
(Bessie Smith, 1925a)

389 *Now in case you want to go,* now let me know
Here now tell me, would you really like to go
(Freddie Spruell, 1935c)

390 *I hate to go,* and I'm really afraid to stay
But I won't be around here, mama, and let you have your way
(Roosevelt Sykes, 1931a)

391 You didn't mean it, baby; you hadn't no right to lie
So go, baby, go, and stay until you die
(Ruth Willis, 1931a)

leave me all lowdown and blue (line 8, r-formula)

Akers was the only singer in the corpus to use the phrase *lowdown and blue* in this formula. In the other manifestations, the "feeling" is simply described as "blue," or in one case (example 394) as *sad and blue.* Akers also chose to delete the deep-level verb *feel* from his surface-level manifestation.

392 You going to leave me, you going to leave me; *you going to leave me blue*
I want some of your loving; don't care what you do
(Leroy Carr, 1934a)

393 When you left me, baby, *you left me feeling so blue*
You know, babe, I didn't love no one but you
(Lonnie Chatman, 1932c)

394 Nobody knows what the sheik will do
They'll spend all their money; *leave you sad and blue*
(Bertha Chippie Hill, 1925b)

395 When you left me, *you left me feeling so blue*
You know, babe, I didn't love no one but you
(Walter Vincson, 1931a)

Ohhhh that's the last word you said (line 9, r-formula)

Akers is the only singer in the corpus to add the Adj *last* to *word,* and in fact the more common surface manifestation of this formula uses the pronoun *what* in place of *word* or *words.*

396   I asked the lady for a drink; *this is what she said*
      I don't have the white, but I have the red
      (Blind Ben Covington, 1928)

397   *Lord, I remember what my big fat mama said*
      She so big and fat, got to put ashes all in my bed
      (Smoky Harrison, 1929)

398   I went out last night; I got drunk; I was in whisky up to my head
      A young lady, she walked up to me, *and this is what she said*
      (Alec Johnson, 1928b)

399   Put both hands on her hips, *and these is the words she said*
      Said, big boy, I couldn't miss you if the good Lord told me you
      was dead
      (Hambone Willie Newbern, 1929a)

400   Lord, I woke up this morning with the blues all around my baby's
      bed
      I turned my face to the wall; *baby, these are the words I said*
      (Frank Stokes, 1927a)

And I just can't remember, babe, the last old words you said (line 10, r-formula)

This is the same formula as in the preceding line, except that Akers added the Emb *remember* to the beginning of the line—as in example 397.

Dough Roller Blues

There can be little doubt that Akers copied this song from a recording titled "Roll and Tumble Blues," which Willie Newbern (1929b) recorded almost a year prior to Akers's 1930 session. Akers's version is almost word-for-word (or at least formula-for-formula) the same as Newbern's, although he sang the lyrics to a different tune. The following is the Newbern version:

401   And I rolled and I tumbled, and I cried the whole night long
      And I rosed this morning, mama, and I didn't know right from
      wrong

      Did you ever wake up, and find your dough-roller gone
      And you wring your hands, and you cry the whole day long

And I told my woman, Lord, before I left her town
And I told my woman, Lord, just before I left her town
Don't she let nobody tear her barrelhouse down

And I fold my arms, Lord, and I walked away
And I fold my arms, Lord, and I slowly walked away
Says that's all right, sweet mama; your trouble going to come
some day
(Willie Newbern, 1929b)

Of course, the possibility exists that Newbern and Akers both learned this song independently from some third source, but there are at least two indications that Akers memorized this song verbatim from Newbern's recording. The verb *rose* in the second line of both songs is the rarest predicate manifestation of the formula +*human woke up*, as shown in the preceding chapter; in addition, Akers's use of the conjunction *and* to preface entire lines—the same lines as in the Newbern song with the exception of line 4—as well as to join formulas in a line, is not entirely consistent with the style of his other three recorded songs, but it is an important stylistic feature of Newbern's song. If Akers had used Newbern's songs only as a formulaic model for his own blues, one might expect the verb *woke up* or *got up* in line 2, as well as a poetic style somewhat closer to that of Akers's other three songs.

Robert Johnson also copied Newbern's song when he recorded "If I Had Possession over Judgment Day" (1936i). He used Newbern's tune, but unlike Akers, he did not memorize Newbern's lyrics. In fact, only two couplets in Johnson's song are from Newbern, and they occur consecutively in the middle of Johnson's blues:

402 And I rolled and I tumbled, and I cried the whole night long
When I woke up this morning, my biscuit-roller's gone

Had to fold my arms, and I slowly walked away
I said in my mind, your trouble going to come some day
(Robert Johnson, 1936i)

Although Johnson retained Newbern's *and* preface in the first line, he adapted the lyrics to his own style in several ways. Note, for example, that Johnson chose the much more common verb *woke up*, rather than *rose*, in the first couplet. As well, Johnson, transferred the formula +*human is gone* to the r-position in the second line of the stanza in which both Newbern and Akers sang manifestations of the +*human didn't know right from wrong* formula. His *I said in my mind* x-formula is an absolute substitution for the *that's all right* formula chosen by the other two singers. While Johnson used the Newbern lyrics as a launching point for his own poetry, Akers accepted the Newbern lyrics in their entirety and concentrated on the subtle variations that he produced in his surface manifestations of the "Newbern" formulas.

Obviously, the following analysis is as much of the Newbern song as of the Akers composition. For this reason, I do not list the Newbern song in the analogues to Akers's formulas, and I describe as "unique" any phrase that is peculiar in the corpus to both the Newbern and the Akers songs.

And I rolled and I tumbled (line 1, x-formula)

This formula could be considered two separate formulas: *I rolled* and *I tumbled.* But it is more profitable to see this phrase as an idiom, not unlike "toss and turn," which should not be further broken down. The following examples seem to confirm the idiomatic nature of this phrase, although some variation—as in example 410—did occur.

403   *Said you roll and you tumble,* till it almost make you blind
       When you get to thinking about your good gal; well you almost
       to lose your mind
       (Kokomo Arnold, 1935b)

404   Did you ever lie down at night, thinking about your brown
       You commence rolling and tumbling; I guess I'm Tampa bound
       (Blind Blake, 1926d)

405   *And I rolled and I tumbled,* and I cried the whole night long
       When I woke up this morning, my biscuit-roller's gone
       (Robert Johnson, 1936i)

406   *Blues, you made me roll and tumble;* you made me weep and
       sigh
       Made me use cocaine and whisky, but you wouldn't let me die
       (Sara Martin, 1928)

407   How do you think a poor man feels; one he loves stays out all
       night long
       Oh Lord, he's rolling and he's tumbling; know he just can't sleep
       alone
       (Will Shade, 1928b)

408 *My girl rolled and tumbled;* cried the whole night long
     She received that message that the man she loved was gone
     (Edward Thompson, 1929c)

409 *I rolled and I tumbled* from side to side
     I was trying so hard to be satisfied
     (Peetie Wheatstraw, 1936d)

410 *I twisted and I tumbled;* I rolled the whole night long
     I didn't have no daddy to hold me in his arms
     (Geeshie Wiley, 1931)

And I cried the whole night long (line 1, r-formula)

411 Lord, I cried last night, mama; *then I cried the whole night long*
     Going to do right, mama; then I won't have to cry no more
     (Kokomo Arnold, 1930)

412 Now don't you hear your mother crying; *weeping and moaning all night long*
     Because old man Wild Water done been here; he took her best
     friends and gone
     (Kokomo Arnold, 1937a)

413 I moaned, I moaned; *I cried the whole night long*
     I was wondering where in the world my man done gone
     (Nellie Florence, 1928)

414 I can't stay away; *I cried the whole night long*
     The good woman I love, she packed her trunk and gone
     (Blind Lemon Jefferson, 1926g)

415 *How many times have I cried all night long*
     You know I must love you, baby, when I beg you to come back
     home
     (Lonnie Johnson, 1929b)

416 And I rolled and I tumbled, *and I cried the whole night long*
     When I woke up this morning, my biscuit-roller's gone
     (Robert Johnson, 1936i)

417 I walked and I wandered, *crying the whole night long*
     Crying wonder will I ever get back home
     (Joe McCoy, 1934c)

418 I just stay and suffer; *sigh and cry all night long*
     Because the way I'm worried; Lordy, it sure is wrong
     (Gertrude Ma Rainey, 1923d)

419 My girl rolled and tumbled; *cried the whole night long*
     She received that message that the man she loved was gone
     (Edward Thompson, 1929c)

420 I am a little boy; *I'm crying all night long*
     I am a little boy; *I cried the whole night long*
     My stepfather, he swears he done done me wrong
     (Big Joe Williams, 1935e)

And I rose this morning (line 2, x-formula)

As stated previously, this is the more rare manifestation of +*human woke up*. Only one other example of the verb *rise* occurs in this context in the corpus, but whether this example is actually a member of the same formula is debatable.

421 *I rise* with the blues, and I work with the blues
     Nothing I can get but bad news
     (Charley Lincoln, 1927d)

And I didn't know right from wrong (line 2, r-formula)

The deep-level predicate of this formula usually generates the verb *know*, but there is one case in the corpus (example 431) in which the verb *tell* fills this slot. Whether examples 423, 425, 427, and 433 are also proper members of this formula is questionable. Example 428 also seems to be a member of this latter group, but my transcription of the lyrics is uncertain.

422 If I mistreat you, I don't mean no harm
     Because I'm a motherless child; *don't know right from, don't know right from wrong*
     (Willie Baker, 1929b)

423 Many nights I rambled, and I hid out the whole night long
Trying to teach my women how to do right from wrong
(Billy Bird, 1928)

424 Well, mama, you don't allow me to fool around all night long
Now I may look like I'm crazy; *poor John do know right from wrong*
(John Estes, 1935c)

425 Yes I'm a poor, poor boy, and a great long way from home
I ain't got nobody, *just to teach me right from wrong*
(Bill Jazz Gillum, 1939)

426 If I mistreat you, gal, I sure don't mean no harm
I'm a motherless child, *and I don't know right from wrong*
(Robert Hicks, 1927d)

427 Mmmmm, mmmmm
I ain't got no sweet mama, *teach me right from wrong*
(Sammy Hill, 1929a)

428 I thought I'd send her, *but I'd leave it* at home
Oh she showed a lot of farmer's boys how to right from wrong
(Bo Weavil Jackson, 1926c)

429 Well it ain't no love; sure ain't no getting along
Said my brown treat me so mean *that I don't know right from wrong*
(Charley Lincoln, 1927b)

430 If I mistreat you, mama, I sure don't mean no harm
I'm a honey dripping papa; *I don't know right from wrong*
(Kid Prince Moore, 1936)

431 I'm so far away from my home; *well I can't tell right from wrong*
Now my baby last night, mama, oh well, she said now, black man, I'm going
(Robert Petway, 1942b)

432 Well there ain't no love; there ain't no getting along
My brown treat me so mean, *sometime I don't know right from wrong*
(Clara Smith, 1923a)

433 Mama, when I talk to you, God above know I don't mean no harm
But it's just because I love you, *and I'm trying to teach you right from wrong*
(J.T. Funny Paper Smith, 1930b)

434 If I mistreat you, I sure don't mean no harm
I'm a motherless child; *don't know right from, don't know right from wrong*
(Curley Weaver, 1928b)

435 Well, well the blues in my room; *I don't know right from wrong*
Because the blues in my kitchen; my biscuit-roller's gone
(Will Weldon, 1936)

Have you ever woke up (line 3, x-formula)

This is another manifestation of *+human woke up*. It is somewhat unusual in that the Adv *this morning* is not present, but as the following list shows, when this formula manifests itself as a question, the Adv usually doesn't occur.

436 *Did you ever wake up* between midnight and day
And felt for your rider; she done eased away
(Blind Joe Amos, 1927)

437 *Have you ever waked up, baby* between midnight and day
Turn over and grab the pillow, where your great gal used to lay
(Wiley Barner, 1927)

438 *Have you ever woke up in the morning;* *you weep and moan*
Your best girl quit you; left you all alone
(Ishman Bracey, 1930d)

439 *Did you ever wake up in the morning,* and find your rider gone
I know just how it feels; that's why I composed this song
(Clifford Gibson, 1929d)

440 *Did you ever wake up* with the blues, and didn't have no place to go
And you couldn't do nothing, but just walk from door to door
(Otis Harris, 1928)

441 *Have you ever woke up* with them bullfrogs on your mind
(William Harris, 1928)

442 *Did you ever wake up in the morning, baby;* same thing all on your mind
Something keep you bothered, mama; honey, worried all the time
(Sammy Hill, 1929a)

443 *Did you ever wake up* twixt night and day
Had your arm around your pillow, where your good gal used to lay
(Charley Lincoln, 1927c)

444 *Have you ever woke up* with whisky-drinking on your mind
You send away to that bootlegger, and you did not have a dime
(Jenny Pope, 1929)

445 *Did you ever wake up* just at the break of day
With your arms around the pillow, where your daddy used to lay
(Gertrude Ma Rainey, 1923a)

446 *Have you ever woke up in the morning;* your bed going around and around
You know about that, baby; you have done throwed me down
(Johnnie Temple, 1937a)

447 *Well, well, well did you ever wake up, mama,* baby, now between midnight and day
Oh with your head on your pillow, babe, where you good man he once have lay
(Peetie Wheatstraw, 1930b)

448 *Did you ever wake up* lonesome all by yourself
And the one you love off loving someone else
(Henry Williams, 1928)

449 *You ever wake up* just about the break of day
    With your arms around the pillow, where Mr. so-and-so used to
    lay
    (Sonny Boy Williamson, 1937b)

And found your dough-roller gone (line 3, r-formula)

This is one of the ten most frequent r-formulas in the corpus: +*human
is gone*. In one of its more common manifestations, the formula is prefaced by the Emb *find*, as in the following examples.

450 I got four feet to walk on; tail shake if it's all night long
    Lord, at daybreak call me, mama; *you'll find your bull-cow gone*
    (Big Bill Broonzy, 1932b)

451 Did you ever wake up in the morning, *and find your rider gone*
    I know just how it feels; that's why I composed this song
    (Clifford Gibson, 1929d)

452 I hate to turn over, *and find my rider gone*
    Walked across my floor; Lordy, how I moan
    (Blind Lemon Jefferson, 1928d)

453 She stays out all night long
    She's going to come home, *and find me gone*
    (Buddy Moss, 1933a)

454 And I got up this morning; a light all in my room
    And I looked behind me, *and I found my faro gone*
    (James Yank Rachel, 1929)

455 He'll stay with you in the winter, whilst your money is long
    Come out in the summer; *you'll find your pig will be gone*
    (Gertrude Ma Rainey, 1926c)

456 Now you will wake up in the morning, *and find me gone*
    Because I'm a rambling man; I can't stay at one place long
    (Ramblin' Thomas, 1928g)

Then you wring your hands (line 4, x-formula)

457   *I wrung my hands,* and I wanted to scream
      But when I woke up, I found it was only a dream
      (Mattie Hite, 1923)

458   *I wring my hands;* baby, and I want to scream
      And I woke up; I found it was all a dream
      (Skip James, 1931f)

And you cry the whole day long (line 4, r-position)

This line is unique in the corpus, although it has obvious parallels with
the formula in the first line of this song, *and I cried the whole night long.*
Again, whether this is another manifestation of the *whole night long* formula is problematic.

And I told my woman (line 5, x-formula)

This is another manifestation of *+human tell +human* previously seen
in "Cottonfield Blues—Part 2," line 1. If this particular manifestation
is interpreted as *+human tell (+human/+female/+loved one),* then this
phrase has the following analogues:

459   I woke up this morning about half past four
      Told my girl I couldn't use her no more
      (C.J. Anderson, 1930)

460   *I told my wife,* if you want me to wait
      You better stop your sister from doing her *gait*
      (Willie Baker, 1929a)

461   *Says I told my baby* about half past two
      Wake up, mama; loving ain't half through
      (Blind Boy Fuller, 1940c)

462   *I told my gal* the week before last
      I had to *take these canned beans* most too fast
      (Samuel Jones, 1927)

463   *I told my mama,* mama, you don't know
      Women in Shreveport kill me; why don't you let me go
      (Huddie Leadbetter, 1935g)

464 *Told my mama;* fell on my knees
   Crying oh Lordy, mama, will you forgive me please
   (Huddie Leadbetter, 1935g)

465 *Lord, I told my old lady,* no longer than a week before last
   I told when I staying all night long, baby, mama, it's done come
   to pass
   (Will Shade, 1928b)

466 *I told my old lady,* so long *as poker* last
   If I gets on Beale Street then, mama, things will come to pass
   (Will Shade, 1929b)

467 *And I told my gal* the week before last
   The gait she's carrying me is most too fast
   (Samuel Jones, 1927)

468 *Yes I told my gal* to bring me bail
   Get some money if she have to sell a little coal
   (Kid Wesley Wilson, 1929)

just before I left your town (line 5, r-formula)

This is one of the ten most frequent r-formulas in the corpus, *+human leave town* (see the preceding chapter for examples). Akers's manifestation is quite common, but his use of the conjunction *before* to link this formula with the x-formula is unique in the corpus.

Don't let nobody tear your barrelhouse down (line 6, r-formula)

This is one manifestation of a formula that might be represented as *+human tear down +juke joint*, where the word *down* is always placed at the end of the phrase for rhyming purposes. The argument *+juke joint* generates the words *barrelhouse, playhouse,* and *ginhouse,* in this corpus, as well as *sugar barrel.* This last term seems to be a euphemism (as might be the others) that makes use of the juke joint image, rather than being a term for the juke joint itself.

469 Ain't going to marry; either settle down
   I'm going to stay right here, *till they tear this barrelhouse down*
   (Kid Bailey, 1929)

470 *The chief of police done tore my playhouse down*
No use in grieving; I'm going to leave this town
(Maggie Jones, 1924c)

471 What you going to do *when they tear your barrelhouse down*
Going to pack my suitcase; hunt some other town
(Charley Jordan, 1930c)

472 Way, way down, babe, way down in Polack Town
Dirty roaches and the chinches done tore my little ginhouse down
(Kid Stormy Weather, 1935)

473 Hey I believe I'll get drunk; *tear this old barrelhouse down*
Because I ain't got no money, but I can hobo out of town
(Memphis Minnie, 1934b)

474 I said don't take my money; then try to dog me around
Because if you do, *I'm going to tear your playhouse down*
(Walter Roland, 1934)

475 Sugar man, sugar man, you got the best sugar in town
Please don't let some other woman tear your sugar barrel down
(Bessie Mae Smith, 1930b)

476 Way down, way down, way down in Polack Town
There the ??? polices have teared my playhouse down
(Jabo Williams, 1932)

477 I spent all my days down in Polack Town
For the womens and bad whisky have torn my playhouse down
(Jabo Williams, 1932)

And I fold my arms (line 7, x-formula)

478 *I folded up my arms,* and I slowly walked away
That's all right, baby; you going to need my help some day
(Walter Davis, 1935b)

479 Mmm *I fold my arms,* and I walked away
That's all right, mama; your troubles will come some day
(Son House, 1930a)

480   *Hey I'm going to fold my arms;* I'm going to kneel down in prayer
When I get up, I'm going to see if my preaching suit a man's ear
(Son House, 1930c)

481   *Lord, I fold my arms,* and I walked away
Just like I tell you; somebody's got to pay
(Son House, 1930d)

482   *Had to fold my arms,* and I slowly walked away
I said in my mind, your trouble going to come some day
(Robert Johnson, 1936i)

And I begin to walk away (line 7, r-formula)

Akers is unique in the corpus in prefacing this formula with the Emb *begin.*

483   Oh captain, captain, what time of day
Oh he looked at me, *and he walked away*
(Texas Alexander, 1927a)

484   *Sooner or later one of us has got to walk away*
She says I don't mind you going, but please don't go away to stay
(Kokomo Arnold, 1938b)

485   Now listen here, mama; treat me in a lowdown way
But if I get what I want, mama, *you'll see me walk away*
(Bo Chatman, 1934)

486   He looked at me and smiled, but yet they refused to say
I asked him again, *and they turned and walked away*
(Ida Cox, 1925)

487   I folded up my arms, *and I slowly walked away*
That's all right, baby; you going to need my help some day
(Walter Davis, 1935b)

488   Mmm I fold my arms, *and I walked away*
That's all right, mama; your troubles will come some day
(Son House, 1930a)

489 Lord, I fold my arms, *and I walked away*
Just like I tell you; somebody's got to pay
(Son House, 1930d)

490 I woke up this morning between midnight and day
I felt for my rider; *she done walked away*
(Peg Leg Howell, 1926b)

491 Had to fold my arms, *and I slowly walked away*
I said in my mind, your trouble going to come some day
(Robert Johnson, 1936i)

492 Ahhhh ha ha, what's the matter with my man today
I ask him if he love me, *Lord, and he walked away*
(Bessie Tucker, 1928b)

493 Is today the day *that you walked away*
Oh you told me you was going; you was going to stay
(Robert Wilkins, 1928b)

I said that's all right, sweet mama (line 8, x-formula)

This is a common formula in the blues. The following are a few of the more than fifty examples of this formula in the corpus.

494 *But I mean that's all right now, baby;* honey, now that's all right for you
You got me here in all this lowdown trouble, baby, and this lowdown way you do
(Bo Chatman, 1938a)

495 *That's all right, mama;* that's all right for you
Treat me lowdown and dirty; any old way you do
(Arthur Crudup, 1941)

496 You's a cold-blooded murderer, when you want me out your way
Says that's all right, mama; you going to need my help some day
(Blind Boy Fuller, 1938)

497 *That's all right, baby,* about how you run around
But you had to face sorrow, when Bob gets back in town
(Robert Hicks, 1930)

498 *That's all right, baby; *sorry* you drove me away*
Well now you don't think, ooo well, well, that you need my help
some day
(Andrew Hogg, 1937)

499 And I'm going away now; I'm going away to stay
That'll be all right, pretty mama; you going to need my help some
day
(Skip James, 1931b)

500 *That's all right, baby; Lord, that's all right for you*
Now it's all right, baby; Lord, about the way you do
(Kid Stormy Weather, 1935)

501 *That's all right, baby; I won't leave you no more*
For that creeping rattlesnake done crawled up to my door
(Jaydee Short, 1930b)

502 *Says that's all right; I'll see you again*
(Frank Stokes, 1929b)

503 *Now, mama, that's all right; mama, that's all right for you*
I mean now that's all right now, pretty mama; most any old way
you do
(Louis Washington, 1934b)

504 *Daddy, it's all right; how you turn me down*
Mmmmm I ain't got a time
(Washington White, 1940d)

505 *Woman, that will be all right; I know my baby ain't going to stay*
away
Well now she forever stays on my mind; people, she the only
woman I crave
(Sonny Boy Williamson, 1938e)

your trouble's going to come some day (line 8, r-formula)

506 Mmm I fold my arms, and I walked away
That's all right, mama; *your troubles will come some day*
(Son House, 1930a)

507 Had to fold my arms, and I slowly walked away
I said in my mind, *your trouble going to come some day*
(Robert Johnson, 1936i)

Jumpin' and Shoutin' Blues

Lord, I know my baby sure going to jump and shout (line 1, r-formula)

This formula might be considered two formulas: *+human jump* and *+human shout,* but as with the *roll and tumble* formula in the preceding song, this phrase seems fairly idiomatic and coherent as it stands. There are examples in which the verb *jump* is not included (511, 514, and 516), but it might be argued that these phrases are members of another formula, because they do not conform to the structure of the idiom.

508 What you going to do, mama, when your thing give out
I'm going to telephone you; *we all* jump and shout
(Texas Alexander, 1934)

509 *I know my baby, she going to jump and shout*
When the train rolls up, and I come walking out
(Ed Bell, 1929)

510 *Says I know my baby she sure going to jump and shout*
When I get down to the bank, and draw my money out
(Big Bill Broonzy, 1930d)

511 Too tight; stepping out
Too tight; *hear me shout*
(Blind Blake, 1929a)

512 *I know my baby, I know my baby, and she's bound to jump, and she's bound to jump and shout*
Now when she gets over to Atlanta; I, I done rolled them few, I done rolled them few days out
(John Estes, 1935h)

513 When I reach old Los Angeles, California, *you ought to hear me jump and shout*
Now the people in Los Angeles, they don't know what it's all about
(Lane Hardin, 1935)

514 I'm going to preach these blues now, *and I want everybody to shout*
I'm going to do like a prisoner; I'm going to roll my time on out
(Son House, 1930b)

515 *I know my baby, she's going to jump and shout*
When she gets a letter from Lemon I wrote her two days out
(Blind Lemon Jefferson, 1926a)

516 I want to see, I want to see the girl I'm *for painted* about
I be so glad, *I sure can't help but shout*
(Furry Lewis, 1927c)

517 Drove so many piles, my hammer's all worn out
That's when I do my driving, *they began to jump and shout*
(Joe McCoy, 1930e)

518 There'll be one of these mornings; *you going to jump and shout*
Open the jailhouse door, and you come walking out
(Joe McCoy, 1935)

519 I saw the Baptist sister jump up, *and began to shout*
But I'm so glad that the whisky vote is out
(Frank Stokes, 1927d)

520 Well when my baby come out and see me, *I know she's going to jump and shout*
Well well well if that don't draw a crowd, ooo people going to know what all this racket about
(Sonny Boy Williamson, 1937c)

When the train get here (line 2, x-position)

This phrase is unique in the corpus, although it might well be considered one manifestation of a formula *train move toward some place.* The two following examples (as well as example 509) are possible analogues.

521 *Just as sure as the train come in San Antone;* then ease up in the yard
It's going to take two dollars and a quarter, I declare to send me a postal card
(Little Hat Jones, 1930c)

522 I went down to the railroad; I laid my head on the track
The train come along, and it broke my back
(Walter Vincson, 1932a)

I come a-rolling out (line 2, r-position)

This phrase is unique in the corpus, although examples 509 and 518 might be considered to contain analogues.

Lord, I tell you it wasn't no need of, mama, trying to be so kind (line 3, r-formula)

This line is remarkable for the number of extraformulaic embellishments that Akers inserted into the formula: Ex (*Lord*); Loc (*I tell you*); Aux, Neg, and Aux (*it wasn't no need of*); Voc (*mama*); Emb (*trying to*); and Adv (*so*). The phrase *I tell you,* however, might be considered a formula in its own right. Other manifestations of the formula sometimes expand the argument *kind* to *nice and kind, loving and kind,* or *good and kind.*

523 He's gone, he's gone; and he's forever on my mind
And I want to see my man, *because, because he's so good and kind*
(Lucille Bogan, 1934c)

524 *I tried to be nice and kind*
Oh she was evil; would not change her mind
(Joe McCoy, 1934b)

525 When I first met you, mama, *you were so nice and kind*
You done got reckless, and change your mind
(Blind Willie McTell, 1931c)

526 But I tried to be nice; *tried to be nice and kind*
But every man I love don't seem like he want to pay me no mind
(Memphis Minnie, 1936b)

527 *What's the use of trying, I said trying, trying to be kind*
When the one you love haven't got you on his mind
(Clara Smith, 1924d)

528 Now listen at me, mama; *mama, if you'll only be kind*
I do everything, mama, to try to satisfy your mind
(Frank Stokes, 1929d)

529 I know he's good; *I know he's nice and kind*
Have a talk with him, before you start to buying
(Robert Wilkins, 1935b)

530 Oh Lord ah she's gone, she's gone; she's forever on my mind
Now she was a sweet little woman; *she just wouldn't be loving and kind*
(Sonny Boy Williamson, 1937a)

Ah you know you don't love me (line 4, x-formula)

This is one of the ten most frequent x-formulas in the corpus: +*human love* +*human*. There are, however, only a few examples of this formula that are prefaced by the Emb *know* and include a Neg.

531 *And you know you didn't love me;* you fell across my bed
Full of your moonshine whisky; mama, talking all out of your head
(Chasey Collins, 1935)

532 Said it's mmm, baby, mmm, baby, mmm
Say you know you do not love me like I say I love you
(Walter Roland, 1933)

533 Well I said look a-here woman; I ain't going to fool around with you no more
I know you don't love me; you wild about Mr. so-and-so
(Sonny Boy Williamson, 1937b)

534 Lord, my baby, my baby, she don't treat me good no more
Now I know the reason she don't love me, she's wild about Mr. so-and-so
(Sonny Boy Williamson, 1938a)

535 Now fare you well; baby, yes I'm going away
Well I know you didn't love me; now I'm going to find me some other place to stay
(Sonny Boy Williamson, 1938e)

536 *Now but I know you don't love me;* baby, you don't love me no more
I know the reason you don't love me, woman, because you is crazy about Mr. so-and-so
(Sonny Boy Williamson, 1940a)

you ain't got me on your mind (line 4, r-formula)

This is one of the ten most frequent r-formulas: *some thing is on +human's mind*. The particular manifestation, wherein the *some thing* has the feature *+human*, is quite common, although it can take a somewhat inverted form—*+human can't get +human off +human's mind*. Akers's addition of a Neg to the uninverted formula, however, is found only one other time in the corpus—example 554. Two other examples, 559 and 563, seem midway between the usual sense of this formula and the negative sense that Akers and Clara Smith chose; that is, "actively trying to forget a loved one." Considering the surface-structure similarities between Akers's r-formula in the first line of this stanza, as well as his manifestation of this formula, and Clara Smith's couplet (examples 527 and 554), the possibility exists that Akers was directly influenced by Smith's earlier recording.

The following list includes all those manifestations of the formula in which the *some thing* is *+human*.

537 Lord, she went up the country, *but she's on my mind*
(Texas Alexander, 1927b)

538 I can't sleep no more; *can't get her off my mind*
Know I wants to see my baby, and only one more time
(Ed Bell, 1930a)

539 *Black dog, black dog, you forever on my mind*
If you only let me see my baby one more time
(Blind Blake, 1927c)

540 Hey, hey your daddy's feeling blue
I'm worried all the time; *I can't keep you off my mind*
(Blind Blake, 1927c)

541 I met a gal; *I couldn't get her off my mind*
She passed me up; says she didn't like my kind
(Blind Blake, 1929b)

542 He's gone, he's gone, *and he's forever on my mind*
And I want to see my man, because, because he's so good and kind
(Lucille Bogan, 1934c)

543 Boo hoo, I just can't keep from crying
     I'm worried about my baby; *she's on my mind*
     (Gene Campbell, 1930)

544 I lay down last night *with that gal all on my mind*
     (Sam Collins, 1927c)

545 I can hear my back door slamming; I can hear a little baby crying
     I can hear my back door slamming; seem like I can hear a little baby crying
     Lord, I wonder, baby, have you got me on your mind
     (Walter Davis, 1940a)

546 Blues ain't nothing; *good man on your mind*
     Well it keep you worried, bother all the time
     (Tom Dickson, 1928b)

547 When you see me with my head hung down
     I ain't got the blues, *but another gal on my mind*
     (Tom Dickson, 1928b)

548 Mmmmm, black snake is so hard to find
     I am worried about my mama; *I can't keep her off my mind*
     (Blind Lemon Jefferson, 1929b)

549 I think I will use ??? poison *to get my brownie off my mind*
     This long distance moan about to worry me to death this time
     (Blind Lemon Jefferson, 1929e)

550 You can't give your sweet woman everything she want in one time
     Well, boys, she get rambling in her brain; *mmm some other man on her mind*
     (Robert Johnson, 1937b)

551 *Oh, babe, you is on my mind*
     I hope to see you some of these days; you know I sure ain't lying
     (Tommy McClennan, 1942b)

552   Girl, I lay down dreaming; woman, I woke up crying
      Since my bird-dog fly away, *poor girl is on my mind*
      (Willie Reed, 1928a)

553   My man's on the ocean, bobbing up and down
      He belongs to Uncle Sam, *but he's always on my mind*
      (Clara Smith, 1924c)

554   What's the use of trying, I said trying, trying to be kind
      When the one you love haven't got you on his mind
      (Clara Smith, 1924d)

555   *Now a brownskin woman always on my mind*
      She keeps me troubled; worried all the time
      (Vol Stevens, 1927b)

556   Now if you love me, baby, I'll treat you good and kind
      I will start being nice, *and keep you on my mind*
      (Frank Stokes, 1929a)

557   I got a gal named Yola; she treats me nice and kind
      I don't care what she do; *Louise is on my mind*
      (Johnnie Temple, 1937b)

558   *You know, baby, you know, baby, you always forever on my mind*
      (Walter Vincson, 1931a)

559   If you have a woman, and she don't do kind
      Pray to the Good Lord *to get her off your mind*
      (Walter Vincson, 1931b)

560   She's the onliest woman I ever loved; *I can't get her off my mind*
      Now I may not find her in the next twenty years, ooo, Lord, but
      I'll be forever trying
      (Washboard Sam, 1941b)

561   Yes I was walking down the street the other day; *my Hattie on my
      mind*
      A woman walked with me, baby, to buy me one drink of shine
      (Louis Washington, 1934a)

562 It's getting so I can't sleep for dreaming, and I can't laugh for
crying
Because the man I love is forever on my mind
(Ethel Waters, 1923b)

563 Stay out all night long, *babe, now to keep you off my mind*
Well now you keep me worried, baby; honey, now and bothered
all the time
(Peetie Wheatstraw, 1934a)

564 Now you done got me so, I hate to see that evening sun go down
I wake up in the morning; *peach orchard woman in my mind*
(Joe Williams, 1938)

565 Oh, Lord, ah she's gone, she's gone; *she's forever be on my mind*
Now she was a sweet little woman; she just wouldn't be loving
and kind
(Sonny Boy Williamson, 1937a)

566 I had an evil-hearted woman; she mistreated me all the time
She went away and left me, *but she's forever on my mind*
(Oscar Woods, 1936)

Mmmmm you ain't got me on your mind (line 5, r-formula)

See line 4 of this song.

And what is the need of, baby, trying to be so kind (line 6, r-formula)

See line 3 of this song.

Mmmmm tried to treat her right (line 7, r formula)

This is another of the most frequent r-formulas in the corpus: +*human
treat* +*human right*. This formula, prefaced by the Emb *try*, is one common manifestation.

567 My baby love me; *tried to treat me right*
Give me her loving both day and night
(Lonnie Chatman, 1932b)

568 Let me tell you, mama, what you said last night
Lay down on my bedside; *try to treat me right*
(Sam Collins, 1927b)

569   Well now I have a woman; *I try to treat her right*
      Well now she will get drunk, ooo well, well and fuss and fight all
      night
      (Andrew Hogg, 1937)

570   I often tell my honey, don't have a fight
      The gal that gets you *has got to try to treat you right*
      (Bo Weavil Jackson, 1926a)

571   Went out with you, baby; *trying to treat you right*
      I drinking whisky, woman, and drunk all night
      (Blind Willie McTell, 1935d)

572   Folks, I love my man; I kiss him morning, noon, and night
      I wash his clothes and keep him clean, and *try to treat him right*
      (Bessie Smith, 1924b)

573   I brought my man here; *tried to treat him right*
      Started fighting over a woman; stayed out every day and night
      (Clara Smith, 1924d)

574   I tried hard all my life
      But you wouldn't try to treat me right
      (Washboard Sam, 1940)

But you started with another man (line 8, x-position)

This phrase is unique in the corpus. Perhaps Akers meant to insert a
gerund after the verb *started*, such as *fighting*, in example 573.

And stayed out every day and night (line 8, r-formula)

Some manifestations of this formula include the words *day* and *night*,
while others use only the rhyme word *night* in the time-adverbial. The
appearance in this couplet of two (or possibly three) analogues from the
Clara Smith song (1924d) (see example 577) adds further weight to the
possibility that Akers was aware of Smith's "Texas Moaner Blues."

575   When I had you, baby, you wouldn't act right
      You with your man, honey, *staying out every night*
      (Bill Jazz Gillum, 1941b)

576 You know you don't treat me right, *when you stay out both day and night*
And I must stop you now, because you got to consider somehow
(Lonnie Johnson, 1927a)

577 I brought my man here; tried to treat him right
Started fighting over a woman; *stayed out every day and night*
(Clara Smith, 1924d)

578 Honey, allow me a-one more chance; I only will treat you right
Honey, won't you allow me a-one more chance; *I won't stay out all night*
(Henry Thomas, 1927b)

579 I'm a real good woman, but my man don't treat me right
He takes all my money, *and stays out all night*
(Sippie Wallace, 1927b)

580 Well the next woman I had, she do nothing but fuss and fight
Well now you know, baby, that will make a barrelhouse man, ooo well well, stay out each and every night
(Peetie Wheatstraw, 1936f)

Says I ain't going down this big road by myself (line 9, r-formula)

581 *Lord I ain't going down that big road by myself*
If I don't carry you, mama, I'm going to carry somebody else
(Kokomo Arnold, 1935h)

582 *I can't go down that big road by myself*
If I can't carry you, I carry someone else
(Mattie Delaney, 1930a)

583 *Crying I ain't going down this big road by myself*
If I don't carry you, going to carry somebody else
(Tommy Johnson, 1928b)

584 *Crying I ain't going down that dark road by myself*
Crying if I don't carry you, carry somebody else
(Willie Lofton, 1935)

585 *Can't go down this dark road by myself*
I don't carry my rider, going to carry me someone's else
(Charley Patton, 1929b)

586 *I ain't going to travel this big road all by myself*
If I don't take my baby, I sure want to have nobody else
(Victoria Spivey, 1927)

587 *I ain't going down, baby, that long road by myself*
If I can't carry you, baby, carry somebody else
(Curley Weaver, 1935)

If I can't get you, mama (line 10, x-formula)

This is a manifestation of one of the ten most frequent x-formulas in the corpus: +*human* get/have +*human*, where the second +*human* is usually the lover or potential lover of the first +*human*. The present tense of the verb *get* implies an active hunt or chase, whereas the past tense *got* implies actual possession. The present tense form is the rarer of the two manifestations, a list of which follows.

588 Lord, but you can't be mine, and someone else's too
Lord, but you can't be my baby, and someone else's too
There can no one get you, baby, Lord until I get through
(Tommie Bradley, 1931b)

589 How long now will I have to wait
Can I get you now; honey have to hesitate
(Sam Collins, 1927e)

590 Tell me how long does I have to wait
Can I get you now, honey, or must I hesitate
(Walter Buddy Boy Hawkins, 1929b)

591 I often tell my honey, don't have a fight
The gal that gets you has got to treat you right
(Bo Weavil Jackson, 1926a)

592 Tell me how long will I have to wait
Can I get you now, or must I hesitate
(Jim Jackson, 1930)

593 Look a-here, mama, just a word or two
Said I get you to let's go loo loo
(Blind Willie McTell, 1933a)

594 Woke up this morning to get my tie
I can't get you, woman, because you let me die
(Marshall Owens, 1932b)

595 Women in Cairo will treat you kind of strange
Get your rider, and take you off that thing
(Henry Spaulding, 1929a)

596 *When I get you, mama,* we going to move out on the outskirts of town
Because I don't want nobody, ooo always hanging around
(Washboard Sam, 1937b)

I'm going to get somebody else (line 10, r-formula)

This r-formula, which has obvious semantic links to the previous x-formula, also allows several different verbs and verb tenses to fill its predicate. Note the verb *have* and the verb *find* in the following examples. The sense of the verb *find* is a bit different from that of *get* or *have,* so that whether example 597 is actually a member of this formula is debatable.

597 Yeah locked up in jail, and I just can't help myself
Yeah when I get out, *I'm going to find me someone else*
(Blind Boy Fuller, 1940d)

598 You won't act right, when I tried to do right myself
Now it's no, no, baby; *I've got somebody else*
(Bill Jazz Gillum, 1941a)

599 Baby, what's the matter; why don't you be yourself
If I didn't love you, *I'd get somebody else*
(Lil Green, 1941c)

600 But you are so dull and rotten; you think everybody like yourself
If I didn't love you, *I'd get somebody else*
(Lil Green, 1941c)

601 Because I love you, baby, and I want you for myself
If I didn't love you, *I'd get somebody else*
(Lil Green, 1941c)

602 I've got a woman now, that I love better than I love myself
She treats me so cold sometimes, *I think she got somebody else*
(Lonnie Johnson, 1937b)

603 Mmmmm, chained down in this dark cell by myself
And my gal, she skipped; *guess she got somebody else*
(Blind Willie McTell, 1933b)

604 Says I'm almost crazy, and I'm all here by myself
If my man don't have me, *he won't have nobody else*
(Alice Moore, 1929a)

Mmmmm what you want your babe to do (line 11, r-formula)

This is another manifestation of one of the ten most frequent r-formulas in the corpus, previously discussed in line 1 of "Cottonfield Blues—Part 1." Here the formula is prefaced by the Emb *want*.

605 Oh, babe, don't mean your bull no good
Why don't you rub your bull-cow and pet him; *tell him what you want your bull to do*
(Big Bill Broonzy, 1932b)

606 Look a-here, mama; *what you want me to do*
I work all the time; bring my money home to you
(Blind Blake, 1927b)

607 *Brownskin mama, what in the world you want me to do*
You keep my poor heart aching; I'm blue through and through
(Blind Blake, 1927d)

608 Now look here, man; *what you want me to do*
Give you my stew meat and credit you too
(Lucille Bogan, 1935b)

609 *I said, Lord, what you want me to do*
I took all my money, and I brought it home to you
(Tommie Bradley, 1931a)

610 Tell me, cruel-hearted mama, *what you want your daddy to do*
     I'd rather see you murder me, baby, and leave me too
     (Kid Cole, 1928a)

611 *Oh, babe, what you want poor me to do*
     Driving a coal wagon, babe; give all my money to you
     (Joe Dean, 1930)

612 Come and tell your papa, *what you want me to do*
     Now just before I go from you
     (Joe Edwards, 1924)

613 *Now what you want poor John to do*
     Lord, I done everything; tried to get along with you
     (John Estes, 1930b)

614 *Vernita, honey, what do you want me to do*
     Now I've done everything, but I can't get along with you
     (John Estes, 1935d)

615 Oh, Alberta, oh, Alberta, don't you hear me calling you
     If Alberta hear you calling, *what you want Alberta to do*
     (Huddie Leadbetter, 1935c)

616 *Baby, what do you want me to do*
     Baby, what do you want your papa to do
     Beg, borrow, and steal; bring it all home to you
     (Furry Lewis, 1927b)

617 Look a-here, look a-here; *what you want me to do*
     Give you my jelly; then I die for you
     (Memphis Minnie, 1929b)

618 *Now, papa, what you want me to do*
     I did everything in this world, trying to get along with you
     (Ollie Rupert, 1927a)

619 *Now, pretty papa, what you want me to do*
     I did everything in this world, trying to get along with you
     (Ollie Rupert, 1927b)

620 *Hey, baby, what do you want your papa to do*
Want me to beg, rob, and steal; bring it all home to you
(Will Shade, 1927a)

621 *Hey what you want your man to do*
Said I rob and steal, and make everything for you
(Frank Stokes, 1927b)

622 *Hey, hey what you want me to do*
Johnny it with you, and eat those narrow-face too
(Washboard Walter, 1930)

623 Look a-here, look a-here; *what you want me to do*
You knew my jelly didn't die for you
(James Boodle It Wiggins, 1929b)

624 Now tell me, baby; *what you want me to do*
Think I can love you, and be your dog too
(Sonny Boy Williamson, 1938c)

625 Now tell me, Red; *what you want me to do*
Now do you think I can love you, and be your little dog too
(Sonny Boy Williamson, 1938g)

626 Now tell me, babe; *what do you want me to do*
I did everything I could, baby, to try to get along with you
(Sonny Boy Williamson, 1941b)

Says I know it's something (line 12, x-formula)

627 You show your linen to any man
And that's something, mama, that I just can't stand
(Walter Davis, 1935c)

628 *Now there is something,* you say that you expect
Now come and tell me what it is that I neglect
(Joe Edwards, 1924)

629 You can't love me, baby, and love my brother too
Because that's, that's something; it will never do
(Robert Hicks, 1929c)

630   *This is something* I never seen before
      You broke down my bed; got a pallet on my floor
      (Washboard Sam, 1937a)

gal, it ain't no use (line 12, r-formula)

631   I chew my bacca, and I spit my juice
      I tried to love you so hard, *but I found out there's no use*
      (Lonnie Johnson, 1927b)

632   Went to the henhouse; looked on the roof
      Looking for my stuff, *but it was no use*
      (Joe McCoy, 1930b)

633   Would go to bed, *but it ain't no use*
      They pile up on the bed like chickens on a roost
      (Blind Willie McTell, 1929d)

* * *

The most striking feature of Akers's songs is that they are highly formulaic. Of the seventy-two phrases analyzed, sixty-two have analogues in the rest of the corpus; this means that more than 86 percent of Akers's recorded repertoire is formulaic. Such a percentage is remarkably high, especially when compared with percentages in other formulaic poetries. Even in blues poetry, Akers probably ranks higher than most of his contemporaries in his reliance on formulas for his compositions.

Akers was also rather conservative—if that is the proper word—in his choice of formulas; twenty-one of the sixty-two formulas he chose are among the twenty most frequently used formulas in the corpus. In other words, one-third of the formulas in Akers's songs are the most common formulas in the repertoires of blues singers in general. Of the other two-thirds, many of the formulas are quite common, occurring more than thirty times each in the corpus.

What do these statistics mean? Certainly, Akers could be called a conservative, traditional composer of blues lyrics. The facts that one of his four recorded songs is a copy from an earlier recording by Newbern (and another seems to have been influenced by one of Clara Smith's recordings) and that Akers repeated a considerable number of formulas from one recording to the next—and even within the same song—seem to indicate that Akers's compositional scope was rather narrow. His talent might have lain in the reinterpretation of other singers' material, because he clearly changed the tune of Newbern's song to fit his own free-form style of singing. My observations are, however, quite speculative here, given the lack of information on this performer; perhaps in other performance contexts Akers was not so conservative, traditional, or derivative.

Is it fair, however, to say that Akers was noninnovative? Innovation can take many forms, and, as I explain in the next chapter, formulaic poetry demands a different kind of innovation from nonformulaic poetry. Akers does show signs of originality in certain aspects of his lyrics. First, one cannot overlook the ten phrases in his songs for which there are no clear formulaic analogues in the corpus. Some of these phrases might indeed be formulaic, but the corpus is not representative enough to reveal this; as Rosenberg wrote, "Any formulas which one claimed to be unique might be variants of systems which have not been collected: the theoretical possibility must be admitted" (1970a, p. 104). Some of these phrases might be entirely the invention of Akers. Without examining all blues recorded in Akers's lifetime (as well as all blues Akers heard in nonrecording contexts), it is impossible to say which phrases fall into which of these two categories.

Whatever the source of the ten "nonformulaic" lines, no simple statistical count accurately reflects the innovative features of Akers's songs. Although he was highly formulaic, the ways in which he used his formulas were often quite original. Akers was most innovative in his use of extraformulaic elements, especially the Emb. For example, his prefacing of the formula *make me love you* with the Emb *want* ("Cottonfield Blues— Part 1," line 2) or his use of the Emb *know* with the formula *you'll go* ("Cottonfield Blues—Part 2," line 8) are found nowhere else in the corpus. His use of the extraformulaic elements in the line *Lord, I tell you it wasn't no need of, mama, trying to be so kind* ("Jumpin' and Shoutin' Blues," line 3) is highly innovative.

Akers's originality is also reflected in his juxtaposition of formulas. If one discounts "Dough Roller Blues," a direct copy of the Newbern song, eleven of Akers's seventeen stanzas are entirely formulaic. In seven of these eleven stanzas, however, Akers's combinations of formulas are unique in the corpus.

The best example of this type of inventiveness is the fifth stanza of "Jumpin' and Shoutin' Blues":

634 Says I ain't going down this big road by myself
   If I can't get you, mama, I'm going to get somebody else
   (Garfield Akers, 1930b)

This stanza is one variant of the "core" of the "Big Road Blues" song complex that Evans analyzed in considerable detail (1982, pp. 265–311). Although the origins of this song complex have been attributed by Evans, among others, to Tommy Johnson's "Big Road Blues" (Tommy Johnson, 1928b), the "core" stanza was actually recorded by Victoria Spivey nine months before Johnson's version (Spivey, 1927).

Regardless of the origins of this song complex, virtually all singers in the corpus sang the first line of the stanza with only very minor variations. Kokomo Arnold's version is typical:

635 Lord, then I ain't going down that big road by myself
 If I don't carry you, mama, I'm going to carry somebody else
 (Kokomo Arnold, 1935h)

Only Spivey's version is substantively different—using the verb *travel* instead of *go down*, in the first line of the stanza:

636 I ain't going to travel this big road all by myself
 If I don't take my baby, I sure want to have nobody else
 (Victoria Spivey, 1927)

The second line of this core stanza has been subject to more variation by singers, but its x-formula is usually *+human carry +human* or *+human take +human*. Evans's examples of this stanza from nonrace record versions maintain the *carry/take* imagery. Akers was alone in substituting the verb *get* in this formula—giving the stanza a more active or aggressive tone. Considering the highly "ossified" nature of this core stanza, Akers's change is both unexpected and original.

Similarly, Akers employed the image of mailing a letter "in the air" in the second and third stanzas of his "Cottonfield Blues—Part 2."

637 I'm going to write you a letter; I'm going to mail it in the air
 Then I know you going to catch it, babe, in this world somewhere

 I'm going to write you a letter; I'm going to mail it in the sky
 Mama, I know you going to catch it, when the wind blows on the line
 (Garfield Akers, 1929b)

In the second stanza, he kept to the general structure employed by other singers, although the first phrase in the second line of this stanza, "Then

I know you going to catch it," is unique in the corpus. In the third stanza, however, Akers deliberately played with the image that he established in the preceding stanza—an image that both the blues singers and their audience understood as a traditional poetic image—by substituting the rhyme word *sky* for *air* in the first line. As in the "Big Road Blues" core stanza, Akers consciously altered a juxtaposition of formulas and images to create a stanza that was original while still within the tradition of blues composition.

It is therefore a mistake to call Akers noninnovative. His choice of formulas was not original, but his choice of extraformulaic elements and formula juxtapositions was distinctive. His inventiveness lay not in the grosser aspects of blues composition but in the more subtle nuances of extra- and interformulaic structures. Whether this type of innovation was appreciated by blues audiences is another question, but my point here is that there was more than one road to innovation in blues composition. The paradox of a formulaic system is that the singer could be both original and traditional at the same time.

Looking at Akers's songs as a whole, there is an explanation for his lack of formulaic originality. His songs are typical of the blues in terms of their themes and treatment of those themes. All four songs are concerned with one or another aspect of love, travel, and anxiety—the major themes of the blues. His treatment of these subjects is almost entirely nonnarrative with little if any chronological sequence from one verse to the next. It is in just such a poetic context that the traditional formulas of the blues work best.

Whenever blues singers decided to compose a song along the lines of Akers's compositions, they had an immediate and large storehouse of formulas from which choose. Patterned, formulaic language naturally accrues to those topics and themes that are most often articulated. Lord recognized this phenomenon in Yugoslavian epic poetry: "The most stable formulas will be those for the most common ideas of the poetry" (1960, p. 34).

A nonnarrative blues song facilitates the use of traditional formulas, because a chronological sequence in a song automatically limits the choice of formulas that can be used in any one section of the song—the singer would have to worry about the temporal logic and progression of the narrative. The singer would also be more restricted in the use of imagery or symbolism, in adhering to a set plot or an inflexible theme. Nonsequential thoughts on the nature of love, travel, and anxiety, however, would allow the singer maximum freedom in the choice and placement of traditional formulas, because one line or stanza need not bear any direct thematic or sequential relationship to any other line or stanza in a song. Because Akers's songs fit these criteria so well, they lent themselves to a traditional, formulaic construction.

By contrast, there were singers who composed narrative songs on topics that were rather unusual in the blues context. One such singer was John Estes, who composed a number of autobiographical blues (as well as more traditional, nonthematic songs). His "Floating Bridge" (1935f), for example, tells of the time he almost drowned in an auto accident. Although the song conforms to blues stanzaic and prosodic structure, it is highly narrative and sequential, and its topic is not at all typical of the blues. In the following transcription, those phrases with analogues in the corpus are italicized:

638   Now I never will forget the floating bridge
      Tell me five minutes time under water I was hid

      When I was going down, *I throwed up my hands*
      Please take me on dry land

      Now they carried me in the house, and they laid me across the bank
      About a gallon and a half of muddy water I had drank

      They dried me off, *and they laid me in the bed*
      Couldn't hear nothing, but muddy water running through my head

      Now my mother often taught me, quit playing a bum
      Go somewhere; settle down and make a crop

      Now people standing on the bridge, *screaming and crying*
      Lord, have mercy, where we going
      (John Estes, 1935f)

Note that much of this song is nonformulaic, and even those formulas that Estes did use, he used in strange ways. The phrase *I throwed up my hands* is usually an image of emotional release, but Estes used it for the more specific image of a drowning man asking for help; the formula *laid me in the bed* usually has sexual connotations, lacking in the Estes song. The most formulaic parts of the song are the last two stanzas, in which Estes turned away from his narrative and toward a more general commentary on the dangers of being unsettled and the uncertainties of life—two topics well served by blues formulas.

The frequency of formulas in a song might well depend on whether a singer kept firmly to the traditions of the blues or used the blues structure to tell a more individualistic kind of story. But whatever the case, the singer was not totally dependent on the formula, nor, however, could the singer completely escape the formula. Akers relied heavily on traditional formulas, but he did not rely entirely on them; Estes, despite his idiosyncratic blues narrative, still felt compelled to use some traditional formulas. In this chapter, I have demonstrated that the formula is clearly an important compositional feature in the blues—that in an examination of blues performance, the reality of the formula is manifest. But a question remains: why use formulas at all?

Conclusion:
Why Is the Blues Formulaic?

As I have shown, if there is such a thing as formulaic poetry, then the blues clearly falls within this prosodic genre. Yet the question remains: why is the blues formulaic? As twentieth-century North American poets, the blues singers had a number of options for the structure of their songs. Elite, European-based poets—the contemporaries of the blues singers—shunned formulaic repetitions in their work, and certainly blues singers were not unaware of the traditions of mainstream, modern poetry. Yet they chose to adapt a traditional, formulaic form of expressiveness to their race record compositions.

The reasons that scholars have given for the formulaic nature of long, narrative poetry—whether valid or not—certainly do not hold for the blues. Epic poetry, especially when performed orally in a spontaneous fashion, requires special skills of memory, and as many scholars have demonstrated, the formula functions quite well as a mnemonic device—an aid to the impromptu composition of the kind of epic poetry that might take several hours to perform. In these poetic contexts, singers need only remember the theme or plot outline of the narrative, because the formulaic system establishes *a priori* the poetic framework on which the story is built. The formula is a labor-saving device that enables singers to recite an epic without relying on rote memorization.

Although this theory might hold true for much of epic poetry, Finnegan has convincingly argued that rote memorization still has a place in these types of performance (1976, p. 151; and 1977, pp. 52–87). But does the same argument hold for short poetic forms? O'Neil studied the formulaic nature of Old English elegiac verse (1960b), while James Ross (1959) showed that short Gaelic poems are also formulaic. O'Neil rightly concluded that "formulaic structure is not a necessary function of length" (1960b, p. 13). The blues, as a short poetic form, needs no special mnemonic devices in its composition; as the repertoire of Akers clearly demonstrates, this form of poetry allows rote memorization while, at the same time, it has a structure that is highly formulaic.

Another argument of formula scholars is that the formula is a mark of orality—an inherent part of the structure of orally composed folk poetry. Magoun, for example, saw an absolute correlation between the formula and orality: "Oral poetry, it may safely be said, is composed entirely of formulas, large and small, while lettered poetry is never formulaic" (1953, p. 447). Lord was equally adamant about the nature of Yugoslavian epic poetry:

> The two techniques [oral and written composition] are, I submit, contradictory and mutually exclusive. Once the oral technique is lost it is never regained. The written technique, on the other hand, is not compatible with the oral technique, and the two cannot possibly combine, to form another, a third, a "transitional" technique. (1960, p. 129)

Although, in all fairness, Lord later modified his stand on this issue (see his comments in Finnegan, 1976, p. 175).

Yet, as I have previously shown, the race record blues is more often than not a written and rehearsed form of poetry. Beatie claimed that the "formula-density necessary to assume an orally-composed text seems, on the basis of previous studies, to be above fifty percent" (1963, p. 99), yet the blues seems to be at least fifty percent formulaic. There are those scholars, of course, who saw no conflict between formulaic structure and written literature. Benson, on the basis of his study of literate Old English verse, claimed that "we can reject any lingering suspicion that the relative percentages of formulas might be used to distinguish between oral and lettered productions" (1966, p. 336), and Schaar (1956) and H.L. Rogers (1966) made similar claims in regard to Old English poetry; Finnegan (1976) and Holzapfel (1974) applied the same logic to the broader spectrum of oral poetry. The formulaic structure of the blues substantiates these observations.

If the commercially recorded blues is not a form of oral poetry, it is nevertheless closely allied to the orally composed blues performed in noncommercial contexts. As well, though the blues was usually written and rehearsed before being set in wax, it was still transmitted aurally to its audience, rather than presented to its audience as a written text. In this sense, the blues is—to use Foley's term—a "voice text" (Foley, 2002, pp. 43–45), similar to medieval literature that was written to be read or recited aloud. As Bäuml, among others, has pointed out, reception of a text is as important as composition in determining the function of formulaic structures (Bäuml, 1987), and the reception of the blues by the record-buying public included a shared understanding and expectation of a formulaic structure inherited from oral traditions (see also Renoir, 1981, p. 320). Blues singers and their audience were clearly working within a shared tradition of formulaic poetry, which may answer the question of why this tradition retained its strength against other twentieth-century popular song forms, such as Tin Pan Alley compositions and stage musicals that seemed to owe very little to formulaic structure.

But if audience reception explains the retention in commercially recorded blues of a formulaic structure, what in fact was being received? The fascination of the blues audience with formulas was not derived from simple conservatism or some love of structure for its own sake. The answer to this question lies partly in the definition of the formula that I gave at the beginning of this study: the formula is a semantic, rather than syntactic, unit. It is, by definition, laden with meaning, rather than merely a mechanical device for composing poetry (see Zumthor, 1982, p. 390). Foley has rightly described the function of the formula by its *immanence:* "the set of metonymic, associative meanings institutionally delivered and received through a dedicated idiom or register either during or on the authority of traditional oral performance" (Foley, 1995, p. 7), and he has shown how immanence applies to oral epics (Foley, 1991).

While Foley implies that immanence is a feature of orally composed poetry, I believe that it applies equally to written traditions such as the blues. The "dedicated idiom or register" shared by blues singers and their audiences was undoubtedly a result of the aural, rather than printed, presentation of the songs, as well as the poetic conventions of oral song forms that were the immediate predecessors—and contemporaries—of the commercially recorded blues. The answer to why the blues is formulaic can be found in the special context in which the race record blues were composed and performed and ultimately relates to the aesthetics of the blues. When recording the blues, singers were confronted with certain constraints and freedoms that shaped the way they composed the blues, and these factors worked to make the commercial blues especially concise, aphoristic, and ultimately formulaic in their composition. In addition, the special context of race record blues, as I demonstrate, actually enhanced the aesthetic value of the formula.

The Constraints and Freedoms of Race Record Blues Composition

As implied earlier, folksong antecedents to the commercial race re-cord blues employed repetition, if not their own formulaic systems; work songs, ballads, minstrel songs, dance songs, game songs, religious songs—all relied on the formula to some extent. As well, nonrace record blues—performed both before and during the race record era, and in-cluding both commercially derived and locally composed blues—were perhaps even more formulaic and repetitive in their structures than were race record blues. The race record blues was certainly an outgrowth of (as well as an influence on) these other forms of songs and thus shared their reliance on the formula.

My contention is that the nonspontaneous, somewhat confined conditions under which singers recorded their race record songs en-couraged, rather than discouraged, their use of formulas. Recording the blues required singers to direct their energies toward composing lyrics rather than toward other aspects of blues performance, to an extent not necessary in most of the nonrace record performance contexts of the blues.

Being performers, blues singers were largely concerned with how to entertain their audience. They had to make sure that their playing and singing were suitable to the audience and to the context in which they were performing. They had to be aware of their overall "stage presence," for in most performance contexts their audiences not only heard them but saw them as well. The singers were "actors" in the literal sense of the word.

As might be expected, in situations where audience–performer in-teraction was low, or where the audience's expectations of the performer were not great, there was less overt acting on the part of singers than when such interactions and expectations were high. In terms of stance while performing, this means that at a house party or juke joint, where singers simply supplied the background music for dancing and social-izing, blues singers could sit in a chair or slouch in a corner while per-forming without feeling the need to call attention to themselves or to their music. When singers were at the center of their audience's atten-tion, however, or where they had to please their audience with high-quality performances, they had to make every effort to keep themselves in the spotlight. Simply sitting in a chair and singing would not sell tick-ets at a tent show or vaudeville performance—such contexts demanded a more animated style from blues singers.

Goldstein noted this difference in the physical performance of one of his informants: "a traditional Negro folksinger from whom I had collected performed almost offhandedly when singing in his kitchen for his own family and friends, and very animatedly when singing before street audiences for money" (1964, p. 98n). On the street, in a cabaret, or on the stage, singers enlivened their performances with all sorts of body language and stunts. I recall the 1972 Mariposa Folk Festival in Toronto where pianist Roosevelt Sykes, when onstage, rocked his body to the rhythm of his music, continually looked around to establish eye contact with members of the audience, made sweeping motions with his hands as he ran his fingers up and down the keyboard, and pointed above with one hand while he played with the other whenever he sang the words *sky* or *heaven*. On at least two occasions, Booker White hopped on stage and danced and clapped his hands while Sykes was playing. These animated displays were in sharp contrast to the other blues singers, who could be seen unobtrusively hunched over their guitars, rehearsing for their stage appearances. The difference in performing styles was a difference in performing contexts.

In highly animated performances, singers often performed what might be called stunts with their instruments. Tommy Johnson would "throw the guitar in the air, flip it, straddle it, stand it on the floor, sit on it, lie on the floor with it and play it behind his head, all without missing a note" (Evans, 1971, p. 100). In addition, he could perform the truly amazing feat of standing on the guitar while playing it with his toes (Evans, 1971, p. 100). Charley Patton would dance around his guitar, bang it while he played it, and, like Johnson, play it behind his head (Fahey, 1970, p. 26). Playing the guitar behind the head seems to have been a common stunt in the repertoire of blues singers: Blind Blake also performed this feat (Calt, n.d.), and I saw Booker White do the same trick at Mariposa.

Gus Cannon was a master of animated performance because of his long career in medicine shows—a context in which the performer was very much the center of his audience's attention. While on stage, he

> would suddenly swing the head of the banjo out over the heads of the people standing by the wagon. He was still holding it with his left hand, and as the banjo swung back he would change the chord with his left hand and pick the strings with his right; then swing it out again. He would finish playing the song with the banjo swaying wildly in front of him. (Charters, 1959, p. 119)

The Chapel Hillbillies, a black string band that included Floyd Council at one time, performed a two-man stunt that is still a favorite of performers, both black and white. George Letlow explained,

We clowned, you might call it, when we were playing ... I would take the guitar and the mandolin, Floyd was playing the guitar and I was playing the mandolin. I would play the guitar and "note" the mandolin. He would play the mandolin and "note" the guitar. We would get close together so that we could cross-hand it. (Lornell, 1975, p. 45)

Keil noted that such stunts symbolize the mastery of humans over machines (1966, p. 176). The function of these stunts, however, was to maintain the attention of the audience in contexts where this was of prime importance. But such feats also highlighted the skill and dexterity of the performer and could be used to impress a particular member of an audience. A bluesman might have wished to show off in front of a woman or to dazzle a potential competitor. Given this function of the stunts, they might also have been performed in certain low-profile contexts, such as at the juke joint or the jam session.

There were those contexts, however, where clowning was definitely counterproductive. If a performer misjudged his or her audience, such antics could provoke an unwelcome response. Such was the case that Eddie Green remembered concerning Allen Shaw:

On one occasion Allen played at a small community called Rialto for a white party. Rialto is on the bank of the Hatchie River. Allen got drunk and started clowning instead of playing, and the people that were paying him didn't like it. So they picked him up, guitar and all, and threw him in the river with his guitar around his neck. (Keil, 1966, p. 176)

Of course stage shows presented a highly animated performance of the blues, including dancing, posing, and acting out the lyrics, but they also added a new dimension to the physical performance of the blues: a flashy costume. For example, Bessie Smith's favorite costume was "a white and blue satin dress with a moderate hoop skirt, adorned with strands of pearls and imitation rubies. With it she wore headgear that looked like a cross between a football helmet and a tassled lamp shade" (Albertson, 1972, pp. 67–68).

In the context of the recording studio, however, animated performances were virtually nonexistent. Guitar flipping, dancing, or even rhythmic body movements were prohibited because of the rather rigid position the singer had to maintain; technicians wanted as little extraneous movement as possible to avoid unnecessary noise or fluctuations in the sound level. But even if such movements had been allowed, the recording context would not, in most cases, call for such animation. There was no audience to attract and no one to impress. The disembodied and future audience that eventually bought the recording would neither know nor care how the singer acted or dressed.

Singers in the recording context, unburdened of the need to act, could devote their full energies to singing and playing—which would probably enrich the quality of these aspects of their performance. Son House was of the opinion that the recorded performances of Charley Patton were "better" than his live performances, because Patton's habit of grandstanding in front of live audiences tended to obscure his singing and playing (Wilson, 1965, p. 12).

There was, however, one aspect of physical performance that was probably unique to the recording context: only in the recording studio could singers read or refer to printed lyrics as they sang. Broonzy recalled having difficulty in sticking his head into the recording horn and reading his song at the same time (1955, p. 47). There were, in fact, many cases in which performers read their songs. In the case of blind singers, assistants could stand behind them and whisper the lyrics into their ears. This method was observed a number of times when Blind Lemon Jefferson recorded: Art Satherly recalled whispering the words to Jefferson during one recording session (Cohen, 1972, p. 19), while John and Emery McClung—two hillbilly singers—remembered seeing Jefferson's "daughter" acting the role of prompter in another session (Nelson, 1974, p. 72). Such a method might also have been used for illiterate singers; sighted singer Charlie Jackson also used a prompter when recording a new song (Charters, 1959, p. 52).

Only in a context in which the singer was unseen could written aids and prompters be used. Race record artists often needed these aids because of the continual demand by the recording companies for innovative material, as well as for the covering of previously recorded songs by other singers. I describe in more detail these two aspects of recorded blues shortly, but it is important to note that, in such a situation, singers sometimes had neither the time nor the inclination to memorize their lyrics.

Different performance contexts also affected the duration of any given song. There is little information on how long the average blues song performance lasted outside of the recording context. Perry Bradford wrote of a particularly long rendition of "Harlem Blues," performed in a cabaret, that lasted twelve minutes (1965, p. 123), and a description of Alberta Hunter's nightclub performance described how she repeated the song "He May Be Your Man, but He Comes to See Me Sometimes," ten or fifteen times to lengthen it, as she serenaded one table after another (Mezzrow and Wolfe, 1946, p. 34). Ferris (1970, p. 43) claimed that in dancing contexts, songs had to be much longer than the three-minute race record blues corroborated by Son House, who said that Patton would sing a song for up to a half an hour at dances (Titon, 1977, p. 32). Middleton's claim, however, that singers would "often sing one song for hours" is probably an exaggeration (1972, p. 45).

It is likely that in contexts in which singers were the center of their audiences' attention, their songs tended to be of shorter duration than when they served in background roles. Dancers would not have been satisfied with a three-minute song, whereas nightclub goers would probably have become restless if one song went on for half an hour. Street singers probably had the greatest freedom in this respect, because their audiences' attention was momentary and fleeting, no matter how long or short the song performance was.

By contrast, the recording context allowed singers little freedom in choosing the length of their songs. The average 78rpm disc permits about two hundred seconds of performance per side. Singers had to come as close to this maximum as possible without going over the limit, which involved a type of precision not necessary in other performance contexts. In a letter to hillbilly artist Fred Stanley, the Columbia Record Company instructed him to work on his songs so that they would not be "less than 2 minutes and 45 seconds and not more than 3 minutes and 15 seconds" (Reif, 1972, p. 15); undoubtedly the same advice was given to race record artists.

To keep to the time limit, singers employed two methods: self-regulation and signals from the control room. Most singers would consciously work to fit their songs into the time limit. Tommy Johnson apparently sang short songs in nonrecorded contexts and had to pad out his works for recordings (Evans, 1971, p. 50), but most singers had the opposite problem of shortening their songs to fit the allotted three minutes. Booker White used a clock to time his songs when practicing for recording sessions (Evans, 1966a, p. 8), and similar methods were undoubtedly used by the perfectionist Will Shade (Charters, 1959, p. 115) or by conscientious urban singers such as Thomas A. Dorsey, Tampa Red (O'Neal and O'Neal, 1975, p. 26), and Leroy Carr (Rosenbaum, 1961).

For artists who had not budgeted their time, the studio technicians had a system of lights to warn them of the impending limit: "There were two lights on top of the window, one green and one red. When the green light came on the performer would begin, and when the red light came on the performer was to end the verse as quickly as possible and stop" (Perls, 1965, p. 4). For blind artists, a prompter would give the signal: "It was Willie [Trice]'s job to tell [Blind Boy] Fuller when to start and when to conclude a number, by touching him on the arm, which he did whenever Mayo Williams was ready to record" (Bastin,

1971, p. 19). By whatever means singers managed this time limitation on their performances, Szwed was certainly correct in pointing out that such a limit affected the form of the blues (1968, p. 274).

Time was not the only limiting factor in race record blues composition. Singers had to be aware of the effects on their audiences of the content or subject matter of their songs. Different contexts required different restrictions on the content of blues songs. As already discussed, the blues is predominantly a love lyric, but the topic of love can be approached in any number of ways, not all of which are suitable for every situation. Charters was probably justified in writing that when Blind Lemon Jefferson played at that picnic for the General Association of the Baptist Church, his audience "would not have stood for 'Black Snake Moan' or 'Piney Woods Money Mama'" (1959, p. 70).

Odum and Johnson long ago pointed out that profanity "is inserted in songs in proportion as the singer is accustomed to use it, or as the occasion demands or permits its use" (1925, p. 174). Most blues singers were adept at singing profane or obscene songs; both Skip James and Son House were quite capable in this respect (Calt, Perls, and Stewart, n.d.a), and the female vaudeville singers such as Mattie Hite, Mary Stafford, Edith Wilson, Josephine Beaty, and Josie Miles all sang obscene material at suitable occasions (Oliver, 1968, p. 205).

Such occasions tended to be those informal, in-group contexts, such as in jam sessions, juke joints, or house parties. In describing the occasions when his brother Tommy Johnson sang obscene material, Mager Johnson said, "He sang them over in the night or something, in other words, just somebody out there, people just out joking around. They don't care where they be" (Evans, 1971, p. 92). Before white audiences, or other outsiders, or before certain groups of women and children, such songs were taboo. Evans wrote that Tommy Johnson

> would occasionally sing songs with obscene lyrics, even before women and white people, which could sometimes be dangerous. Ishman Bracey recalls an occasion when One Legged Sam had to put his hand over Johnson's mouth to keep him quiet. (1971, p. 96)

While there are a few examples of obscene material on race records—perhaps the most graphic example being Lucille Bogan's unissued recording of "Shave 'Em Dry" (issued on Stash ST-101)—in general, the recording context was definitely one in which overtly obscene lyrics were taboo. Speckled Red clearly made the distinction between proper and improper contexts for performing obscene songs:

They used to have a word they say "playin' the dozens." It was talkin' dirty you know. ... So I made up a kind of song out of the words and I called it "The Dirty Dozens." But they was real bad words you see; I was playin' in one of them turpentine jukes where it didn't matter. Anything I said there was all right in there you see. I had to clean it up for the record. (Oliver, 1965, p. 61)

To the singer it was not simply a matter of impropriety to sing taboo lyrics in the wrong place; it was a matter of self-protection. Buster Pickens's comment on Kokomo Arnold's song "Sissy Man Blues"—a blues song about homosexuality—was not that it was improper but that "God, I thought they'd put him inside for that!" (Oliver, 1968, p. 188). Overt social commentary, especially concerning racism, was definitely limited to in-group contexts where performers were sure that their songs would neither offend nor antagonize any portion of their audience. For example, according to Bill Broonzy, Tommy McClennan misjudged the sensitivity of northern blacks to the word *nigger*, which he insisted on using in a song he sang at a Chicago house party:

So I just stayed close to him [McClennan] because I knew there would be some trouble when he would get to that verse. And there was. I had to put Tommy out the window and me and him ran about five miles to another friend of mine's house where we got a drink. (Broonzy, 1955, pp. 103–104)

In the context of the recording studio, where the immediate audience was made up of white technicians and company officials, and where the sensibilities of the faceless record-buying public could not be entirely judged, singers naturally avoided overt social commentary in their songs.

A major influence on the composition of race record blues lyrics, however, involved the expectations, assumptions, needs, and aesthetics of record company officials. Before singers were recorded, they had to convince A&R (artist and repertoire) men and other company officials that their material and styles of performance were marketable. For example, the Edison Record Company auditioned Bessie Smith and rejected her with the note, "Bessie Smith. Voice N.G. [no good]" (Oliver, 1959, p. 25). She had no better luck at the studios of the black-owned Pace Phonograph Company:

Whilst the recording engineers and the accompanying group of musicians waited, the tall, plump, copper-skinned young woman broke off in the middle of her song and expectorated. Harry Pace, the President of the Pace Phonograph Company, which issued Black Swan records, was disgusted and summarily ended the recording test, dismissing the girl on the spot. (Oliver, 1959, p. ix)

A&R men carefully scrutinized the repertoires of those singers who were accepted for a recording contract, and any material that did not fit the company's criteria would not be recorded. As stated earlier, any obscene or socially sensitive songs usually did not meet these criteria and neither did songs that the record company felt did not portray the proper image of the blues singer to the public. "As late as the early 1940s, when Brownie McGhee asked to record some hillbilly songs he regularly performed, he was told that it was not '[his] kind of music'" (Titon, 1977, p. 55).

In general, the songs that the record companies wanted were original blues compositions. Odum and Johnson were the first to recognize this when they wrote that "phonograph artists are encouraged by their employers to sing blues of their own making" (1926, p. 24), and talent scout Sam Ayo corroborated this statement:

They [the blues singers] had all their own material—in other words we wouldn't record anyone else's tunes—they'd have their own originals. You have better luck recording a person's own originals than by recording someone else's tunes. Blues—mostly blues, and it was all original stuff. (Oliver, 1965, p. 117)

This meant that before singers could record, they had to prove to the record company that they indeed had original songs:

The companies want [A&R man] Speir to be sure that each singer to be recorded had at least four different songs of his own composition. Many of them could sing plenty of songs, but they were not original. In other words, they were either traditional or had already been recorded in variant form, or they were interpretations of hit records. (Evans, 1972, p. 120)

This could present a problem to those blues singers who relied heavily on traditional material or other singers' compositions to fill out their repertoire. But a worse problem was that the record company's concept of "original" might have been very different from that of the singers, which meant that songs that singers considered their own creations might be rejected by the record company as "unoriginal." For example, Clifford Gibson, like many other blues singers, felt that a change in lyrics constituted a new song, even if the accompanying music remained the same (Calt, Perls, and Stewart, n.d.b); an A&R man, however, might have considered all of Gibson's songs the same and thus dub them "unoriginal" for the very reason that Gibson sang all of them to the same tune.

More often, however, it happened that A&R men did not consider the lyrics different enough from one song to another in the singers' repertoires. Such was the case with Tommy Johnson:

> Speir wanted to make certain that Johnson had at least four different original songs, as this was the requirement of the companies then. He claims that Johnson had only two and that they had to spend some time together before they could meet the requirements. This may seem strange in a professional musician like Tommy Johnson, who must have had an extensive repertoire of songs. Yet ... Johnson, like many folk blues singers, had the habit of using some of the same lyrics and musical ideas in different songs. Thus his pieces may not have sounded "different" to Speir's ears. (Evans, 1971, p. 46)

In their quest for original material, record companies would often instruct singers to make up blues songs especially for the recording session, which meant that singers had to increase their repertoires on rather short notice. Booker White's experience in this respect was typical:

> When he came to the recording session he had songs like "Prowling Ground Hog" and "Sitting on Top of the World." The recording engineer liked Booker's voice but didn't want to record these old songs. So he gave Booker a meal ticket and a room for two weeks and told him to make up some original songs. Booker thought about this and came up with "Pinebluff Arkansas" and "Shake 'Em on Down." (Evans, 1966a, p. 7)

This is not to say that record companies recorded nothing but original compositions. There are many traditional songs and ballads, as well as covers of other people's songs, on race records. But the main staple of the companies was original blues compositions. Even when they wanted traditional songs, they actively sought those pieces that had not already been overdone on record. Note the following letter from T.G. Rockwell to John Hurt:

> We would like to have you get together about eight selections at least four of them to be old time tunes, similar to selections "Frankie" and "Nobody's Business." There are a great many tunes like these, which are known throughout the South. (Spottswood, n.d.)

The repertoires and compositional skills of blues singers were severely tested under these conditions, and the record companies helped them to compose their songs in a number of ways. Quite often they suggested topics or ideas that singers could work with. Sometimes the companies wanted singers to compose songs in the style of already successful artists; Son House, for example, was told to compose a song in the style of Blind Lemon Jefferson, and the result was "Mississippi County Farm Blues" (Fahey, 1970, p. 12). When Skip James wanted to record a song composed by another singer, the company suggested that he compose his own song on the same theme:

> James attempted to record a song which he had learned from another Paramount record, the "Forty-Four Blues" by James Wiggins, Paramount 12860. [Arthur] Laibley suggested that James do a song about a gun with a different size calibre, and so James recorded his "22-20 Blues." When Laibley requested that James make up a song about the depression, the singer recorded "Hard Time Killin' Floor Blues." (Fahey, 1970, p. 12)

Some veteran recording artists were asked to write topical songs, in the same way that a newspaper might order one of the staff writers to pen a feature article. Such was the case with Brownie McGhee:

> I went back to Tennessee, and I've still got the telegram he [J.B. Long] wrote me and said: "Brownie, write me a song. [Blind Boy] Fuller's very sick, 'Please Mister Fuller Don't Die.' " I started writing on that, and before I could finish, before anything materialized, I got a call from him … Fuller was dead! Said: "Brownie, why don't you work on a song 'The Death of Blind Boy Fuller.' And be sure to mention his women in there because he was very fond of women." And that's where the song "Death of Blind Boy" comes in. (Elmes, 1973, p. 20)

A record company might ask several singers to write songs on a single topic, if they thought that topic was particularly remarkable. The October 31, 1935, Decca session saw several artists sing blues on a Christmas or New Year theme, probably at the direction of the company that was preparing their Christmas promotion for that year (Oliver, 1968, p. 36). In fact, companies went to considerable lengths if they felt a topic was especially worthwhile:

> Between April and June thousands of people were victims of the floods [of the Mississippi River in 1927] and according to Big Bill Broonzy the talent scout, Mayo Williams, chartered a boat for a number of the blues singers to witness them. Including Lonnie Johnson, Kansas Joe McCoy, Springback James, Sippie

Wallace and Broonzy himself the party was joined by Bessie Smith. (Oliver, 1959, p. 47)

For those who were new to the recording context, or who were not imaginative composers, record companies would supply more direct help in composing songs. They might employ a veteran artist to coach the inexperienced singer, as was apparently the case with Arthur Crudup, when he first began his recording career:

He [Melrose] say, "You reckon you can get me a couple more songs?" I said "I don't know." Tampa [Red] said, "Come on over to my house tomorrow afternoon and I'll help you." So I went over there and he gave me a little instruction on it, you know, how to get my words together and he told me don't have no fear, 'cause that's the way I done and that's the way the rest of them done—he says nobody perfect, and I just went from there. (Leadbitter, 1970, p. 17)

Joe Williams and Charley Jordan fulfilled a similar role at their rehearsal hall in St. Louis:

Williams said that he and Jordan would work closely with various singers and instrumentalists, preparing them for recording sessions for which Jordan had arranged. The two men would select and re-work songs for the performers and drill them in their execution; when all was ready, Jordan would pile the musicians into his car and drive them to Chicago or wherever the recordings were being made, working closely with the record company officials charged with supervising the recordings. (Welding, n.d.b)

Sometimes the white A&R men helped the singers:

It appears that [J.B.] Long frequently wrote or rewrote songs for [Blind Boy] Fuller and would write down the verses that Fuller had sung, to prevent him from forgetting them. He would carefully rehearse Fuller for some three or four days, having him stay at his home or at a hotel in Burlington. (Bastin, 1971, p. 23)

Bastin also reported that while in Memphis, "Long heard an elderly man sing 'Touch It Up and Go' which he rewrote for Fuller and which he had Fuller cut" (1971, p. 22).

Besides helping singers to write their songs, the record companies also supplied compositions that were not from the performers' repertoires at all. Especially in the early years of the race record era, if one female vaudeville singer recorded a big-selling song, other companies would cover this song; that is, they would have another artist record the same song in the hope that they could exploit its popularity (see Godrich, 1969). In fact, the songs of the female vaudeville blues singers were often written for them by Tin Pan Alley–type blues writers such as Perry Bradford, Clarence Williams, Porter Granger, and Thomas A. Dorsey.

Covering or singing other artist's songs was not practiced solely by the early female singers; blues singers in general expanded their recorded repertoire with outside material. Blues such as "Sitting on Top of the World," "Big Road Blues," and "Tight Like That" were often covered by different singers. As well, record companies sometimes gave newly composed pieces to their male, rural-based singers. The following letter from the Okeh Record Company to white singer Land Norris was probably similar to ones sent to black blues singers:

> … asking you to be in New York 27th and 28th [1926] to make some recordings and at which time we suggest you making eight selections so that we would suggest your picking out the best eight numbers that you now have and when you arrive here, we will undoubtedly be able to give you one or two which you can learn in a very short time. ("Commercial Music Documents," 1971, p. 125)

Even highly individualistic singers such as Blind Lemon Jefferson and Peetie Wheatstraw sung other writers' compositions (see Bastin and Cowley, 1974, p. 13, and Garon, 1971, pp. 107–11, respectively). Alex Moore recalled that "Blind Norris McHenry recorded some songs I wrote for Decca Records in Chicago" (Moore, 1974, p. 14); the young Andrew Hogg, who after World War II became famous as Smokey Hogg, began his recording career in 1937 with two Wheatstraw compositions (Paulsen, 1968, p. 3), while Roosevelt Scott had several sources for his blues: "Joe McCoy, one 'Robert' (not a musician) and Willie Townsend (a Yazoo City trumpet player) wrote some of his songs" (Eagle, 1972, p. 12).

The result of the record companies' needs for original material, as well as their penchant for supplying already composed songs to their artists, broadened the repertoires of these singers. The juke joint, house party, street, or even cabaret context did not make such heavy demands on the singer's ability to compose and cover songs as did the recording context. The record companies' demands for originality, especially, had implications for blues composition in general. Calt viewed this influence as devolutionary:

The introduction of blues on phonograph brought a new emphasis to blues lyrics, if only because a passive rather than participatory audience now awaited them. That the country bluesman who obtained recording sessions in the middle and later Twenties were so often unequal to the challenge of the new medium that would reap dividends for the facile songwriters like Leroy Carr and Barbecue Bob is probably indicative of the fact that they could not have realistically anticipated their discovery by commercial talent scouts. But by the same token many country bluesmen made only a hack's response to the novelty presented by the blues recording, copying its verses as they came down to him. (1973, p. 14)

As stated earlier, Calt had a rather low opinion of the use of the formula in the blues (1973, p. 25); he believed that singers were "unequal to the challenge" because they relied so heavily on previously recorded material in composing their songs. But if one takes a positive view of formulaic structure, then the fact that singers constantly dipped into the storehouse of phrases to which race records gave them access can be viewed as resourcefulness on their part. The pressure exerted by record companies was largely responsible for this resourcefulness; they forced singers to reexamine the blues tradition—as found both on recordings and from other sources—to compose new songs that were "original" from the companies' points of view, as well as satisfying to the singers' sensitivities and the understanding they shared with their audience of the blues tradition.

Evans demonstrated a more balanced view of the implications of the race record blues than did Calt. He placed the traditionally composed, nonrace record blues and the race record compositions at different points on an aesthetic continuum:

A double folk aesthetic of blues performers and audiences has thus gradually developed with the older values of "truth," tradition, and familiarity on one side, and the more recent commercially influenced values of lyric originality, thematic coherence, and standardization of musical structure on the other. Since both types of blues can be performed by the same singer, and since a number of blues seem to share the characteristics of both types, we ought to view this double folk aesthetic as a spectrum rather than as a set of opposing values. Blues performers and audiences have much less difficulty in accepting and enjoying all kinds of blues than have songwriters and record company executives who were responsible, in large part, for broadening the aesthetic spectrum. (1973, p. 20)

The constraints on style, duration, and subject matter of the performance, as well as the freedom to read the lyrics or be prompted, compelled singers to produce concise, coherent, forceful songs. Energy otherwise spent on "stage presence" went into lyric writing. The time limit forced singers to tighten their material and to cut out what was not essential to the message of the song. Constraints on subject matter, while limiting the range of thematic material, enriched the poetic imagery of that more limited range. Print and prompting kept the poetry tight and spare.

The pressure to be "original" forced singers to be self-reliant, linguistically articulate, and continually innovative. At the same time, the phenomenon of covering and composing in the style of other singers added to singers' compositions literary precedent, borrowing, and a generally heightened awareness of the blues lyric tradition. The result of these contextual restraints and freedoms was a highly complex and compact form of song, relying heavily on short, aphoristic pronouncements and concise poetic imagery. Singers either consciously or semiconsciously understood that the surest way of meeting the demands of the recording situation was not to be continually innovative in the way that elite, literary poets were but to draw on the blues lyric tradition for their originality; in other words, to exploit and broaden the formulaic system inherent in other blues and blues-related songs.

Thus did the recording context add a new dimension to blues composition and aesthetics—a dimension that, as Evans explained, grew out of the folk blues tradition and that was complementary with that tradition. Yet the question of aesthetics that Evans raised is a complex one, and perhaps it is in the realm of aesthetics, rather than merely in the context of commercial recording, that the value and function of the blues formula more properly lies.

The Aesthetics of the Blues Formula

Lord has written that the formula is a matter not of aesthetics but of verse making (1986, pp. 491–93), while Basgoz, in exploring a specific form of Turkish folk literature, has described the formula as a purely aesthetic device (1978, p. 21). The reality undoubtedly lies somewhere between these two extremes, and the relative functions of structure and pleasure will certainly vary from one poetic tradition to the next.

Aesthetics, however, is definitely a factor in the use of the formula, whether in Yugoslavian epic, Old English verse, or blues compositions.

If there is one defining quality of the formula—or formulaic poetry, for that matter—it is repetition. The formula, as I have described it, is a concise, semantic message that singers consciously employed and that their audiences consciously heard and understood as repetitions. As Foley has pointed out for oral poetic traditions, "The traditional oral society educates its members—that is, it provides them with necessary information—through the repeated and collective experience of performed epic poetry, by presenting them time and again with a verbal montage of the group's poetic models and thereby with the data which these models encode" (1977, p. 134). The same was true of the blues audience. Each singing of a formula was a reworking of something that was familiar and recognizable from its appearance in other, previous singings.

The context of the race record blues cannot entirely explain the reality of the repetitive nature of this song form. As poets, the singers could have chosen other strategies in meeting the constraints and freedoms of the recording situation. They could have broken away from whatever traditional formulaic systems they knew from noncommercial blues or other contemporary song forms. They could have composed their lyrics along the lines of Tin Pan Alley composers, who certainly used repetitive themes, images, and rhyme schemes but whose songs lack the overwhelmingly formulaic structure of the race record blues.

That the singers chose to compose their blues as they did was ultimately a matter of aesthetics. There is something essentially pleasing and fulfilling in formulaic poetry. Its repetitive and derivative nature—when composed and performed in an "artistic" fashion (however that is to be defined)—is stimulating rather than tedious. The aesthetics of repetition have been understood for a long time; Horace, for example, pointed out that a good poem might be heard many times and still give pleasure (1971, p. 68). The very act of repeating the poem heightens and maintains this pleasure.

This pleasure derives partly from the common language of the blues immediately understood by singer and audience—what Foley termed the "communicative economy" of formulaic poetry (2002, p. 117). Rosenberg wrote that "in traditional art there is no suspense and no surprise; one is satisfied aesthetically because of a sense of the logic and justness of procedure, the inherent dignity of it, and because of the fulfillment of traditional expectations" (1975, p. 93). But the aesthetic is more complicated than Rosenberg allows; although formulaic poetry fulfills "traditional expectations," it is not entirely derivative and repetitive. The very act of repetition brings a new perspective to that which is repeated.

"A rose is a rose is a rose," by the very nature of its repetitiveness, forces one to reconsider the idea of "rose" anew with each repetition and to understand another meaning of "rose" with every restatement of the proposition. Repetition compels the listener to reevaluate a statement in the light of its restatement. In Kierkegaard's terms, a repetition forces a recollection:

> Repetition and recollection are the same movement, only in opposite directions; for what is recollected has been, is repeated backwards, whereas repetition properly so called is recollected forwards. (1946, pp. 3–4)

This "remembrance of things past" enriches the repeated statement, because it calls up the original and previously repeated times when the statement was uttered. In discussing the three repeated scenes in Poe's *The Purloined Letter*, Felman explored this phenomenon: "The second scene, through repetition, allows for an understanding, for an *analysis* of the first" (1980, p. 138, emphasis in the original). The formula similarly evokes nostalgia, but at the same time, it provokes a reevaluation of itself in a new context.

Because each repetition adds something to the overall understanding and analytical possibilities in a text, Kierkegaard was right in wondering if there was indeed any such thing as "repetition"; his examples of never being able to make the same trip twice to Berlin, or see—in exactly the same way twice—the same theatrical production speak to this point (1946). Given this understanding, is the formula a repetition? If one considers the entire corpus of race record blues as a single text, then each resinging of a formula in that extended text is not a repetition, because in each new context the listener must reinterpret the formula in a new way. Once the singer abstracts the formula from one song and introduces it into another song, it becomes, in Bateson's terms, a part divorced from the whole: "The 'part' may take on special ritual or metaphoric meanings in contexts where the original whole to which it once referred is no longer relevant" (1973, p. 393).

Yet the formula remains relevant to its original song context at the same time that it gains new relevance in another song context. Thus, from the listener's point of view (the ideal audience being aware of all songs in the blues corpus), the singing of a particular formula is both a repetition and not a repetition. The way around this quandary is to redefine repetition according to its actual, paradoxical qualities. Repetition embodies difference, as well as sameness; Felman went so far as to assert, "Repetition is not of *sameness* but of *difference,* not of independent terms or of analogous themes but of a structure of differential interrelationships" (1980, p. 139, emphasis in original).

To express this paradox, Robert Rogers used the term *redundancy* to replace repetition: while all waves that crash on a beach are redundant in relation to each other, they are still different from each other in their specific qualities (1987, p. 585). For Rogers, the distinction lies between "repetition"—an ideal concept—and "repetition with a difference"—the reality. Suleiman (1980), likewise, preferred the term *redundancy* and stressed the necessity of redundancy in all literature. There is no originality in literature—indeed no literature at all— without repetition:

> When originality in seriousness is acquired and conserved, then there is succession and repetition. ... The serious man is serious precisely through the originality with which he comes back to repetition. (Kierkegaard, 1957, p. 96)

The formula, then, is a commentary on the necessity of repetition in literature. It makes manifest what is perhaps only implied in nonformulaic literatures. Because the formula so clearly speaks to the question of the nature of repetition, it raises this question to the level of aesthetics; the singer and audience celebrate repetition through their shared understanding of the formula.

The aesthetic of repetition involves new contexts for old material. As Parry wrote,

> One oral poet is better than another not because he has by himself found a more striking way of expressing his own thought but because he has been better able to make use of the tradition. He strives not to create a new ideal of poetry, but to achieve that which everyone knows to be best. (1932, p. 334)

Because the audience recognized the formula, whether consciously or unconsciously, from previous poetic contexts, the formula accrued meaning; it gathered thematic and psychological associations around itself from one repetition to the next, in the way that a snowball gathers more snow as it rolls down a hill. With each new singing of a formula, the audience recalled all of that formula's past lyrical contexts and all of the other formulas with which it was juxtaposed. With each repetition, the formula gained meaning and significance beyond its inherent semantic structure.

Greenfield recognized this phenomenon in Old English poetry:

> A highly stylized poetry like Anglo-Saxon, with its many formulas and presumably many verbal conventions, has certain advantages in comparison with a less traditional type of poetry. The most notable advantage is that the very traditions it employs lend extra-emotional meaning to individual words and phrases. That is, associations with other contexts using similar formula will inevitably color a particular instance of a formula so that a whole host of overtones springs into action to support the aesthetic response. (1955, p. 205)

And Rosenberg, in discussing a particular sermon formula, also raised this point:

> One can say with certainty that Brown has associated the formula "Same man" with particular events in the life of Jesus, and that this particular descriptive passage intuitively calls this formula, and its variants, out of Brown's word-hoard. In certain psycholinguistic situations the reverse may be true: the formula calls forth the theme. (1970a, p. 61)

This evocative quality is as present in nonaphoristic formulas as it is in those that are particularly proverbial. "Whether or not a given formula embodies an actual metaphor, it is nevertheless always imagistic, and appeals directly to the senses" (Whitman, 1958, p. 110). Repetition, rather than any inherent quality in the formula, provokes an aesthetic response from the audience. Thus, Foley is justified in asserting that the formula "is finally not metrical-compositional but aesthetic" (Foley, 1991, p. 245).

The precedent for this aesthetic in the blues comes not only from other formulaic poetries, not only from other forms of black folksong, but also from the African American literary tradition. Snead's discussion of repetition in black culture accords with the views outlined earlier: "Repetition [in African American culture] has occurred, but that, given a 'quality of difference' compared to what has gone before, it has become not a 'repetition' but rather a 'progression'" (1984, p. 59). His concept of the "cut" in black culture—wherein texts return "to another beginning which we have already heard" (1984, p. 69)—is pervasive in African American expressive forms.

Gates's understanding of African American literary traditions also centers on the aesthetics of formulaic repetition. His description of the toast "Signifying Monkey" as an indicator of black literary style might work just as well for a description of the blues: "It is as if a received structure of crucial elements provides a base for poesis, and the narrator's technique, his or her craft, is to be gauged by the creative (re)placement of these expected or anticipated formulaic phrases and formulaic events rendered anew in unexpected ways" (1988, p. 61).

Only two scholars have applied these theories of aesthetics directly to the blues formula. Evans (n.d.) made his point in trying to show how the aesthetics of audiences change over time and how different cultures apply different aesthetic criteria to the same songs:

> If the lack of unity or novelty in the lyrics, taken by themselves, makes them seem monotonous to today's listener, this was not the case for either the Negro audiences of the time or for the performers themselves at country parties. Each verse or line could stand on its own having its own built-in response; the very familiarity of the phrases (and to some extent of the music) making them pleasurably easy to recognize and identify with.

Welding was the only blues scholar to make any connection between this blues aesthetic and literary traditions in general, in his use of the theories of Edmund Wilson (1955):

> The blues is most accurately seen as a music of re-composition. That is, the creative bluesman is the one who imaginatively handles traditional elements and who, by his realignment of commonplace elements, shocks us with the familiar. He makes the old newly meaningful for us. His art is more properly viewed as one of providing the listener with what critic Edmund Wilson described as "the shock of recognition," a pretty accurate description, I believe, of the process of re-shaping and re-focusing of traditional forms in which the blues artist engages. (Welding, n.d.a)

Yet the aesthetic of repetition does not entirely explain the overall aesthetics of the blues formula. Evans and Welding, as well as others cited previously, concentrated on repetition—whether with or without difference—to the exclusion of nonformulaic, nonrepeated parts of formulaic poetry. Although the blues, like much other formulaic poetry, is aphoristic and even sometimes proverbial (see Taft, 1994), it differs from the proverb in terms of the nature of its repetition. Like the formula, the proverb is a recognized, linguistic entity repeated under a variety of contexts; thus incorporating an infinity of meanings within its repeated usage. But unlike the proverb, the formula is part of a larger poetic structure that includes both other formulas and nonformulaic, innovative phrases.

These innovative phrases, by their very presence, enhance the aesthetics of the formula. They complement the "difference" of the repeated formula with their own "difference"—a difference that is other than that of the formula. When an audience listens to the blues, it is shocked (to use Welding's and Wilson's term) in two ways: by the new use of familiar phrases and by the use of unfamiliar phrases. The innovative or unfamiliar phrases might become formulas in subsequent texts (see Jarrett, 1984, pp. 160–61, on this point), but their initial use by singers heightens the pleasure of the blues lyric by adding another level of expectation to the song. As Snead pointed out in his discussion of African American music: "[It] sets up expectations and disturbs them at irregular intervals: that it will do this, however, is itself an expectation" (1984, p. 69).

If the blues was nothing more than a series of formulas, it would be stagnant and mechanical. Without the added feature of innovative phrases, the "pool" of formulas would not grow. Without this counterbalance to the repetition aesthetic of the formula, singers would undoubtedly have had to rely on other song forms in meeting the constraints and freedoms of race record blues composition. But to think of any formulaic poetry as *entirely* formulaic is probably a misconception. Folk literature, if not all literature, consists of an interplay between repetitive and innovative elements. As Cawelti pointed out,

> All culture products contain a mixture of two kinds of elements: conventions and inventions. Conventions are elements which are known to both the creator and his audience beforehand— they consist of things like favorite plots, stereotyped characters, accepted ideas, commonly known metaphors and other linguistic devices, etc. Inventions, on the other hand, are elements which are uniquely imagined by the creator, such as new kinds of characters, ideas, or linguistic forms. (1969, pp. 384–85)

Similarly, Middleton has shown that the source of "pleasure" in popular song stems from a combination of repetition and variation (1983). The formula is "convention," while the innovative phrase is "invention."

Toelken has best expressed this phenomenon as it applies to folklore in his formulation of the "twin laws" of conservatism and dynamism. These two forces act in varying degrees on all forms of folklore and describe, in Toelken's term, the "behaviour" of the text (1979, pp. 32–39). In the songs of Garfield Akers, the small number of innovative, invented, "dynamic" lines shock us with pleasure, just as the autobiographical blues of John Estes shocks us with its sprinkling of formulaic, conventional, "conservative" phrases. These different "differences" make up, to a large extent, the aesthetic component of the blues; Gates might well have been writing of the blues, rather than toasts, when he observed, "There is no fixed text of these poems; they exist as a play of differences" (1988, p. 61).

Another aspect of the aesthetic of the blues concerns the evocative power of the formula—a power that extends beyond the evocative nature of repetition within the poetic tradition of the blues. The blues formula not only reestablished and redefined a poetic phrase in the minds of the audience but also brought to mind a larger, nonblues repertoire of language and images. As Miller discussed in relation to the sermons of Martin Luther King Jr., preachers added authority to their talks by reciting passages from scripture, hymns, and philosophical writings (1990, p. 78). Similarly, blues singers added outside authority to their songs by using formulas.

From where does this authority stem in the blues? Although a few examples of the use of scripture, proverbs, and even nursery rhymes can be found in the corpus, the major source of authority for the blues formula comes from everyday African American speech. The conversational use of "signifying," as discussed by Gates (1988), and the broader expressive behavior of "talking black," as discussed by Abrahams (1976), among others, are the source of blues formulas. Blues lyrics evoked the kind of conversational banter that African American audiences heard and used themselves in certain situations: talk between lovers or between rivals, bragging and insulting, rapping, talking shit, testifying, talking sweet, and signifying.

Most blues formulas grew out of such expressive talk, although it is impossible to show exactly how this process took place. Willie Borum's description of how he was inspired to compose gives some hint, however:

> It was working that give me my ideas. I walk around the plant at night, when it's quiet, you know, and I can hear the men talking. Some of them is crying that their wife has left them or that she isn't doing them right, and somebody else is saying that his girl's took up with somebody else. I hear all that and that's what I put in my blues. I come back here and write down the things, rhymed up, of course. I make the verses and things right when I'm still there walking around the job. (Charters, 1961)

Borum's rhyming up and juxtaposing of formulas grew out of conversations he heard, especially conversations on the blues themes of love, travel, and anxiety.

There are few examples of recorded conversation of this type from the race record era, but one bit of dialogue collected by Charles S. Johnson gives some indication of how formulas arose from everyday speech. In the following example, I have matched phrases from the Johnson quote with formulas from the corpus:

Tom Bright was my husband, but he fight me (a) so I just couldn't live with him (b). He treat me so bad (c). I didn't do nothing a-tall (d). I uster cook his breakfast (e) and he'd come home with a big stick and beat me (f). Said I didn't have no breakfast done. He drank but he wa'n't drunk (g) when he beat me. One time I went away to mama's (h) and come back I found some woman in my house (i). When I come in (j) he got mad and went to cussin', so I packed up (k) and went back home (l). (1934, p. 53)

(a)   *Wife and I just had a fight*
      (Joe McCoy, 1934d)

(b)   *Lord if you don't live with me, mama,* you ain't going to live with
      nobody else
      (Kokomo Arnold, 1937e)

(c)   *She don't have to treat me so bad,* because she lives in Tennessee
      (Blind Willie McTell, 1933f)

(d)   There's no need of you dogging me; *mama, I ain't done nothing to
      you*
      (Blind Blake, 1928)

(e)   *But she cooked my breakfast;* brings it to my bed
      (Johnnie Temple, 1937b)

(f)   *I beat my girl with a singletree*
      (Henry Thomas, 1928b)

(g)   *Because you see me staggering, daddy, don't you think I'm drunk*
      (Rosie Mae Moore, 1928a)

(h)   *So I went back to my mama;* nothing else I could do
      (Roosevelt Sykes, 1929e)

(i)   Says I sorry for you, woman; *another woman has taken your
      place*
      (Alice Moore, 1929b)

(j) *When you come in,* your rider she's out and gone
(Peg Leg Howell, 1926b)

(k) *I packed my suitcase;* Lord, I started to the train
(Will Shade, 1927b)

(l) *Said I'm going back home, mama,* and I'm going back there to stay
(Kokomo Arnold, 1935e)

Such everyday conversation is the source for much of African American literature, as Baker observed:

> Afro-American ordinary discourse is, in fact, *continuous with* Afro-American artistic discourse and that an investigation of the Afro-American oral tradition must finally concern itself, not simply with a lexicon, but also with a grammar (in the fit linguistic sense) adequate to describe the syntax and phonology of *all* Afro-American speech. (1984, p. 104, emphases in original)

But it is the blues, perhaps more than any other form of African American literature, that so clearly evokes ordinary discourse. Bluesman J.D. Short spoke to this point: "What I think about what made the blues really good is when a fellow writes a blues and then writes it with a feeling, with great harmony, and there's so many true words in the blues, of things that have happened to so many people, and that's why it makes the feeling in the blues" (Charters, 1963, p. 12). Truth and harmony, as Short said, are what make the blues "really good." Not the truth of personal experience but the truth of shared experience expressed in the shared discourse of singer and audience.

Evans wrote that the "main aesthetic criterion then for early folk blues was truth. But it was a truth based in universal human experience or at least one that was relevant to singer and audience" (1973, p. 15). The same can be said for race record blues, wherein the formula expressed this truth. Short's idea of "great harmony" was expanded by Baker: "Rather than a rigidly personalized form, the blues offer a phylogenetic recapitulation—of a nonlinear, freely associative, nonsequential meditation—of species experience" (1984, p. 5).

The "meditation" shared by singer and audience was aesthetically rich. Through repetition and difference, through formula and nonformula, through truth and harmony, the blues replayed and played with the fundamental concerns of African American society. "The blues is like a discourse that comprises the 'already said' of Afro-America" (Baker, 1984, p. 206).

Singers and Their Songs

Singers, dates, songs, and matrix numbers are as identified in Dixon, Godrich, and Rye (1997).

Akers, Garfield
1929a Cottonfield Blues—Part 1 (M-201-)
1929b Cottonfield Blues—Part 2 (M-202-)
1930a Dough Roller Blues (MEM-776-)
1930b Jumpin' and Shoutin' Blues (MEM-777-A)

Alexander, Texas
1927a Section Gang Blues (81224-B)
1927b Levee Camp Moan Blues (81225-B)
1928a No More Woman Blues (400446-A)
1928b Work Ox Blues (401330-A)
1928c I Am Calling Blues (401349-A)
1929 Ninety-Eight Degree Blues (402640-A)
1930 Seen Better Days (404112-B)
1934 Easy Rider Blues (FW-1138)

Amos, Blind Joe
1927 C & O Blues (C-1009/10)

Anderson, C. J.
1930 Thirty-Eight and Plus (16266-B)

Anderson, Jelly Roll
1927 Free Woman Blues (12718-B)

Arnold, Kokomo
1930 Rainy Night Blues (59938-2)
1934 Milk Cow Blues (C-9428-B)
1935a Sissy Man Blues (C-9654-A)
1935b Back Door Blues (C-9656-A)
1935c Slop Jar Blues (C-9776-A)
1935d Black Annie (C-9777-A)
1935e Southern Railroad Blues (C-9921-A)
1935f Let Your Money Talk (C-9924-)
1935g Policy Wheel Blues (90158-A)
1935h Stop Look and Listen (90201-A)
1936 Mister Charlie (90958-A)
1937a Wild Water Blues (91134-A)
1937b Laugh and Grin Blues (91135-A)
1937c Buddie Brown Blues (91299-A)
1937d Rocky Road Blues (91300-A)
1937e Head Cuttin' Blues (91331-A)
1937f Broke Man Blues (91332-A)
1938a Tired of Runnin' from Door to Door (67346-A)
1938b Midnight Blues (63750-A)
1938c Bad Luck Blues (63753-A)

Bailey, Kid
1929 Rowdy Blues (M-211)

Baker, Willie
1929a Mama, Don't Rush Me Blues (14666)
1929b No No Blues (14667)
1929c Weak-Minded Blues (14668)
1929d Bad Luck Moan (14892)
1929e Weak-Minded Blues (14896)
1929f Sweet Patunia Blues (14897)

Barner, Wiley
1927 If You Want a Good Woman—Get One Long and Tall (GEX-804-A)

Batts, Will
1933 Highway No. 61 Blues (13729-1)

Beaman, Lottie
1928 Goin' Away Blues (14163-A)
1929 Rollin' Log Blues (KC-605-)

Bell, Ed
1927a Mamlish Blues (4816-3)
1927b Mean Conductor Blues (4820-1)
1929a Shouting Baby Blues (488-A)
1929b From Now On (149357-2)
1930a One More Time (150305-1)
1930b Carry It Right Back Home (151037-2)

Bird, Billy
1928 Mill Man Blues (147323-2)

Black, Lewis
1927a Rock Island Blues (145361-3)
1927b Gravel Camp Blues (145366-2)
1927c Corn Liquor Blues (145367-2)

Black Boy Shine
1936 Sugarland Blues (SA-2551-1)

Blackwell, Francis Scrapper
1928a Kokomo Blues (IND-624-)
1928b Penal Farm Blues (IND-625-)
1931a Rambling Blues (18216)
1931b Blue Day Blues (18217-A)
1931c Down South Blues (18218)
1931d Back Door Blues (18221)

Blake, Blind
1926a Early Morning Blues (3057-1)
1926b Early Morning Blues (3057-2)
1926c Blake's Worried Blues (3060-2)
1926d Tampa Bound (3062-2)
1927a One Time Blues (4363-2)
1927b Bad Feeling Blues (4443-1)

1927c Hey Hey Daddy Blues (20801-1)
1927d Brownskin Mama Blues (20106-2)
1927e You Gonna Quit Me Blues (20110-1)
1928 Doggin' Me Mama Blues (20517-3)
1929a Too Tight Blues—No. 2 (15460)
1929b Police Dog Blues (15463)
1929c Georgia Bound (15466)
1930 Righteous Blues (L-648-1)
1932 Depression's Gone from Me Blues (L-1476-2)

Blind Percy
1927 Fourteenth Street Blues (20180-2)

Bogan, Lucille
1927a Levee Blues (4324-1)
1927b Jim Tampa Blues (4672-2)
1929 Pot Hound Blues (C-3462-)
1930a Alley Boogie (C-5563-A)
1930b Black Angel Blues (C-6847-A)
1930c Tricks Ain't Working No More (C-6848-A)
1933 Baking Powder Blues (13569-1)
1934a My Man Is Boogan Me (15487-2)
1934b I Hate That Train Called the M. and O. (15491-1)
1934c Sweet Man, Sweet Man (15506-2)
1934d Down in Boogie Alley (15508-2)
1935a Barbeque Bess (16984-1)
1935b Stew Meat Blues (17013-1)

Bolling, Pillie
1930a I Don't Like That (150301-1)
1930b She's Got a Nice Line (150302-1)

Boyd, Georgia
1933 Never Mind Blues (76835-1)

Bracey, Ishman
1928a Leavin' Town Blues (45458-2)
1928b My Brown Mamma Blues (45459-2)
1928c Trouble-Hearted Blues (45460-1)
1928d Trouble-Hearted Blues (45460-2)
1928e The Four Day Blues (45461-2)

1930a Woman Woman Blues (L-239-2)
1930b Suitcase Full of Blues (L-240-1)
1930c Bust Up Blues (L-241-2)
1930d Pay Me No Mind (L-242-2)

Bracey, Mississippi
1930 I'll Overcome Someday (404767-B)

Bradley, Tommie
1931a Please Don't Act That Way (17884)
1931b Four Day Blues (17886-A)
1932 Window Pane Blues (18326)

Broonzy, Big Bill
1928 Starvation Blues (20923-2)
1930a Grandma's Farm (9600-1)
1930b Skoodle Do Do (9601-2)
1930c Skoodle Do Do (16573)
1930d The Banker's Blues (17281)
1932a Mr. Conductor Man (18392)
1932b Bull Cow Blues (11610-2)
1932c How You Want It Done? (11611-2)
1935a C and A Blues (C-1020-B)
1935b Keep Your Hands Off Her (96230-1)
1935c Good Liquor Gonna Carry Me Down (96232-1)

Brown, Hi Henry
1932 Skin Man (11509-A)

Brown, Richard Rabbit
1927 James Alley Blues (38000-1)

Bryant, Laura
1929 Dentist Chair Blues—Part 2 (323-A)

Burse, Charlie
1932 Tappin' That Thing (18648)
1934 Boodie Bum Bum (C-792-1)

Byrd, John
1930a Billy Goat Blues (L-289-2)

Calicott, Joe
1930 Traveling Mama Blues (MEM-779-)

Campbell, Charlie
1937 Goin' Away Blues (B-32-2)

Campbell, Gene
1930 Wandering Blues (C-5701-A)

Cannon, Gus
1928 Heart Breakin' Blues (47001-2)

Carr, Leroy
1929 Gettin' All Wet (C-4034-)
1932a I Keep the Blues (11497-A)
1932b Midnight Hour Blues (11499-A)
1934a Hold Them Puppies (SL-6-3)
1934b Take a Walk around the Corner (15604-2)
1934c My Woman's Gone Wrong (15626-1)
1934d Southbound Blues (15627-2)
1934e Barrel House Woman (15628-2)
1934f Bo Bo Stomp (15649-1)
1934g You Left Me Crying (16418-2)
1934h Eleven Twenty-Nine Blues (16429-1)
1934i You've Got Me Grieving (16430-2)
1934j Tight Time Blues (16433-1)
1934k Shinin' Pistol (16438-)

Chatman, Bo
1931 The Law Gonna Step on You (404935-A)
1934 Howlin' Tom Cat Blues (82630-1)
1935 Let Me Roll Your Lemon (87624-1)
1936 Rolling Blues (99237-1)
1938a Some Day (027877-1)
1938b Country Fool (027879-1)
1940 Honey (047657-1)

Chatman, Lonnie
1932a It's a Pain to Me (L-1545-2)
1932b The New Sittin' on Top of the World (L-1556-2)
1932c Please Baby (L-1562-2)

Chatman, Peter
1940 I See My Great Mistake (053595-1)
1941 You Gonna Worry Too (070435-1)

Clark, Lonnie
1929 Broke Down Engine (15660)

Clayton, Jennie
1927 I Packed My Suitcase, Started to the Train (40312-1)

Cole, Kid
1928a Hard Hearted Mama Blues (C-1997-)
1928b Niagara Falls Blues (C-1998-)

Coleman, Bob
1929 Sing Song Blues (15167)

Coleman, Jaybird
1927a Man Trouble Blues (GEX-771)
1927b Mistreatin' Mama (GEX-801-A)
1930 Man Trouble Blues (150631-1)

Coleman, Lonnie
1929 Old Rock Island Blues (148258-2)

Collins, Chasey
1935 Walking Blues (96248-1)

Collins, Sam
1927a The Jail House Blues (12736)
1927b Devil in the Lion's Den (12737-A)
1927c Loving Lady Blues (12739)
1927d Riverside Blues (12740)
1927e Hesitation Blues (13033)
1927f Midnight Special Blues (13035)
1931a New Salty Dog (10837-1)
1931b Slow Mama Slow (10839-2)
1931c I'm Sitting on Top of the World (10842-2)
1931d My Road Is Rough and Rocky (10843?)

Cooksey, Robert
1927 Dollar Blues (E-22051/52/53)

Covington, Blind (Bogus) Ben
1928 It's a Fight Like That (C-4630-)

Cox, Ida
1923 Ida Cox's Lawdy, Lawdy Blues (1488-3 or 4)
1924 Wild Women Don't Have the Blues (1842-4)
1925 Rambling Blues (2294-1 or 2)

Crawford, Rosetta
1939 My Man Jumped Salty on Me (64972-A)

Crudup, Arthur
1941 If I Get Lucky (064876-1)

Daddy Stovepipe
1924 Sundown Blues (11861-A)

Darby, Blind
1929 Lawdy Lawdy Worried Blues (15566)
1931a Deceiving Blues (67583-1)
1931b Built Right on the Ground (67584-1)

Davis, Carl
1935 Elm Street Woman Blues (DAL-103-2)

Davis, Walter
1931 Howling Wind Blues (67579-1)
1935a Travelin' This Lonesome Road (85480-1)
1935b Sad and Lonesome Blues (85481-1)
1935c I Can Tell by the Way You Smell (91433-1)
1935d Ashes in My Whiskey (96237-1)
1936 Jacksonville—Part 2 (100338-1)
1940a Can't See Your Face (049320-1)
1940b Please Don't Mistreat Me (049323-1)
1940c Why Shouldn't I Be Blue (049325-1)
1941 Don't You Want to Go (070448-1)

Day, Bill
1929 Goin' Back to My Baby (149512-1)

Day, Will
1928a Central Avenue Blues (146186-2)
1928b Sunrise Blues (146191-2)

Dean, Joe
1930 I'm So Glad I'm Twenty-One Years Old Today (C-5991-)

Delaney, Mattie
1930a Down the Big Road Blues (MEM-785-)
1930b Tallahatchie Blues (MEM-786-)

Dickson, Pearl
1927 Little Rock Blues (145371-2)

Dickson, Tom
1928a Death Bell Blues (400355-B)
1928b Happy Blues (400359-B)
1928c Labor Blues (400360-A)

Dorsey, Thomas A.
1930a Maybe It's the Blues (16222)
1930b Where Did You Stay Last Night? (17277-A)
1930c Been Mistreated Blues (17290)
1931 Come on In (L-719-2)
1932 If You Want Me to Love You (11242-A)

Easton, Amos
1932 I'm Waitin' on You (11503-A)

Edwards, Frank
1941 Terraplane Blues (C-3811-1)

Edwards, Joe
1924 Construction Gang (72817-B)

Edwards, Susie
1924 Construction Gang (72817-B)

Edwards, Teddy
1934 Louise (80608-1)

Estes, John
1929a The Girl I Love, She Got Long Curly Hair (55581-1)
1929b Black Mattie Blues (56335-1)
1930a Watcha Doin'? (59967-)
1930b Poor John Blues (59968-)
1930c My Black Gal Blues (62548-2)
1935a Down South Blues (90094-A)
1935b Who's Been Tellin' You Buddy Brown Blues (90097-A)
1935c Drop Down Mama (90176-A)
1935d Vernita Blues (62463-A)
1935e I Ain't Gonna Be Worried No More (62464-A)
1935f Floating Bridge (62465-A)
1935g Need More Blues (62466-A)
1935h Airplane Blues (62482-A)
1938a Liquor Store Blues (63648-A)
1938b Easin' Back to Tennessee (63649-A)
1938c Fire Department Blues (63650-A)
1938d Clean Up at Home (63651-B)
1938e New Someday Blues (63652-A)
1940 Drop Down (93009-A)

Evans, Joe
1931 New Huntsville Jail (10651-2)

Florence, Nellie
1928 Midnight Weeping Blues (146175-2)

Fox, John D.
1927 The Worried Man Blues (GEX-1011-A)

Fuller, Blind Boy
1935 I'm a Rattlesnakin' Daddy (17862-2)
1938 Pistol Snapper Blues (22674-1)
1940a Step It Up and Go (26592-A)
1940b Somebody's Been Talkin' (26599-A)
1940c Good Feeling Blues (26616-A)
1940d Crooked Woman Blues (26619-A)
1940e Thousand Women Blues (WC-3142-A)

Gibson, Clifford
1929a Beat You Doing It (482-A)
1929b Stop Your Rambling (486-A)

1929c Don't Put That Thing on Me (57174-2)
1929d Old Time Rider (57176-2)
1929e Keep Your Windows Pinned (57757)
1929f Jive Me Blues (57758-1)

Gillum, Bill Jazz
1938 She Won't Treat Me Kind (030826-)
1939 Got to Reap What You Sow (034810-1)
1940 Key to the Highway (044972-1)
1941a I Got Somebody Else (064739-1)
1941b It's All Over Now (070440-1)
1941c You Drink Too Much Whiskey (070445-1)
1942 Woke Up Cold in Hand (074651-1)

Glaze, Ruby
1932 Lonesome Day Blues (71604-1)

Glover, Mae
1929a Pig Meat Mama (15933)
1929b I Ain't Giving Nobody None (15395-A)

Grant, Bobby
1927a Nappy Head Blues (20204-3)
1927b Lonesome Atlanta Blues (20212-2)

Green, Lil
1941a Knockin' Myself Out (059152-1)
1941b How Can I Go On? (064135-1)
1941c If I Didn't Love You (064728-1)
1942 I'm Wasting My Time on You (070803-1)

Hannah, George
1930 Freakish Man Blues (L-562-1)

Hardin, Lane
1935 California Desert Blues (91450-1)

Harris, Otis
1928 Waking Blues (147608-1)

Harris, William
1927 I'm Leavin' Town (GEX-743-B)
1928 Bull Frog Blues (14318)

Harris, Willie
1930 Lonesome Midnight Blues (C-5551-)

Harrison, Smoky
1929 Hop Head Blues (L-79-1)

Hart, Hattie
1929 Memphis Yo Yo Blues (56345-2)
1934 Coldest Stuff in Town (15952-1)

Hawkins, Walter Buddy Boy
1927a Snatch It Back Blues (4420-2)
1927b Awful Fix Blues (20034-1)
1929a How Come Mama Blues (15213)
1929b Voice Throwin' Blues (15219)

Henderson, Bertha
1928a Lead Hearted Blues (20560-2)
1928b Let Your Love Come Down (20562-2)

Henderson, Katherine
1928a St. Louis Blues (236-A)
1928b Have You Ever Felt That Way? (257-A)

Henry, Hound Head
1928 Low Down Hound Blues (C-2451-)

Henry, Lena
1924 Low Down Despondent Blues (13596)

Hicks, Robert
1927a Barbecue Blues (143757-1)
1927b Cloudy Sky Blues (143758-2)
1927c Easy Rider Don't Deny My Name (144284-3)
1927d Motherless Chile Blues (145134-1)
1927e Crooked Woman Blues (145198-1)
1928a Blind Pig Blues (146050-1)
1928b Hurry and Bring It Back Home (146055-2)

1928c She's Gone Blues (147306-1)
1929a Freeze to Me Mama (149345-2)
1929b Me and My Whiskey (149346-2)
1929c Unnamed Title (149347-1)
1930 Atlanta Moan (151054-2)

Hill, Bertha Chippie
1925a Low Land Blues (9456-A)
1925b Kid Man Blues (9457-A)

Hill, King Solomon
1932a Whoopee Blues (L-1252-1)
1932b Whoopee Blues (L-1252-2)
1932c Down on My Bended Knee (L-1253-2)
1932d Tell Me Baby (L-1258-2)

Hill, Sammy
1929a Cryin' for the Blues (55319-1)
1929b Needin' My Woman Blues (55320-2)

Hite, Mattie
1923 Graveyard Dream Blues (70413)

Hogg, Andrew
1937 Family Trouble Blues (61856-A)

Hollins, Tony
1941 Stamp Blues (C-3843-1)

House, Son
1930a My Black Mama—Part 2 (L-409-2)
1930b Preachin' the Blues—Part 1 (L-410-1)
1930c Preachin' the Blues—Part 2 (L-411-1)
1930d Dry Spell Blues—Part 1 (L-425-4)
1930e Dry Spell Blues—Part 2 (L-426-2)

Howell, Peg Leg
1926a Coal Man Blues (143116-2)
1926b Tishamingo Blues (143117-1)
1927 Doin' Wrong (145184-2)
1929 Ball and Chain Blues (148270-2)

Hull, Papa Harvey
1927a Gang of Brownskin Women (12689)
1927b Mama You Don't Know How

Hurt, Mississippi John
1928a Ain't No Tellin' (401471-A)
1928b Big Leg Blues (401474-B)
1928c Got the Blues Can't Be Satisfied (401484-B)

Jackson, Bo Weavil
1926a You Can't Keep No Brown (2678-2)
1926b Poor Boy Blues (E-3872/73W)
1926c Jefferson County Blues (E-3874/75W)

Jackson, Jim
1930 Hesitation Blues (MEM-804-)

Jackson, Papa Charlie
1925a The Faking Blues (2121-1 or 2)
1925b I'm Alabama Bound (2144-2)
1925c Take Me Back Blues (2208-2)
1925d Maxwell Street Blues (2288-2)
1925e Texas Blues (11031-1)
1926a Up the Way Bound (2547-1)
1926b Your Baby Ain't Sweet Like Mine (2613-4)
1927a Fat Mouth Blues (2769-3)
1927b She Belongs to Me Blues (4243-1)
1927c Coal Man Blues (4244-2)
1927d Skoodle Um Skoo (4670-1)

James, Jesse
1936a Sweet Patuni (90760-A)
1936b Southern Casey Jones (90761-A)

James, Skip
1931a Devil Got My Woman (L-746-1)
1931b Cypress Grove Blues (L-747-2)
1931c Cherry Ball Blues (L-748-2)
1931d Hard Time Killin' Floor Blues (L-752-2)
1931e Special Rider Blues (L-760-2)
1931f Little Cow and Calf Is Gonna Die Blues (L-763-1)
1931g 22-20 Blues (L-765-1)

1931h If You Haven't Got Any Hay Get on Down the Road
(L-766-1)

Jaxon, Frankie Half Pint
1929 It's Heated (C-3585-)

Jefferson, Blind Lemon
1926a Got the Blues (2471-1)
1926b Booster Blues (2474-1)
1926c Dry Southern Blues (2475-1)
1926d Black Horse Blues (2543-1)
1926e Corinna Blues (2544-2)
1926f Old Rounders Blues (2018-?)
1926g Stocking Feet Blues (3066-1)
1926h That Black Snake Moan (3067-2)
1926i Broke and Hungry (3076-1 or 2)
1926j Shuckin' Sugar (3077-2)
1926k Rabbit Foot Blues (3089-1)
1927a Black Snake Blues (80523-B)
1927b Match Box Blues (80524-B)
1927c Easy Rider Blues (4423-2)
1927d Match Box Blues (4424-2)
1927e Match Box Blues (4446-4)
1927f Right of Way Blues (4515-2)
1927g Black Snake Dream Blues (4577-2)
1927h Struck Sorrow Blues (20039-2)
1927i Rambler Blues (20040-2)
1927j Chinch Bug Blues (20064-1)
1927k Deceitful Brownskin Woman (20065-2)
1928a Blind Lemon's Penitentiary Blues (20363-2)
1928b Lemon's Worried Blues (20375-3)
1928c Balky Mule Blues (20381-3)
1928d Prison Cell Blues (20388-2)
1928e Competition Bed Blues (20749-2)
1928f How Long How Long (20788-1)
1929a Eagle Eyed Mama (21095-3)
1929b That Black Snake Moan—No. 2 (21202-1)
1929c Bed Springs Blues (15664)
1929d Mosquito Moan (15666)
1929e Long Distance Moan (15670-A)

Johnson, Alec
1928a Sundown Blues (147381-1)
1928b Next Week Sometime (147382-2)

Johnson, Edith North
1929a Good Chib Blues (15559)
1929b Honeydripper Blues (15561)

Johnson, Elizabeth
1928 Sobbin' Woman Blues (401280-B or C)

Johnson, James Stump
1932 Barrel of Whiskey Blues (70680-1)

Johnson, Lil
1929 You'll Never Miss Your Jelly Till Your Jelly Roller's Gone
(C-3356-)

Johnson, Lonnie
1925 Mr. Johnson's Blues (9435-A)
1927a Sweet Woman You Can't Go Wrong (81189-B)
1927b Low Land Moan (82043-A)
1928 New Black Snake Blues—Part 1 (401222-A)
1929a Sundown Blues (402438-A)
1929b Baby Please Don't Leave Me No More (402441-A)
1937a Flood Water Blues (91341-A)
1937b It Ain't What You Usta Be (91342-A)
1938a Blue Ghost Blues (63523-A)
1938b South Bound Backwater (63524-A)
1941 Crowin' Rooster Blues (059205-1)

Johnson, Louise
1930a All Night Long Blues (L-398-1)
1930b Long Way from Home (L-399-2)
1930c By the Moon and Stars (L-420-2)

Johnson, Robert
1936a Kind Hearted Woman Blues (SA-2580-1)
1936b I Believe I'll Dust My Broom (SA-2581-1)
1936c Come on in My Kitchen (SA-2585-1)
1936d 32-20 Blues (SA-2616-1)

1936e Dead Shrimp Blues (SA-2628-2)
1936f Walkin' Blues (SA-2630-1)
1936g Preachin' Blues (SA-2632-1)
1936h Preachin' Blues (SA-2632-2)
1936i If I Had Possession over Judgement Day (SA-2633-1)
1937a Stones in My Passway (DAL-377-2)
1937b I'm a Steady Rollin' Man (DAL-378-1)
1937c Hell Hound on My Trail (DAL-394-2)
1937d Malted Milk (DAL-396-1)

Johnson, Tommy
1928a Cool Drink of Water Blues (41836-2)
1928b Big Road Blues (41837-2)
1928c Maggie Campbell Blues (41839-2)
1928d Canned Heat Blues (45462-2)
1928e Lonesome Home Blues (45463-1)
1928f Lonesome Home Blues (45463-2)
1928g Big Fat Mama Blues (45465-1)
1929a Lonesome Home Blues (L-230-2)
1929b Black Mare Blues (L-245-2)

Jones, Anna
1923 Trixie Blues (1473-1)

Jones, Jake
1929 Southern Sea Blues (DAL-474-)

Jones, Little Hat
1929a Two String Blues (402648-A)
1929b Corpus Blues (402701-B)
1930a Bye Bye Baby Blues (404198-B)
1930b Cross the Water Blues (404199-B)
1930c Cherry Street Blues (404300-A)

Jones, Maggie
1924a Jealous Mamma Blues (140105-1)
1924b If I Lose, Let Me Lose (140187-1)
1924c Good Time Flat Blues (140191-2)
1924d You May Go, but You'll Come Back Some Day (140192-2)
1925a North Bound Blues (140534-2)
1925b Dallas Blues (140952-3)
1926 The Man I Love Is Oh So Good (142165-3)

Jones, Samuel
1927 Bed Slats (80760-B)

Jordan, Charley
1930a Stack o' Dollars Blues (C-5834-)
1930b Big Four Blues (C-5837-)
1930c Hunkie Tunkie Blues (C-5841-)
1931 You Run and Tell Your Daddy (VO-143-)
1936a I Couldn't Stay Here (18980-)
1936b Got Your Water On (18982-2)

Jordan, Luke
1927a Church Bell Blues (39819-1)
1927b Church Bell Blues (39819-2)
1929 My Gal's Done Quit Me (57703-1)

Kelly, Eddie
1937 Poole County Blues (013023-1)

Kelly, Jack
1933a Highway No. 61 Blues (13712-1)
1933b Believe I'll Go Back Home (13715-2)
1933c Ko-Ko-Mo Blues (13721-2)
1939 Betty Sue Blues (MEM-143-1)

Kid Stormy Weather
1935 Short Hair Blues (JAX-179-2)

King David
1930 Rising Sun Blues (404665-A)

Kyle, Charlie
1928 Kyle's Worried Blues (45468-2)

Lasky, Louie
1935 Teasin' Brown Blues (C-945-B)

Leadbetter, Huddie
1935a Roberta—Part 2 (16684-1)
1935b C.C. Rider (16686-)
1935c Alberta (16692-)
1935d Baby, Don't You Love Me No More? (16693-)

1935e Death Letter Blues—Part 1 (16695-1)
1935f Red River Blues (16704-)
1935g Mr. Tom Hughes' Town (16808-)
1935h Shorty George (16814-2)

Lee, Bertha
1934 Mind Reader Blues (14636-1)

Leecan, Bobby
1927 Macon Georgia Cut-Out

Lewis, Furry
1927a Mr. Furry's Blues (C-750/1)
1927b Sweet Papa Moan (C-752/3)
1927c Good Looking Girl Blues (C-1246/47)
1927d Falling Down Blues (C-1250/51)
1928a Furry's Blues (45424-1)
1928b I Will Turn Your Money Green (45425-2)
1928c Mistreatin' Mama (45428-2)
1928d Dry Land Blues (45429-1)
1929a Black Gypsy Blues (M-185-)
1929b Creeper's Blues (M-186-)

Lewis, Noah
1929 Pretty Mama Blues (56342-2)
1930a Ticket Agent Blues (64736-2)
1930b Bad Luck's My Buddy (64739-2)

Lincoln, Charley
1927a Hard Luck Blues (145104-2)
1927b My Wife Drove Me from My Door (145106-1)
1927c Country Breakdown (145107-1)
1927d Chain Gang Trouble (145108-2)

Lockwood, Robert
1941a Little Boy Blue (064640-)
1941b Take a Little Walk with Me (064641-)

Lofton, Cripple Clarence
1935 Brown Skin Girls (C-1074-A)
1936–38 I Don't Know

Lofton, Willie
1934 My Mean Baby Blues (C-9387-A)
1935 Dark Road Blues (96257-1)

Lucas, Jane
1930 Double Trouble Blues (17285)

MacFarland, Barrel House Buck
1934 I Got to Go Blues (C-9321-)

Martin, Carl
1935a Badly Mistreated Man (C-881-2)
1935b Let's Have a New Deal (90294-A)

Martin, Sara
1923 Blind Man Blues (71711-B)
1928 Death Sting Me Blues (278-A)

Mason, Moses
1928 Molly Man (20283-2)

McClennan, Tommy
1939 Brown Skin Girl (044243-1)
1940a New Highway No. 51 (044986-)
1940b My Little Girl (044988-)
1940c My Baby's Doggin' Me (044991-)
1940d Love with a Feeling (053740-1)
1940e Drop Down Mama (053741-1)
1940f Black Minnie (053742-1)
1940g Elsie Blues (053743-)
1941a Cross Cut Saw Blues (064885-)
1941b Deep Blue Sea Blues (064889-)
1941c I'm a Guitar King (064890-)
1942a Mozelle Blues (074100-)
1942b Bluebird Blues (074107-)

McCoy, Charlie
1929 Last Time Blues (M-176)
1930 That Lonesome Train Took My Baby Away (404726-A)

McCoy, Joe
1929a Goin' Back to Texas (148709-2)
1929b When the Levee Breaks (148711-1)
1930a I'm Going Back Home (59992-)
1930b I'm Wild about My Stuff (C-5820-A)
1930c My Mary Blues (C-5830-)
1930d Cherry Ball Blues (C-5864-A)
1930e Pile Drivin' Blues (C-6012-)
1931a Beat It Right (C-7246-)
1931b My Wash Woman's Gone (VO-110-A)
1934a Someday I'll Be in the Clay (C-9290)
1934b Evil Devil Woman Blues (C-9299-A)
1934c Going Back Home (C-9300-A)
1934d You Got to Move—Part 1 (C-9380-)
1935 Something Gonna Happen to You (96262-)
1936a Southern Blues (90913-A)
1936b We Gonna Pitch a Boogie Woogie (90982-A)

McCoy, Robert Lee
1940 Friar's Point Blues (93037-A)

McCoy, William
1928 Central Tracks Blues (147611-1)

McPhail, Black Bottom
1932a My Dream Blues (11513-A)
1932b Whiskey Man Blues (11514-A)

McTell, Blind Willie
1927a Writin' Paper Blues (40308-1)
1927b Mama, 'Tain't Long Fo' Day (40310-1)
1928 Statesboro Blues (47187-3)
1929a Atlanta Strut (149299-2)
1929b Travelin' Blues (149300-1)
1929c Come on around to My House (149302-2)
1929d Kind Mama (149319-2)
1929e Drive Away Blues (56599-1)
1930 Talking to Myself (150257-2)
1931a Southern Can Is Mine (151904-1)
1931b Broke Down Engine Blues (151905-1)
1931c Stomp Down Rider (405002-1)
1933a It's a Good Little Thing (14010-1)

1933b Death Cell Blues (14049-1)
1933c B and O Blues—No. 2 (14066-1)
1933d Weary Hearted Blues (14067-1)
1933e Southern Can Mama (14069-2)
1933f Runnin' Me Crazy (14070-1)
1935a Bell Street Blues (C-9946-A)
1935b Ticket Agent Blues (C-9954-A)
1935c Cold Winter Day (C-9956-A)
1935d Your Time to Worry (C-9957-A)

Memphis Minnie
1929a Goin' Back to Texas (148709-2)
1929b 'Frisco Town (148710-2)
1930a Bumble Bee Blues (59993-2)
1930b Meningitis Blues (59994-)
1930c Memphis Minnie-Jitis Blues (C-5822-)
1930d I'm Talking about You—No. 2 (C-6010-A)
1930e I Called You This Morning (C-6013-)
1930f Grandpa and Grandma Blues (C-6082-)
1930g Garage Fire Blues (C-6083-)
1931a Crazy Cryin' Blues (VO-112-A)
1931b Soo Cow Soo (VO-151-A)
1934a Stinging Snake Blues (CP-1069-1)
1934b Drunken Barrelhouse Blues (CP-1070-1)
1935 Reachin' Pete (90018-)
1936a Black Cat Blues (C-1386-1)
1936b It's Hard to Be Mistreated (C-1671-1)

Miller, Lillian
1928 Dead Drunk Blues (13718-A)

Mississippi Moaner
1935 Mississippi Moan (JAX-201-1)

Montgomery, Eurreal Little Brother
1935a Pleading Blues (94419-1)
1935b Mama You Don't Mean Me No Good (94421-1)
1936a The First Time I Met You (02642-1)
1936b Leaving Town Blues (02650-1)

Moore, Alice
1929a Black and Evil Blues (15447)
1929b My Man Blues (15449-A)
1929c Broadway St. Woman Blues (15452)
1930a Lonesome Dream Blues (L-170-2)
1930b Kid Man Blues (L-171-2)

Moore, Kid Prince
1936 Honey Dripping Papa (18999-2)

Moore, Rosie Mae
1928a Staggering Blues (41830-2)
1928b School Girl Blues (41832-2)
1928c Mad Dog Blues (NOR-760)

Moore, Whistlin' Alex
1929 It Wouldn't Be So Hard (149562-2)

Moore, William
1928a One Way Gal (20309-1)
1928b Midnight Blues (20312-2)

Moss, Buddy
1933a Daddy Don't Care (12908-1)
1933b Hard Road Blues (12946-1)

Nelson, Blue Coat Tom
1928 Blue Coat Blues (400258-B)

Newbern, Hambone Willie
1929a Hambone Willie's Dreamy-Eyed Woman's Blues (402305-B)
1929b Roll and Tumble Blues (402306-B)

Nickerson, Charlie Bozo
1930a Going Back to Memphis (62583-)
1930b You May Leave but This Will Bring You Back (64733-)

Noble, George
1935 The Seminole Blues (C-897-2)

Oden, Jimmy
1941 Going Down Slow (070409-1)

Owens, Big Boy George
1926 Kentucky Blues (12571)

Owens, Marshall
1932a Texas Blues (L-1238-2)
1932b Try Me One More Time (L-1240-1)

Palmer, Sylvester
1929 Broke Man Blues (403305-B)

Patton, Charley
1929a Screamin' and Hollerin' Blues (15214)
1929b Down the Dirt Road Blues (15215)
1929c Pony Blues (15216)
1929d It Won't Be Long (15220)
1929e Tom Rushen Blues (15222-A)
1929f Going to Move to Alabama (L-37-1)
1929g Hammer Blues (L-47-2)
1929h When Your Way Gets Dark (L-49-1)
1929i Heart Like Railroad Steel (L-50-1)
1930a Dry Well Blues (L-429-2)
1930b Moon Going Down (L-432-1)
1934a Jersey Bull Blues (14723-)
1934b High Sheriff Blues (14725-2)
1934c Love My Stuff (14746-)
1934d Revenue Man Blues (14747-)
1934e Poor Me (14757-1)

Perkins, Gertrude
1927 No Easy Rider Blues (145340-1)

Petties, Arthur
1928 Two Time Blues (41906-2)
1930 Good Boy Blues (C-5921-B)

Petway, Robert
1941 Catfish Blues (059476-1)
1942a My Baby Left Me (074114-1)
1942b Cotton Pickin' Blues (074115-1)

Pickett, Charlie
1937 Crazy 'bout My Black Gal (62467-A)

Poor Jab
1928 Whitewash Station Blues (47036-2)

Pope, Jenny
1929 Whiskey Drinkin' Blues (M-193-)
1930 Bull Frog Blues (MEM-757-A)

Pullum, Joe
1934 Black Gal What Makes Your Head So Hard?—No. 2 (82786-?)

Rachel, James Yank
1929 Little Sarah (55597-2)
1930 Sweet Mama (62550)
1934 Gravel Road Woman (14793-2)

Rainey, Gertrude Ma
1923a Bad Luck Blues (1596-2)
1923b Bo-Weavil Blues (1597-)
1923c Barrel House Blues (1598-2)
1923d Those All Night Long Blues (1599-)
1923e Moonshine Blues (1608-)
1923f Walking Blues (1613-2)
1924a Honey Where You Been So Long (1701-2)
1924b Those Dogs of Mine (1703-1)
1925a Rough and Tumble Blues (2210-2)
1925b Four Day Honory Scat (2213-1)
1926a Bessemer Bound Blues (2373-2)
1926b Oh My Babe Blues (2374-1)
1926c Trust No Man (2631-1)

Ramey, Ben
1929 Tired of Your Driving Me (56344)

Reed, Willie
1928a Dreaming Blues (147600-2)
1928b Texas Blues (147601-1)

Richardson, Mooch
1928a "Mooch" Richardson's Low Down Barrel House Blues—Part
    1 (400215-A)
1928b Burying Ground Blues (400375-A)

Robinson, Bob
1928 Selling That Stuff (21035-3)

Roland, Walter
1933 T Model Blues (13552-1)
1934 Every Morning Blues (15521-2)

Rupert, Ollie
1927a I Raised My Window and Looked at the Risin' Sun (37963-2)
1927b Ain't Goin' to Be Your Low Down Dog (37964-2)

Schaffer, Ed
1930 Fence Breakin' Blues (59965-2)

Shade, Will
1927a Sometimes I Think I Love You (38657-1)
1927b I Packed My Suitcase, Started to the Train (40312-1)
1927c Kansas City Blues (40315-1)
1928a Snitchin' Gambler Blues (41817-2)
1928b She Stays Out All Night Long (41891-1)
1929a Feed Your Friend with a Long Handled Spoon (55598-1)
1929b I Can Beat You Plenty (55599-)
1929c Taking Your Place (56343)

Shaw, Allen
1934a I Couldn't Help It (15967-1)
1934b Moanin' the Blues (15978-1)

Short, Jaydee
1930a Telephone Arguin' Blues (L-456-1)
1930b Lonesome Swamp Rattlesnake (L-468-1)
1932a Snake Doctor Blues (11474-)
1932b Barefoot Blues (11475-)
1932c Grand Daddy Blues (11479-A)

Sims, Henry
1929 Tell Me Man Blues (L-65-1)

Smith, Bessie
1923a Down Hearted Blues (80863-5)
1923b Jail-House Blues (81226-2)
1924a Ticket Agent Ease Your Window Down (81670-2)

1924b Weeping Willow Blues (140062-2)
1925a Sobbin' Hearted Blues (140249-2)
1925b J.C. Holmes Blues (140629-2)
1926 Young Woman's Blues (142878-3)
1927a Back Water Blues (143491-1)
1927b Send Me to the 'Lectric Chair (143576-2)
1928 Empty Bed Blues—Part ? (14578?-?)
1929 St. Louis Blues—Part ? (NY-??-)
1933 I'm Down in the Dumps (153580-2)

Smith, Bessie Mae
1929 St. Louis Daddy (L-78-)
1930a Sugar Man Blues—Part 1 (C-6167-)
1930b Sugar Man Blues—Part 2 (C-6168-)

Smith, Clara
1923a Every Woman's Blues (81060-5)
1923b All Night Blues (81153-3)
1923c Don't Never Tell Nobody (81198-4)
1923d Uncle Sam Blues (81253-2)
1924a It Won't Be Long Now (81476-1)
1924b 31st Street Blues (81514-2)
1924c Deep Blue Sea Blues (81931-3)
1924d Texas Moaner Blues (81932-1)
1924e Freight Train Blues (140064-3)
1924f Death Letter Blues (140108-1)
1924g Prescription for the Blues (140109-1)
1924h He's Mine, All Mine (140182-1)
1925 Shipwrecked Blues (140491-1)

Smith, Ivy
1927 Third Alley Blues (4094-1)

Smith, J.T. Funny Paper
1930a Howling Wolf Blues—No. 2 (C-6405-A)
1930b Mama's Quittin' and Leavin'—Part 1 (C-7100-)
1930c Mama's Quittin' and Leavin'—Part 2 (C-7107-)
1931a Corn Whiskey Blues (VO-127-)
1931b Before Long (VO-170-A)

Smith, Trixie
1924 Sorrowful Blues (1780-2)

1925 Love Me Like You Used To (2365-)
1938 Freight Train Blues (63866-A)

Spand, Charlie
1929a Good Gal (15453)
1929b Back to the Woods Blues (15456)

Spaulding, Henry
1929a Cairo Blues (C-3449-)
1929b Biddle Street Blues (C-3450-)

Spivey, Victoria
1927 Arkansas Road Blues (80768-B)
1936 T.B.'s Got Me Blues (90790-A)

Spruell, Freddie
1926a Milk Cow Blues (9793-A)
1926b Muddy Water Blues (9908-A)
1935a 4A Highway (85782-)
1935b Your Good Man Is Gone (85784-)
1935c Let's Go Riding (85785-)
1935d Mr. Freddie's Kokomo Blues (85786-)

Stevens, Vol
1927a Beale Street Mess Around (40320-1)
1927b Vol Stevens Blues (40324-1)
1928a Coal Oil Blues (41888-2)
1928b Papa Long Blues (41889-2)
1930a Aunt Caroline Dyer Blues (62541-)
1930b Stonewall Blues (62542-)

Stokes, Frank
1927a Sweet to Mama (4773-1)
1927b Half Cup of Tea (4774-2)
1927c Last Go Round (4777-1)
1927d Mr. Crump Don't Like It (20045-1)
1927e Blues in D (20048-2)
1928a What's the Matter Blues (41826-1)
1928b Nehi Mama Blues (45421-2)
1928c Stomp That Thing (45426-2)
1929a Ain't Going to Do Like I Used to Do (21229-2)
1929b Hunting Blues (21234-1)
1929c Bunker Hill Blues (55574-1)

1929d Right Now Blues (55584-2)
1929e Frank Stoke's Dream (56305-2)
1929f Memphis Rounders Blues (56306-2)

Sykes, Roosevelt
1929a 44 Blues (402451-A)
1929b The Way I Feel Blues (402453-B)
1929c Skeet and Garret (403312-A)
1929d Lost All I Had Blues (403322-A)
1929e Poor Boy Blues (403323-A)
1930 We Can Sell That Thing (L-450-2)
1931a As True as I've Been to You (69403-1)
1931b Hard Luck Man Blues (69404-)

Tampa Red
1928 Through Train Blues (20544-2)
1929a The Duck Yas-Yas-Yas (C-3485-)
1929b What Is It That Tastes Like Gravy? (C-3594-)
1937 Seminole Blues (014333-)

Taylor, Charley
1930a Heavy Suitcase Blues (L-251-2)
1930b Louisiana Bound (L-252-2)

Temple, Johnnie
1935 The Evil Devil Blues (C-987-)
1936 Louise Louise Blues (90981-A)
1937a So Lonely and Blue (91247-A)
1937b New Louise Louise Blues (91248-A)

Thomas, Henry
1927a Cottonfield Blues
1927b Honey, Won't You Allow Me One More Chance? (C-1220)
1928a Texas Worried Blues (C-2002-)
1928b Don't Ease Me In

Thomas, Ramblin'
1928a So Lonesome (20334-2)
1928b Hard to Rule Woman Blues (20335-3)
1928c Lock and Key Blues (20336-3)
1928d Ramblin' Mind Blues (20339-2)
1928e No Job Blues (20343-2)

1928f Hard Dallas Blues (21018-2)
1928g Ramblin' Man (21019-4)
1928h Good Time Blues (21027-1)

Thompson, Ashley
1928 Minglewood Blues (41803-2)

Thompson, Edward
1929a Showers of Rain Blues (GEX-2411-A)
1929b Florida Bound (GEX-2412)
1929c Seven Sister Blues (GEX-2413)

Torey, George
1937a Married Woman Blues (B-64-2)
1937b Lonesome Man Blues (B-65-1)

Townsend, Henry
1929 Henry's Worry Blues (403300-A)

Townsend, Sam
1930 Lily Kimball Blues (150259-2)

Tucker, Bessie
1928a Bessie's Moan (45436-2)
1928b Penitentiary (45441-2)

Turner, Buck
1937a Black Ace (61790-A)
1937b Christmas Time Blues (61793-A)

Unknown artists
1926 String Band Blues
1928a Touch Me Light Mama (20590-2)
1928b Throw Me Down (20998-1)
1930a German Blues (404677-B)
1930b The Wild Cat Squawl (404680-A)
1930c Gettin' Ready for Trial (404682-C)
1930d Giving It Away (404683-A)

Vincson, Walter
1930a Your Good Man Caught the Train and Gone (404710-A)
1930b She Ain't No Good (404783-B)

1930c Ramrod Blues (404784-A)
1930d Stop and Listen Blues—No. 2 (404785-)
1931a Please Baby (405007-1)
1931b The World Is Going Wrong (405009-1)
1932a New Shake That Thing (L-1555-2)
1932b Don't Wake It Up (L-1560-1)

Virgial, Otto
1935a Little Girl in Rome (96240-1)
1935b Bad Notion Blues (96241-1)

Walker, Aaron T-Bone
1929 Trinity River Blues (149548-1)

Walker, Uncle Bud
1928a Look Here Mama Blues (402008-A)
1928b Stand Up Suitcase Blues (402009-B)

Wallace, Minnie
1935 The Cockeyed World (JAX-113-2)

Wallace, Sippie
1926 Special Delivery Blues (9547-A)
1927a Dead Drunk Blues (80837-A)
1927b Have You Ever Been Down? (80838-A)
1927c Lazy Man Blues (80839-B)
1927d The Flood Blues (80840-B)

Washboard Sam
1935 Jesse James Blues (C-1023-B)
1937a Back Door (07616-)
1937b We Gonna Move (07617-)
1940 I'm Goin' to St. Louis (049370-)
1941a I'm Not the Lad (064478-1)
1941b Gonna Hit the Highway (070377-1)
1941c You Stole My Love (070382-1)

Washboard Walter
1930 Narrow Face Blues (L-142-4)

Washington, Louis
1934a Tallahassee Women (14637-1)
1934b Black Snake Blues (14676-1)

Waters, Ethel
1921 Down Home Blues (P-115-1)
1923a You Can't Do What My Last Man Did (A)
1923b Ethel Sings 'Em (B)

Weaver, Curley
1928a Sweet Patunia (147304-2)
1928b No No Blues (147305-2)
1935 Fried Pie Blues (C-9943-A)

Weldon, Will
1927 Hitch Me to Your Buggy, and Drive Me Like a Mule (40323-2)
1936 Blues Everywhere I Go (100323)
1937 Worried about That Woman (C-2032-1)

Welsh, Nolan
1926a The Bridwell Blues (9727-A)
1926b St. Peter Blues (9728-A)

Wheatstraw, Peetie
1930a Mama's Advice (C-6487-A)
1930b Ain't It a Pity and a Shame (C-6488-A)
1930c Don't Hang My Clothes on No Barbed Wire Line (C-6489-A)
1931 C and A Blues (C-6891-A)
1934a All Night Long Blues (C-9315-A)
1934b Doin' the Best I Can (C-9443-)
1935 Cocktail Man Blues (90173-A)
1936a First and Last Blues (C-1257-2)
1936b Sweet Home Blues (C-1261-2)
1936c Good Woman Blues (C-1262-1)
1936d Working Man (60506-A)
1936e When I Get My Bonus (60511-A)
1936f The First Shall Be the Last and the Last Shall Be the First
(60523-A)
1936g Remember and Forget Blues (C-1351-2)
1936h Don't Take a Chance (C-1352-1)
1936i When a Man Gets Down (90961-A)
1937a Crazy with the Blues (91150-A)

1937b Peetie Wheatstraw Stomp (91152-A)
1937c Working on the Project (91164-A)
1938 Sugar Mama (91529-A)

White, Georgia
1938 The Blues Ain't Nothin' but … ??? (91545-A)

White, Joshua
1934 Stormy Weather—No. 1 (14903-1)

White, Washington
1937a Pinebluff Arkansas (C-1996-2)
1937b Shake 'Em on Down (C-1997-1)
1940a Strange Place Blues (WC-2978-A)
1940b When Can I Change My Clothes (WC-2979-A)
1940c Aberdeen Mississippi Blues (WC-2990-A)
1940d Special Stream Line (WC-2992-A)

Wiggins, James Boodle It
1928 Evil Woman Blues (20379-2)
1929a Forty-Four Blues (15768-A)
1929b Frisco Bound Blues (15769-A)
1930 Corrine Corrina Blues (L-103-2)

Wilber, Bill
1935 Greyhound Blues (90199-A)

Wiley, Geeshie
1931 Eagles on a Half (L-826-1)

Wilkins, Robert
1928a Jail House Blues (45499-)
1928b I Do Blues (47000-)
1929 Alabama Blues (M-190-)
1930 I'll Go with Her Blues (MEM-743-)
1935a Dirty Deal Blues (JAX-104-)
1935b New Stock Yard Blues (JAX-107-)

Williams, Big Joe
1935a Little Leg Woman (85487-1)
1935b Somebody's Been Borrowing That Stuff (85488-1)
1935c 49 Highway Blues (85490-)

1935d My Grey Pony (85491-)
1935e Stepfather Blues (85492-1)
1935f Wild Cow Blues (96246-1)
1937 Rootin' Ground Hog (07662-1)
1941a Crawlin' King Snake (053989-2)
1941b Peach Orchard Mama (053991-1)
1941c Highway 49 (070485-1)

Williams, Henry
1928 Lonesome Blues (146149-2)

Williams, Jabo
1932 Polock Blues (L-1406-)

Williams, Joe
1929a I Want It Awful Bad (M-195-)
1929b Mr. Devil Blues (M-196-)
1938 Peach Orchard Mama (020855-1)

Williamson, Sonny Boy
1937a Skinny Woman (07654-)
1937b Early in the Morning (016524-)
1937c Project Highway (016525-)
1938a Down South (020117-1)
1938b You Give an Account (020846-)
1938c You've Been Foolin' Round Town (020848-1)
1938d Deep Down in the Ground (020849-1)
1938e Number Five Blues (030848-1R)
1938f Susie-Q (030850-1)
1938g Goodbye Red (030854-1)
1938h The Right Kind of Life (030855-1)
1939 T.B. Blues (040532-)
1940a Train Fare Blues (049198-)
1940b My Little Machine (053002-)
1941a My Baby Made a Change (064022-)
1941b Shady Grove Blues (064492-)
1941c You Got to Step Back (064495-)
1941d She Don't Love Me That Way (070146-)

Willis, Ruth
1931a Experience Blues (151906-1)
1931b Painful Blues (151907-1)
1933 Man of My Own (12920-1)

Wilson, Kid Wesley
1929 The Gin Done Done It (148977-)

Wilson, Leola B.
1926a Stevedore Man (2616-1)
1926b Down the Country (4012-2)

Woods, Hosea
1929a Fourth and Beale (C-4338-)
1929b The Rooster's Crowing Blues (56340-)

Woods, Oscar
1936 Evil Hearted Woman (60847-)
1937 Don't Sell It (SA-2845-1)

Yates, Blind Richard
1927 I'm Gonna Moan My Blues Away (GEX-577-A)

References

Abrahams, Roger D. (1976). *Talking black*. Rowley, MA: Newbury House.

Abrahams, Roger D., and George Foss. (1968). *Anglo-American folksong style*. Englewood Cliffs, NJ: Prentice Hall.

Ahlstrand, Clas. (1967). Blind Jimmie Brewer. *Blues Unlimited, 48* (Dec.), 11–12.

Albertson, Chris. (1972). *Bessie*. New York: Stein and Day.

Ames, Russell. (1943). Art in Negro folksong. *Journal of American Folklore, 56*, 241–54.

_____. (1950). Protest and irony in Negro folk song. *Science and Society, 14*, 193–213.

_____. (1951). Communications: Implications of Negro folk song. *Science and Society, 15*, 163–73.

_____. (1955). *The story of American folk song*. New York: Grosset and Dunlap.

Ankeny, Jason. (2004). Garfield Akers. *MSN Entertainment/Music*. Retrieved November 4, 2004 from http://music.msn.com/artist/?artist=16107199

Anon. (n.d.). Record notes to *Blues before sunrise: Leroy Carr, piano and vocal* [LP recording]. New York: Columbia C–30496.

Ashby, Genette. (1979). A generative model of the formula in the *Chanson de Roland*. *Olifant, 7*, 39–65.

Austin, J.L. (1975). *How to do things with words*. 2nd ed. Ed. J.O. Urmson and Marina Sbisa. London: Oxford University Press.

Baker, Houston A., Jr. (1984). *Blues, ideology and Afro-American literature: A vernacular theory*. Chicago: University of Chicago Press.

Barnie, John. (1978a). Formulaic lines and stanzas in the country blues. *Ethnomusicology, 22*, 457–73.

_____. (1978b). Oral formulas in the country blues. *Southern Folklore Quarterly, 42,* 39–52.

Basgoz, Ilhan. (1978). *Formula in prose narrative*—hikâye. Folklore Preprint Series, vol. 6 (2). Bloomington, IN: Folklore Forum.

Bastin, Bruce. (1971). *Crying for the Carolines.* London: Studio Vista.

Bastin, Bruce, and John Cowley. (1974). Uncle Art's logbook blues. *Blues Unlimited, 108,* 12–17.

Bateson, Gregory. (1973). *Steps to an ecology of mind.* St. Albans: Paladin.

Bäuml, Fanz H. (1987). The theory of oral-formulaic composition and the written medieval text. In *Comparative research on oral traditions: A memorial for Milman Parry,* ed. John Miles Foley, 29–45. Columbus: Slavica.

Beatie, Bruce A. (1963). Oral-traditional composition in the Spanish *romancero* of the sixteenth century. *Journal of the Folklore Institute, 1,* 92–113.

Benson, Larry D. (1966). The literary character of Anglo-Saxon formulaic poetry. *PMLA, 81,* 334–41.

Blaustein, Richard. (1971). The curative function of the blues: A structural analysis. Paper read at the annual meeting of the Society for Ethnomusicology, Chapel Hill, North Carolina, November 14, 1971.

Blesh, Rudi. (1958). *Shining trumpets: A history of jazz.* 2nd rev. ed. New York: Alfred A. Knopf.

Bolton, W.F. (1985). A poetic formula in *Beowulf* and seven other Old English poems: A computer study. *Computers and the Humanities, 19,* 167–73.

The book of common prayer. (n.d.). London: Society for Promoting Christian Knowledge.

Bradford, Perry. (1965). *Born with the blues.* New York: Oak Publications.

Brakeley, Theresa C. (1949). Blues. In *Funk and Wagnalls standard dictionary of folklore mythology and legend,* ed. Maria Leach, vol. 1, p. 151. New York: Funk and Wagnalls.

Broonzy, William. (1955). *Big Bill blues: William Broonzy's story.* Ed. Yannick Bruynoghe (Orig. pub.: London: Cassell) (Reprinted: New York: Oak Publications, 1964).

Brown, Sterling A. (1930). The blues as folk poetry. In *Folk-say: A regional miscellany,* ed. B.A. Botkin, 324–39, 432–33. (Reprinted: New York: Johnson Reprint Corp., 1970).

_____. (1943). Blues, ballads and social songs. In *75 years of freedom: Commemoration of the 75th anniversary of the proclamation of the 13th Amendment to the Constitution of the United States,* ed. Library of Congress, 17–25. Washington: Government Printing Office.

_____. (1953). The blues. *Phylon, 13,* 286–92.

Buchan, David. (1972). *The ballad and the folk.* London: Routledge and Kegan Paul.

Calt, Stephen. (1972). Record notes to *Mississippi & Beale Street Sheiks 1927–1932* [LP recording]. Canaan, NY: Biograph BLP–12041.

_____. (1973). The country blues as meaning. In *Country blues songbook,* ed. Stefan Grossman, Stephen Calt, and Hal Grossman, 8–35. New York: Oak Publications.

_____. (n.d.). Record notes to *No dough blues, Vol. 3: Blind Blake 1926–1929* [LP recording]. Canaan, NY: Biograph BLP-12031.

Calt, Stephen, Nick Perls, and Michael Stewart. (n.d.a). Record notes to *Bo Carter: Greatest hits 1930–1940* [LP recording]. New York: Yazoo L–1014.

_____. (n.d.b). Record notes to *Clifford Gibson: Beat you doing it* [LP recording]. New York: Yazoo L–1027.

Carruth, Hayden. (1986). *Sitting in: Selected writings on jazz, blues, and related topics.* Iowa City: University of Iowa Press.

Cassidy, Frederic G. (1965). How free was the Anglo-Saxon scop? In *Medieval and linguistic studies in honor of Francis Peabody Magoun, Jr.,* ed. Jess B. Bessinger Jr. and Robert P. Creed, 75–85. London: George Allen and Unwin.

Cawelti, John G. (1969). The concept of formula in the study of popular literature. *Journal of Popular Culture, 3,* 381–90.

Charters, Samuel B. (1959). *The country blues.* New York: Rinehart.

_____. (1961). Record notes to *Hard working man blues: Memphis Willie B.* [LP recording]. Bergenfield, NJ: Bluesville 1048.

_____. (1963). *The poetry of the blues.* New York: Oak Publications.

_____. (1973). An introduction. In *Country blues songbook,* ed. Stefan Grossman, Stephen Calt, and Hal Grossman, 4–6. New York: Oak Publications.

Chase, Gilbert. (1955). *America's music: From pilgrims to the present.* New York: McGraw-Hill.

Chomsky, Noam. (1965). *Aspects of the theory of syntax.* Cambridge: MIT Press.

Clar, Mimi. (1960). Folk belief and custom in the blues. *Western Folklore, 19,* 173–89.

Clough, John, and Jack Douthett. (1991). Maximally even sets. *Journal of Music Theory, 35,* 93–173.

Cohen, Norm. (1972). "I'm a record man"—Uncle Art Satherley reminisces. *JEMF Quarterly, 8,* 18–22.

Commercial music documents: Number Nine. (1971). *JEMF Quarterly, 7,* 124–25.

Conner, Patrick W. (1972). Schematization of oral-formulaic processes in Old English poetry. *Language and Style, 5,* 204–20.

Cook, Bruce. (1973). *Listen to the blues.* New York: Charles Scribner's Sons.

Courlander, Harold. (1963). *Negro folk music, U.S.A.* New York: Columbia University Press.

Creed, Robert P. (1957). The *answarode*-system in Old English poetry. *Speculum, 32,* 523–28.

_____. (1959). The making of an Anglo-Saxon poem. *ELH, 26,* 445–54.

Dankworth, Avril. (1968). *Jazz: An introduction to its musical basis.* London: Oxford University Press.

Diamond, Robert E. (1963). *The diction of the Anglo-Saxon metrical psalms.* The Hague: Mouton.

Dixon, Robert M.W., and John Godrich. (1970). *Recording the blues.* London: Studio Vista.

Dixon, Robert M.W., John Godrich, and Howard Rye, comps. (1997). *Blues & gospel records, 1890–1943.* 4th ed. New York: Oxford University Press.

Duggan, Joseph J. (1969). *A concordance of the* Chanson de Roland. Columbus: Ohio State University Press.

_____. (1973). *The Song of Roland: Formulaic style and poetic craft.* Berkeley: University of California Press.

Eagle, Bob. (1972). Roosevelt Scott remembers. ... *Blues World, 43,* 9, 12.

Elmes, Barry. (1973). Living Blues interview: Sonny Terry & Brownie McGhee. *Living Blues, 13,* 14–23.

Evans, David. (1966a). Booker White—Part 2. *Blues Unlimited, 37,* 7–9.

_____. (1966b). Booker White—Part 3. *Blues Unlimited, 38,* 6–7.

_____. (1967). The Rev. Rubin Lacy—Part 4. *Blues Unlimited, 43,* 13–14.

_____. (1971). *Tommy Johnson.* London: Studio Vista.

_____. (1972). An interview with H.C. Spier. *JEMF Quarterly, 8,* 117–21.

_____. (1973). Folk, commercial, and folkloristic aesthetics in the blues. *Jazzforschung, 5,* 11–32.

_____. (1974). Techniques of blues composition among black folksingers. *Journal of American Folklore, 87,* 240–49.

_____. (1982). *Big road blues: Tradition and creativity in the folk blues.* Berkeley: University of California Press.

_____. (n.d.). Record notes to *The Mississippi blues, no. 3: Transition, 1926–1937* [LP recording]. Berkeley: Origin Jazz Library OJL–17.

Fahey, John. (1970). *Charley Patton.* London: Studio Vista.

Felman, Shoshana. (1980). On reading poetry: Reflections on the limits and possibilities of psychoanalytical approaches. In *The literary Freud: Mechanisms of defense and the poetic will,* ed. Joseph H. Smith, 119–48. New Haven: Yale University Press.

Ferris, William R., Jr. (1970a). *Blues from the Delta.* London: Studio Vista.

_____. (1970b). Creativity and the blues. *Blues Unlimited, 71,* 13–14.

Finlayson, John. (1963). Formulaic technique in *Morte Arthure. Anglia, 81,* 372–93.

Finnegan, Ruth. (1976). What is oral literature anyway? Comments in the light of some African and other comparative material. In *Oral literature and the formula,* ed. Benjamin A. Stolz and Richard S. Shannon III, 127–76. Ann Arbor: Center for the Coordination of Ancient and Modern Studies, University of Michigan.

_____. (1977). *Oral poetry: Its nature, significance and social context.* Cambridge: Cambridge University Press.

Foley, John Miles. (1977). *Beowulf* and the psychohistory of Anglo-Saxon culture. *American Imago, 34,* 133–53.

_____. (1981a). Oral texts, traditional texts: Poetics and critical methods. *Canadian–American Slavic Studies, 15,* 122–45.

_____. (1981b). *Oral traditional literature: A Festschrift for Albert Bates Lord.* Columbus: Slavica.

_____. (1985). Oral narratives and edition by computer. In *Computers in literary and linguistic computing,* ed. Jacqueline Hamesse and Antonio Zampolli, 173–82. Paris: Champion-Slatkine.

_____. (1991). *Immanent art: From structure to meaning in traditional oral epic.* Bloomington: Indiana University Press.

_____. (1995). *The singer of tales in performance.* Bloomington: Indiana University Press.

_____. (2002). *How to read an oral poem.* Urbana: University of Illinois Press.

Fry, Donald K. (1967). Old English formulas and systems. *English Studies, 48,* 193–204.

_____. (1968). Old English formulaic themes and type-scenes. *Neophilologus, 52,* 48–54.

Garon, Paul. (1971). *The devil's son-in-law: The story of Peetie Wheatstraw and his songs.* London: Studio Vista.

Gates, Henry Louis, Jr. (1988). *The signifying monkey: A theory of Afro-American literary criticism.* New York: Oxford University Press.

Gattiker, Godfrey L. (1962). The syntactic basis of the poetic formula in *Beowulf.* Unpublished doctoral dissertation, University of Wisconsin.

Godrich, John. (1965). Postscript (see BU 19): Victoria Spivey. *Blues Unlimited, 20,* 10.

_____. (1969). Record notes to *Clara Smith: Volume three* [LP recording]. N.pl.: Vintage Jazz Mart VLP–17.

Goldstein, Kenneth S. (1964). *A guide for field workers in folklore.* Hatboro, PA: Folklore Associates.

Green, Donald C. (1971). Formulas and syntax in Old English poetry: A computer study. *Computers in the Humanities, 6,* 85–93.

Greenfield, Stanley B. (1955). The formulaic expression of the theme of "exile" in Anglo-Saxon poetry. *Speculum, 30,* 200–206.

Groh, George W. (1972). *The black migration: The journey to urban America.* New York: Weybright and Talley.

Gruver, Rod. (1972). The origin of the blues. *Blues World, 43,* 6–9.

Guralnick, Peter. (1971). *Feel like going home: Portraits in blues & rock 'n' roll.* New York: Outerbridge and Dienstfrey.

Haggo, Douglas, and Koenraad Kuiper. (1983). Review of the book *Conversational routine. Linguistics, 21,* 531–51.

Hainsworth, J.B. (1964). Structure and content in epic formulae: The question of the unique expression. *Classical Quarterly, 14,* 155–64.

_____. (1968). *The flexibility of the Homeric formula.* London: Oxford University Press.

Harris, Sheldon. (1979). *Blues who's who: A biographical dictionary of blues singers.* New Rochelle, NY: Arlington House.

Holzapfel, Otto. (1974). Homer—Nibelungenlied—Novalis: Zur Diskussion um die Formelhaftigkeit epischer Dichtung. *Fabula, 15,* 34–46.

Horace Flaccus, Q. (1971). *Ars Poetica.* In *Horace on poetry: The "Ars poetica,"* C.O. Brink. Cambridge: Cambridge University Press.

Hyman, Stanley E. (1958). Negro literature and folk tradition. *Partisan Review.* (Reprinted in *The promised end: Essays and reviews 1942–1962,* ed. Stanley Edgar Hyman, 295–315. Cleveland: World Publishing, 1963.)

Jackson, Bruce. (1965). Foreword. In *American Negro folk-songs,* Newman I. White, v–xx. Hatboro, PA: Folklore Associates.

Jahn, Janheinz. (1968). *A history of neo-African literature*. Trans. Oliver Coburn and Ursula Lehrburger. London: Faber and Faber.

Jarrett, Dennis. (1978). The singer and the bluesman: Formulations of personality in the lyrics of the blues. *Southern Folklore Quarterly, 42*, 31–37.

_____. (1984). Pragmatic coherence in an oral formulaic tradition: I can read your letters/sure can't read your mind. In *Coherence in spoken and written discourse*, ed. Deborah Tannen, 155–171. Norwood, NJ: Ablex.

Johnson, Charles S. (1934). *Shadow of the plantation*. Chicago: University of Chicago Press.

Johnson, Guy B. (1935). Negro folk songs. In *Culture in the south*, ed. W.T. Couch, 547–69. Chapel Hill: University of North Carolina Press.

Jones, LeRoi. (1963). *Blues people: Negro music in white America*. New York: William Morrow.

Joos, Martin. (1964). *The English verb: Form and meaning*. Madison: University of Wisconsin Press.

Kamin, Jonathan. (1965). The blues: The structure of a tradition. Unpublished M.A. thesis, Wesleyan University.

Keil, Charles. (1966). *Urban blues*. Chicago: University of Chicago Press.

Kennedy, Louise Venable. (1930). *The Negro peasant turns cityward: Effects of recent migrations to northern cities*. New York: Columbia University Press.

Kent, Don. (1971). Record notes to *Feeling lowdown: Washboard Sam* [LP recording]. New York: RCA LPV–577.

Kent, Don, and Michael Stewart. (n.d.). Record notes to *New Deal blues (1933–1939)* [LP recording]. New York: Mamlish S–3801.

Kierkegaard, Soren A. (1946). *An essay in experimental psychology*. Trans. and intro. Walter Lowrie. Princeton, NJ: Princeton University Press.

_____. (1957). *The concept of dread*. Princeton, NJ: Princeton University Press.

Kiparsky, Paul. (1976). Oral poetry: Some linguistic and typological considerations. In *Oral literature and the formula*, ed. Benjamin A. Stolz and Richard S. Shannon III, 73–125. Ann Arbor: Center for the Coordination of Ancient and Modern Studies, University of Michigan.

Lakoff, Robin. (1971). If's, and's, and but's about conjunction. In *Studies in linguistic semantics*, ed. Charles J. Fillmore and D. Terrence Langendoen, 114–49. New York: Holt, Rinehart and Winston.

Leadbitter, Mike. (1970). Big Boy Crudup. *Blues Unlimited, 75*, 16–18.

Leech, Geoffrey. (1974). *Semantics*. Harmondsworth: Penguin Books.

Locke, Alain. (1936). *The Negro and his music*. (Orig. pub.: Washington, D.C.: The Associates in Negro Folk Education) (Reprinted: New York: Arno Press and the *New York Times*, 1969).

Longini, Muriel D. (1939). Folk songs of Chicago Negroes. *Journal of American Folklore, 52*, 96–111.

Lord, Albert B. (1938). Homer and Huso II: Narrative inconsistencies in Homer and oral poetry. *Transactions and Proceedings of the American Philological Association, 69*, 439–45.

_____. (1951). Composition by theme in Homer and Southslavic epos. *Transactions and Proceedings of the American Philological Association, 82,* 71–80.

_____. (1960). *The singer of tales.* Cambridge: Harvard University Press.

_____. (1986). Perspectives on recent work on the oral traditional formula. *Oral Tradition, 1,* 467–503.

Lornell, Christopher. (1972). Record notes to *Leroy Carr: Singin' the blues 1934* [LP recording]. Canaan, NY: Biograph BLP–C9.

_____. (1975). The Chapel Hillbillies. *Living Blues, 24,* 8, 45.

Lowry, Pete. (1973). Some cold rainy day. *Blues Unlimited, 103,* 15.

Magoun, Francis P., Jr. (1953). Oral-formulaic character of Anglo-Saxon narrative poetry. *Speculum, 28,* 446–67.

McCulloh, Judith M. (1970). "In the pines": The melodic-textual identity of an American lyric folksong cluster. Unpublished doctoral dissertation, Indiana University.

Metfessel, Milton. (1928). *Phonophotography in folk music.* Chapel Hill: University of North Carolina Press.

Mezzrow, Milton "Mezz," and Bernard Wolfe. (1946). *Really the blues.* New York: Dell.

Middleton, Richard. (1972). *Pop music and the blues: A study of the relationship and its significance.* London: Victor Gollancz.

_____. (1983). "Play it again Sam": Some notes on the productivity of repetition in popular music. *Popular Music, 3,* 235–70.

Miller, Keith D. (1990). Composing Martin Luther King, Jr. *PMLA, 105,* 70–82.

Minton, W.W. (1965). The fallacy of the structural formula. *Transactions and Proceedings of the American Philological Association, 96,* 241–53.

Moore, Alex. (1974). Yours truly, Whistlin' Alex Moore. *Blues Unlimited, 109,* 14.

Nagler, Michael N. (1967). Towards a generative view of the oral formula. *Transactions and Proceedings of the American Philological Association, 98,* 269–311.

Nagy, Gregory. (1976). Formula and meter. In *Oral literature and the formula,* eds. Benjamin A. Stolz and Richard S. Shannon III, 239–72. Ann Arbor: Center for the Coordination of Ancient and Modern Studies, University of Michigan.

Nelson, Donald L. (1974). The West Virginia snake hunters: John and Emery McClung. *JEMF Quarterly, 10,* 68–73.

Newton, Francis. (1959). *The jazz scene.* London: Macgibbon and Kee.

Nicholas, A.X. (1973). *Woke up this mornin': Poetry of the blues.* Toronto: Bantam Books.

Nicholson, Lewis E. (1963). Oral techniques in the composition of expanded Anglo-Saxon verses. *PMLA, 78,* 287–92.

Niles, Abbe. (1926a). Blue notes. *New Republic, 45* (February 3), 292–93.

_____. (1926b). Introduction. In *Blues: An anthology,* ed. W.C. Handy, 1–40. New York: Albert and Charles Boni.

Odum, Howard W. (1911). Folk-song and folk-poetry as found in the secular songs of the southern Negroes—concluded. *Journal of American Folklore, 24,* 351–96.

Odum, Howard W., and Guy B. Johnson. (1925). *The negro and his songs.* Chapel Hill: University of North Carolina Press.

_____. (1926). *Negro workaday songs.* Chapel Hill: University of North Carolina Press.

Oliver, Paul. (1959). *Bessie Smith.* (Orig. pub.: London: Cassell) (Reprinted: New York: A.S. Barnes, 1961).

_____. (1965). *Conversations with the blues.* New York: Horizon Press.

_____. (1968). *Aspects of the blues tradition.* (Orig. pub.: London: Cassell) (Reprinted: New York: Oak Publications, 1970).

_____. (1969). Record notes to *Mississippi Joe Callicott* [LP recording]. New York: Blue Horizon BM–4606.

Olsson, Bengt. (1970). *Memphis blues and jug bands.* London: Studio Vista.

O'Neal, Jim, and Amy O'Neal. (1975). Living blues interview: Georgia Tom Dorsey. *Living Blues, 20,* 16–34.

O'Neil, Wayne A. (1960a). Another look at oral poetry in *The Seafarer. Speculum, 35,* 596–600.

_____. (1960b). Oral-formulaic structure in Old English elegiac poetry. Unpublished doctoral dissertation, University of Wisconsin.

Oster, Harry. (1969a). The blues as a genre. *Genre, 2,* 259–74.

_____. (1969b). *Living country blues.* Detroit: Folklore Associates.

Parry, Milman. (1928). The traditional epithet in Homer. (Reprinted in *The making of Homeric verse: The collected papers of Milman Parry,* ed. and trans. Adam Parry, 1–190. Oxford: Clarendon Press, 1971.)

_____. (1930). Studies in the epic technique of oral verse-making. I. Homer and Homeric style. *Harvard Studies in Classical Philology, 41,* 73–147. (Reprinted in *The making of Homeric verse: The collected papers of Milman Parry,* ed. and trans. Adam Parry, 266–324. Oxford: Clarendon Press, 1971.)

_____. (1932). Studies in the epic technique of oral verse-making. II. The Homeric language as the language of an oral poetry. *Harvard Studies in Classical Philology, 43,* 1–50. (Reprinted in *The making of Homeric verse: The collected papers of Milman Parry,* ed. and trans. Adam Parry, 325–64. Oxford: Clarendon Press, 1971.)

Paulsen, Gary. (1968). In remembrance of Smokey Hogg. *Blues Unlimited, 55,* 3–5.

Pearson, Barry L. (1972). Review of the book *Blues from the Delta. Journal of American Folklore, 85,* 192–95.

Perls, J. Nicholas. (1965). Notes on Son House and the Paramount days. *Blues Unlimited, 18,* 3–4.

Postal, Paul M. (1966). On so–called "pronouns" in English. In *Report of the seventeenth annual round table meeting on linguistics and language studies,* ed. Francis P. Dineen, 177–206. Washington, D.C.: Georgetown University Press.

Propp, Vladimir. (1928). Reprinted and translated as *Morphology of the folktale.* 2nd rev. ed. Ed. Louis A. Wagner and trans. Laurence Scott. Austin: University of Texas Press, 1968.

Quirk, Randolph. (1963). Poetic language and Old English metre. In *Early English and Norse studies presented to Hugh Smith in honour of his sixtieth birthday,* eds. Arthur Brown and Peter Foote, 150–71. London: Methuen.

Reif, Fred. (1972). Fred Stanley: His story. *Old Time Music, 6,* 15–16.

Renoir, Alain. (1981). Oral-formulaic context: Implications for the comparative criticism of medieval texts. In *Oral traditional literature: A festschrift for Albert Bates Lord,* ed. John Miles Foley. (Orig. pub.: Columbus, OH: Slavica Publishers) (Reprinted in *Oral-formulaic theory: A folklore casebook,* ed. John Miles Foley, 313–35. New York: Garland, 1990.)

Roberts, John S. (1972). *Black music of two worlds.* New York: Praeger.

Rogers, H.L. (1966). The crypto-psychological character of the oral formula. *English Studies, 47,* 89–102.

Rogers, Robert. (1987). Freud and the semiotics of repetition. *Poetics Today, 8,* 579–90.

Rosenbaum, Arthur. (1961). Record notes to *Scrapper Blackwell: Mr. Scrapper's blues* [LP recording]. Bergenfield, NJ: Bluesville 1047.

Rosenberg, Bruce A. (1970a). *The art of the American folk preacher.* New York: Oxford University Press.

_____. (1970b). The formulaic quality of spontaneous sermons. *Journal of American Folklore, 83,* 3–20.

_____. (1975). Oral sermons and oral narrative. In *Folklore: Performance and communication,* eds. Dan Ben-Amos and Kenneth S. Goldstein, 75–101. The Hague: Mouton.

_____. (1978). *The formula: New directions?* Folklore Preprint Series, vol. 6 (4). Bloomington, IN: Folklore Forum.

Ross, James. (1959). Formulaic composition in Gaelic oral literature. *Modern Philology, 57,* 1–12.

Ross, John Robert. (1967). On the cyclic nature of English pronominalization. *To honor Roman Jakobson: Essays on the occasion of his seventieth birthday.* Vol. 3, pp. 1669–82. The Hague: Mouton.

Rowe, Mike. (1975). *Chicago breakdown.* New York: Drake.

Roxin, Charles. (1973). *Aspects of the blues.* Fairport, NY: Space Age Printers.

Rust, Brian. (1962). Record notes to *Blues singers: Jazz sounds of the 20s* [LP recording]. Victoria, Australia: Swaggie S-1240.

Santelli, Robert. (1993). *The big book of blues: A biographical encyclopedia.* New York: Penguin.

Schaar, Clas. (1956). On a new theory of Old English poetic diction. *Neophilologus, 40,* 301–305.

Schwetman, John. (1980). The formulaic nature of Old English poetry: A linguistic analysis. *Linguistics in Literature, 5* (3), 71–109.

Shapiro, Nat, and Nat Hentoff. (1955). *Hear me talkin' to ya: The story of jazz by the men who made it.* New York: Rinehart.

Snead, James A. (1984). Repetition as a figure of black culture. In *Black literature and literary theory,* ed. Henry Louis Gates Jr., 59–79. New York: Methuen.

Spaeth, Sigmund. (1927). *Weep some more, my lady.* Garden City: Doubleday, Page.

Spottswood, Richard K. (n.d.). Record notes to *Mississippi John Hurt 1963* [LP recording]. N.pl.: Piedmont PLP–13157.

Spraycar, Rudy S. (1981). Statistics and the computer in formula analysis of Serbo–Croatian heroic verse. In *Applied systems and cybernetics: Proceedings of the international congress on applied systems research and cybernetics. Vol. V. Systems approaches in computer science and mathematics,* ed. G.E. Lasker, 2576–80. New York: Pergamon.

Spraycar, Rudy S., and Lee F. Dunlap. (1982). Formulaic style in oral and literate epic poetry. *Perspectives in Computing, 2* (4), 24–33.

Suleiman, Susan Rubin. (1980). Redundancy and the "readable" text. *Poetics Today, 1* (3), 119–42.

Szwed, John F. (1968). Negro music: Urban renewal. In *Our living traditions: An introduction to American folklore,* ed. Tristram P. Coffin, 272–82. New York: Basic Books.

_____. (1970). Afro-American musical adaptation. In *Afro-American anthropology: Contemporary perspectives,* ed. Norman E. Whitten Jr. and John F. Szwed, 219–27. New York: Free Press.

Taft, Michael. (1977). The lyrics of race record blues, 1920–1942: A semantic approach to the structural analysis of a formulaic system. Unpublished doctoral dissertation, Memorial University of Newfoundland.

_____. (1978). Willie McTell's rules of rhyme: A brief excursion into blues phonetics. *Southern Folklore Quarterly, 42,* 53–71.

_____. (1984). *Blues lyric poetry: A concordance.* New York: Garland.

_____. (1994). Proverbs in the blues: How frequent is frequent? *Proverbium, 11,* 227–58.

_____. (2005). *Talkin' to myself: Blues lyrics, 1921–1942.* New York: Routledge.

Titon, Jeff Todd, ed. (1974). *From blues to pop: The autobiography of Leonard "Baby Doo" Caston.* Los Angeles: John Edwards Memorial Foundation.

_____. (1977). *Early downhome blues: A musical and cultural analysis.* Urbana: University of Illinois Press.

Toelken, Barre. (1979). *The dynamics of folklore.* Boston: Houghton Mifflin.

Van Vechten, Carl. (1925). The black blues: Negro songs of disappointment in love—their pathos hardened with laughter. *Vanity Fair, 24* (August), 57, 86, 92.

Waldron, Ronald A. (1957). Oral-formulaic technique and Middle English alliterative poetry. *Speculum, 32,* 792–804.

Welding, Peter J. (1968). David "Honey Boy" Edwards. *Blues Unlimited, 54,* 3–12.

_____. (n.d.a). Big Joe and Sonny Boy: The shock of recognition. Record notes to *Big Joe Williams and Sonny Boy Williamson* [LP recording]. Berkeley: Blues Classics BC–21.

_____. (n.d.b). Record notes to *The blues in St. Louis 1929–1939* [LP recording]. Berkeley: Origin Jazz Library OJL–20.

White, Newman I. (1928). *American Negro folk-songs.* (Orig. pub.: Cambridge: Harvard University Press) (Reprinted: Hatboro, PA: Folklore Associates, 1965).

_____. (1928–29). The white man in the woodpile: Some influences on Negro secular folk-songs. *American Speech, 4,* 207–15.

Whitman, Cedric H. (1958). *Homer and the Homeric tradition.* Cambridge: Harvard University Press.

Wilgus, D.K. (1961). Review of the book *The singer of tales. Kentucky Folklore Record, 7,* 40–44.

Wilson, Al. (1965). Son House. *Broadside* (Boston). (Reprinted in *Blues Unlimited Collectors Classics, 14,* 1–12 [1966]).

Wilson, Edmund, ed. (1955). *The shock of recognition: The development of literature in the United States recorded by the men who made it.* 2nd ed. New York: Farrar, Straus and Cudahy.

Windelberg, Marjorie, and D. Gary Miller. (1980). How (not) to define the epic formula. *Olifant, 8,* 29–50.

Wolfe, Charles K. (1971–72). Where the blues is at: A survey of recent research. *Popular Music and Society, 1,* 152–66.

Woodson, Carter G. (1918). *A century of Negro migration.* (Orig. pub.: Washington, D.C.: The Association for the Study of Negro Life and History) (Reprinted: New York: Russell and Russell, 1969).

Woofter, T.J., Jr., ed. (1928). *Negro problems in cities.* (Orig. pub.: Garden City, NY: Doubleday, Doran, & Company) (Reprinted: New York: Negro Universities Press, 1969).

Zumthor, Paul. (1982). Le discours de la poésie orale. *Poétique, 52,* 387–401.

Index